PRAISE FOR INFECTIOUS GREED

"Whether or not you agree with the diagnosis and remedies, you can surely benefit from considering the clear, energetic presentation of these experienced academics."

—**Michael G. Ferri**
Foundation Chair in Finance, George Mason University/
Former Vice President for Economic Research, Nasdaq

"Nofsinger and Kim have written a book that is both timely and important. Encompassing issues from boards of directors to accountants to analysts, it is a clear exposition and analysis of topics that have filled the front pages of daily newspapers for the last year."

—**Erik Sirri**
Babson College/Former Chief Economist
of the U.S. Securities and Exchange Commission

"This book should be compulsory reading for everyone in the investment industry. John Nofsinger and Kenneth Kim have laid bare the causes of the recent stock market bubble and crash, suggesting that the problem lies not only in the malfeasance of a few managers, but also in the whole system of corporate governance in America today. They go into the heart of American corporate culture and issue a stark warning that many things in that culture must change if investor confidence is to be restored and the economy to recover."

—**Morgen Witzel**
Editor-in-Chief, Corporate Finance Review

Infectious Greed

ISBN 0-13-140644-2

FINANCIAL TIMES

In an increasingly competitive world, it is quality
of thinking that gives an edge—an idea that opens new
doors, a technique that solves a problem, or an insight
that simply helps make sense of it all.

We work with leading authors in the various arenas
of business and finance to bring cutting-edge thinking
and best learning practice to a global market.

It is our goal to create world-class print publications
and electronic products that give readers
knowledge and understanding which can then be
applied, whether studying or at work.

To find out more about our business
products, you can visit us at www.ft-ph.com

Infectious Greed

Restoring Confidence in America's Companies

JOHN NOFSINGER
KENNETH KIM

FT Prentice Hall
FINANCIAL TIMES

An Imprint of PEARSON EDUCATION
Upper Saddle River, NJ • New York • London • San Francisco • Toronto • Sydney
Tokyo • Singapore • Hong Kong • Cape Town • Madrid
Paris • Milan • Munich • Amsterdam

www.ft-ph.com

A Cataloging-in-Publication Data record for this book can be obtained from the Library of Congress.

Editorial/production supervisor: *Faye Gemmellaro*
Executive editor: *Tim Moore*
Editorial assistant: *Richard Winkler*
Marketing manager: *Alexis R. Heydt-Long*
Manufacturing buyer: *Maura Zaldivar*
Cover design director: *Jerry Votta*
Cover illustrator: *Tom Post*
Interior design director: *Gail Cocker-Bogusz*

 © 2003 Pearson Education, Inc.
Publishing as Financial Times Prentice Hall
Upper Saddle River, New Jersey 07458

Financial Times Prentice Hall books are widely used by corporations and government agencies for training, marketing, and resale.

For information regarding corporate and government bulk discounts, please contact Corporate and Government Sales at (800) 382-3419 or *corpsales@pearsontechgroup.com*

Printed in the United States of America

10   9   8   7   6   5   4   3   2   1

ISBN 0-13-140644-2

Pearson Education Ltd.
Pearson Education Australia Pty, Ltd.
Pearson Education Singapore, Pte. Ltd.
Pearson Education North Asia, Ltd.
Pearson Education Canada, Ltd.
Pearson Educación de Mexico, S.A. de C.V.
Pearson Education—Japan
Pearson Education Malaysia, Pte. Ltd.

FINANCIAL TIMES PRENTICE HALL BOOKS

For more information, please go to www.ft-ph.com

Contents

CHAPTER 14 REGAINING INVESTOR CONFIDENCE 247

PREFACE

"Why did corporate governance checks and balances that served us reasonably well in the past break down? At root was the rapid enlargement of stock market capitalizations in the latter part of the 1990s that arguably engendered an outsized increase in opportunities for avarice. An infectious greed seemed to grip much of our business community."

—ALAN GREENSPAN, FEDERAL RESERVE CHAIRMAN,
SPEECH TO CONGRESS, JULY 16, 2002

Chairman Greenspan's comments lead to some very intriguing questions. What are the "corporate governance checks and balances" that he spoke of? How and why did they fail us? Can this breakdown ever happen again?

Answering these questions is what this book is all about. We refer to the checks and balances as executive incentives and corporate monitors. Indeed, there are many participants in the corporate governance system. Although the corporate scandals take on specific names and faces (like Andrew Fastow, Martha Stewart, Enron, Arthur Andersen, and World-Com), the problem actually involves a whole system that either allowed the misdeeds or failed to catch them.

It might be convenient to blame one group of people or another. For example, CEOs and other top executives have been blamed for being greedy, but they weren't the only ones who acted greedily. Many politicians and the media have blamed auditors, but they weren't the only ones who failed to monitor the companies. The problem was a breakdown of the *system*. For example, a board of directors, which was elected by the shareholders, gave the CEO and other executives stock options. This motivated them to maximize the stock price at a specific point when they could cash in the options for millions of dollars. The CEO then talked up his or her company to analysts. The captive analysts, impressed with the business, assigned a buy rating and hyped the stock. To meet the expectations, the CEO demanded that the accounting department manufacture paper profits. Solutions also came from consultants and often involved investment bankers. These perilous actions were either okayed or overlooked by the corporate lawyers and the auditors. Any one of these groups could have put a stop to the shenanigans, but didn't. Why not? In this book, we thoroughly discuss the incentives, conflicts, and actions of each of the participants in the corporate system.

Some of the problems had been developing for many years. The Securities and Exchange Commission (SEC) knew about some of the problems but failed to act to stop them. Indeed, in the middle and late 1990s, the government enacted laws that reduced investor protection. When the scandals broke in 2001 and 2002, however, politicians were then lining up to speak against the "evil doers," the greedy corporate executives—a 180-degree turnaround. And, as if by script, they worked fast to enact new laws and to restore investor confidence. New laws were passed, but confidence hasn't been restored. Why not? Is it that the laws that were passed were not as effective as they could have been? People are naturally skeptical of these new laws, and their skepticism may not be unfounded as the participants in the corporate governance system are some of the largest donors to political campaigns. Auditing firms, investment banking firms, corporate lawyers, and the public companies themselves donate tens of millions of dollars to the two major political parties per election cycle. Should we really believe that these politicians are turning their backs on those who have made donations? This book exposes why many of the new laws and policies will only be marginally effective in improving the system.

We recognize that these new proposals are an important part of the process to restore investor confidence, but where the creators of these solutions fall short is their inability to recognize that the American corporate form of business is an integrated system with many parts. We should first realize, however, that this system has allowed the U.S. economy to become the largest and strongest in the world. Therefore, the basic system is a good one that deserves to be preserved, but it does have its problems that can be fixed. The best solutions neither overburden the basic system nor overtax or unnecessarily scare the people. After all, we want our capitalist system to continue to churn out new jobs, wealth, and revenue far into the future. In this book, we propose some incentive-driven solutions that fit within the current system to make it better. Combining our incentive-driven solutions with the punishment and regulation-based solutions that have been proposed from the government should make the system not only whole again, but better.

If you own any stocks, either as an active investor or through your retirement savings, then this book was very much written for you. The group with the greatest interest in monitoring management is the shareholders themselves. The American investor has become disengaged from the company he or she owns. Too often, investors take little interest in the inner workings of the corporation. If something about a company upsets an investor, he or she simply sells the stock and buys a different one. The dramatic decline in commission costs lends itself to this apathy. If shareholders do not take a stand for their own investment, why should executives, the board, or anyone else? Investors need to educate themselves on how this corporate system works and what their role should be. Being more knowledgeable about the system, its failures, and the solutions would also help investors regain some of the trust that was broken. This book aims to provide that education.

Finally, we believe that anyone who is interested in participating in the corporate system in the future (for example, business students) should read this book. To make sure that breakdowns like the ones that occurred recently are never to be experienced again, the future participants in the system need to learn from the past.

Acknowledgments

A book like this cannot be written in a vacuum. We thank all those who helped us formulate our thoughts and ideas. In particular, we are grateful for the contributions by Jon Armstrong, Stephen Bowie, Eric Budin, Dan Deli, Tim Eaton, Al Frakes, Sue Gill, Gordon Graham, Dan Rogers, Jonathan Sokobin, Peter Tsirigotis, Morgen Witzel, and many others who wish to remain anonymous.

1

THE IMPORTANCE OF INVESTOR CONFIDENCE

One scandal rocks investors after another. The problems with Enron, Arthur Andersen, Rite Aid, WorldCom, Adelphia, Global Crossing, Martha Stewart, Merck, etc., have been blamed on greedy accountants, analysts, executives, and directors. The intense media frenzy and investor attention has allowed many people to grab the limelight, and much grandstanding has occurred. Regulators have gone after high-profile companies for fraud. Politicians have suggested and enacted new regulations and laws. Prosecutors have indicted individuals at these scandal-ridden firms. Yet the actions and proposals do not seem to be enough to satisfy investors.

In order to reverse the crisis in investor confidence, investors need to believe that two things will happen. First, those individuals in the corporate system that have misbehaved will be punished. The tough rhetoric from regulators, prosecutors, and politicians makes punishment seem very likely. Second, investors need to see changes in the system that will preclude bad behavior in the future. In general, there are two ways to change behavior—the carrot and the stick. The U.S. government is good with the stick—that is, deterring misbehavior through a fear of legal punishment. The government can make the stick thicker, harder, and more accurate. Indeed, nearly all the proposals have dealt with more laws, better laws, and more regulation. Such measures can change some behavior, but if you really want to change behavior, offer the carrot. In fact, a well-designed incentive system can be a far more powerful motivator than regulation. In a nutshell, this idea has been the triumph of capitalism over socialism. The U.S. government, however, is terrible at offering solutions with the carrot.

When corporate scandals are viewed from an understanding of the corporate system, then solutions can be designed that enhance the system, not drag it down. For example, many view the recent corporate failures as a problem with accountants and auditors. However, the accountants in a firm are operating in an environment created by the company's management in which the accounting department is directed to act like a profit center. Instead of a tracking and evaluation function, accounting departments have also been assigned the task of smoothing earnings and even generating profits. Managers do this to boost the stock price and cash in millions of dollars of stock options. These incentive packages are offered to top managers by the firm's board of directors—the stockholders elect this board of directors. Sure, the accounting profession must share some of the blame for the recent financial meltdowns. But blame can also be shared by managers, the stock option incentive, boards of directors, analysts, and even shareholders. Trying to fix the system by looking at only one piece of it in isolation is a doomed approach. A failure to examine the entire corporate system will only lead to temporary patches and not long-term solutions.

The purpose of this book is to examine the entire corporate system, identify the problems, and propose remedies that both fix the problems and enhance the system without creating more layers of costly government bureaucracy.

ASLEEP AT THE WHEEL

To gain some perspective, it should be noted that these scandals originated from the excesses of the late 1990s. Indeed, there were strong signals in the late 1990s of forthcoming scandals. However, investors did not seem to care. As long as the stock market was going up, investors did not want to ask too many questions about the behavior of the corporate system that was earning them profits.

Consider SEC Chairman Arthur Levitt's speech to CPAs, lawyers, and academics in New York. The chairman attacked accounting chicanery and earnings management practices, and promised that the agency would go on the offensive. Although the speech was given in 1998, it is reminiscent of the post-Enron environment of 2001 and 2002. In the couple of years after the speech was given, the SEC took actions against many firms for accounting manipulation and fraud. Some firms were mega firms like Bankers Trust, Cendant, Sunbeam, Waste Management, and McKesson HBOC. Other well-known firms with accounting problems included Boston Chicken, Mercury Finance, Telxon, and Oxford Health.[1] But were investors upset about these corporate misdeeds? Were Congressional inquiries made? For the most part, no.

Even the largest two firms (in market value) have been under suspicion—General Electric (GE) and Cisco. The media expressed concerns about the earnings management practices of GE, and, while the company is notorious for producing increased profits every year, *Money* magazine claimed that earnings would have been down in 1997 and flat in 1999 had it not been for some accounting maneuvering.[2] *Barron's* questioned the long-term viability of Cisco's practice of financial engineering.[3] The article specifically questioned the accounting used in Cisco's endless string of acquisitions. Indeed, the article went so far as to call Cisco a "modern house of cards." Again, investors did not seem too concerned about the accounting problems. After all, investors had made a lot of money investing in Cisco and GE.

However, the stock market declined (along with the economy) in 2000 and 2001. Then came the failures and collapse at Enron in the fall of 2001. Enron's managers, accountants, analysts, and board of directors all failed the investors and employees of Enron. Investors became angry at the enormous fraud at Enron and at the other firms that have subsequently announced problems. However, the problems have been brewing for a while. It has only been since the Enron debacle that investors, the media, regulators, and politicians have taken notice and demanded accountability.

The outcry against corporate greed and fraud is a manifestation of the failing confidence of investors in the corporate system, which, in turn, is partially caused by the decline in the stock market. The following sections illustrate this crisis in investor confidence and how it affects the stock market. Eventually, the lack of confidence can become a drag on the economy. The crisis needs to be reversed before too much damage is done.

INVESTOR ATTITUDE

A crisis in investor confidence means that the very people who support the corporate system become disillusioned with the system. The corporate form of business relies on investors to fund a company with capital through the purchase of its stock. The dynamics of the corporate system are described in the next chapter. However, the role of investors is a critical component to the corporate system and to capitalism in general. So, is there really a crisis in investor confidence? One way to find out is to simply ask investors.

United States Trust Company frequently surveys Americans deemed to be in the wealthiest 1 percent. Their 21st survey occurred in 2002 and included several questions about confidence in the corporate system.[4] Before we examine the responses, we should get to know the people considered to be in the wealthiest 1 percent of Americans. People are considered to be in the top 1 percent if they either have a net worth of at least $3.75 million or earn at least $300,000 annually. In addition, most of these people created this wealth themselves—only 5 percent inherited wealth. Indeed, nearly 70 percent of respondents said that they grew up in a middle class or lower household. So, how did they create this wealth? Generally, they became wealthy in the business world. For example, 41 percent thought their corporate employment was a very important source of their wealth. Family-owned business was a very important source of wealth for 37 percent of those surveyed. In other words, these people know about business. They have worked in the business world for several decades and were able to create wealth for themselves. They are business insiders.

How do these insiders feel about the corporate system? Figure 1–1 shows the percent of those surveyed who agree with various questions about investor confidence. First, 38 percent are wary of investing in public companies. These affluent Americans mostly obtained their wealth through the business world, yet more than one third of them are wary of public companies! Why are they concerned? The graph shows that 76 percent of those surveyed do not trust public company financial statements, 73 percent do not trust equity analyst recommendations, 66 percent do not trust corporate management, and 58 percent do not trust auditors. If these business insiders lack confidence in the corporate system, then the rest of us should too!

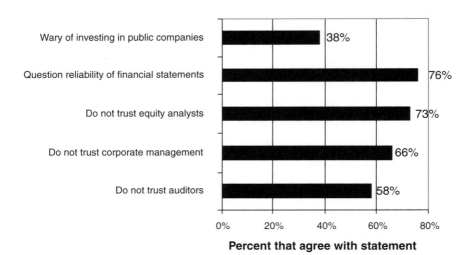

Percent that agree with statement

FIGURE 1–1   This graph shows the percent of affluent Americans who agree with the statement about confidence in the corporate system. Source: U.S. Trust Survey of Affluent Americans, June 2002

These attitudes are bad news for the economy because the wealthy are likely to reduce their spending as a response to their drop in wealth and mistrust of the corporate system. For example, 41 percent of those surveyed stated that they were likely to postpone home improvements, 39 percent will cut back on big-ticket purchases, and 37 percent will postpone the purchase of a new car or boat. If this reduction in spending actually occurs, it will hurt the economy. Both consumer spending and business spending drive the economy. If consumers reduce spending, the economy will be adversely affected.

The average investor also seems to have lost confidence in corporate America. CBS News conducted a poll of 685 people on July 8 and 9, 2002.[5] When asked, 79 percent of the respondents thought questionable accounting practices were widespread, 68 percent thought insider trading was widespread, 67 percent thought American corporate executives were not honest, and 57 percent thought white-collar crimes happen very often. Investor reaction to the scandals can be seen in the media, which often reflects an audience's mood. Print, radio, and TV media frequently bring up the crisis in investor confidence. Newspapers are printing many letters to the editor from readers on the subject, and thousands of messages are being posted on stock-oriented discussion boards. Will the lack of investor confidence also translate into changes in consumer spending?

INVESTOR CONFIDENCE AND THE STOCK MARKET

It seems clear that investors lack confidence in the corporate system. However, does this translate into changes in investing behavior? One way to examine this issue is to look at the stock market's performance. We expect the stock market to decline in conjunction with a decline in the economy. In fact, it usually declines in anticipation of an economic downturn. The economy actually did contract in the third quarter of 2001. Since that time, the economy has been growing. Shouldn't the stock market be rising along with the expansion of the economy?

The following analysis describes the stock market reaction to the last four instances of economic contraction.

Consider the four graphs of the stock market and the economy in Figure 1–2. They illustrate that the bear market in the 2002 stock market is not related to the economy. Each of the four graphs is structured the same. The bar graph shows the real GDP growth rate in the economy in several quarters (the term "real" means that inflation has been removed). The scale for the growth rate is on the left-hand side and is the same in all four graphs. Therefore, the height of each bar is comparable between graphs. The line represents the level of the Standard & Poor's (S&P) 500 Index at the end of each quarter. The level is denoted on the right-hand side of the graph. Since the level of the stock market changes over time, the right-hand scale is not the same among graphs.

The figure shows the last four times the economy has shrunk for at least one quarter. The period between the second quarter of 1980 and the third quarter of 1982 experienced several quarters of recession. This is depicted in Panel A of the figure. The graph begins with three quarters of growth starting in the third quarter of 1979. Then, in the second quarter of 1980, the economy experiences a severe recession that continues for six months. Note that the stock market anticipates the recession and declines before the recession begins. Indeed, by the middle of the recession, the stock market has predicted the ensuing recovery and has already moved upward. While the recovery was strong, it was also short. By the second quarter of 1981, the economy was shrinking again. Real economic growth was negative in four out of six quarters between the second quarter of 1981 and the third quarter of 1982. The stock market declined through the tough times and again predicted a recovery and started moving up during the third quarter of 1982. The graph ends with three quarters of continued economic expansion. At the end of the three quarters of expansion, the stock market was well higher than when it started three quarters before the beginning of the economic decline. In fact, the S&P 500 Index was up nearly 60 percent from before the recession to after it.

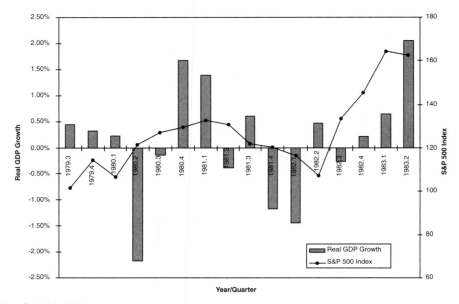

Panel A Early 1980s recession.

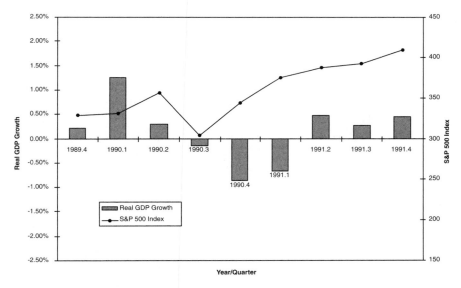

Panel B Early 1990s recession.

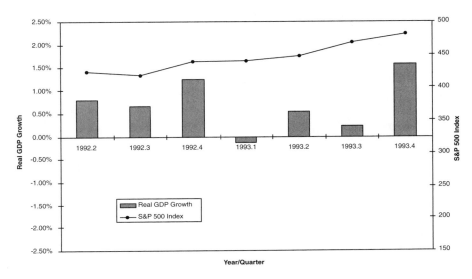

Panel C Mid-1990s recession.

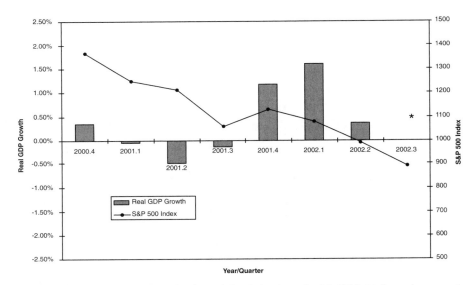

Panel D Recent recession. (S&P 500 Index data ended on Friday, September 13, 2002. * indicates that economic growth data for the quarter was unavailable at the time of printing.)

Figure 1–2 The four figures show the real GDP growth by quarter for the past four recession periods. The level of S&P 500 Index for the periods is also shown.

The next economic recession occurred in the early 1990s. Panel B of the figure illustrates what happened. The real economic growth rate for the economy was negative in the three consecutive quarters starting in the third quarter of 1990. The stock market declined early in the recession and then rose higher in anticipation of the recovery. Three quarters into the recovery, the stock market had risen nearly 25 percent from its pre-recession levels.

The next interruption in the growth of the economy occurred in first quarter of 1993. Note from Panel C of the figure that the economy only shrunk for one quarter and only by a small amount. The stock market hardly noticed the economic decline and continued to rise during the period.

That brings us to the most recent period of economic contraction. Panel D shows the economic growth and stock market level around 2001. The real growth in the fourth quarter of 2000 was modest. Beginning with the first quarter of 2001, the economy contracted. However, the recession was small compared to the contractions of the early 1980s (Panel A) and early 1990s (Panel B). The stock market anticipated the decline in the economy and trended downward before it started to decline. The stock market also anticipated the recovery that began in the fourth quarter of 2001. Indeed, the growth of the economy in the three quarters after the recession was large compared to the three previous recessions depicted in Panels A through C. Yet the stock market did not recover.

The stock market has continued its decline in the face of the economic recovery. The S&P 500 Index fell to less than 800 in July 2002. Why? If the stock market had recovered as strongly as in previous recessions, the S&P 500 could have been more than 1,500 in June 2002. At the beginning of 2002, Jeffrey Applegate, strategist at Lehman Brothers, forecast the S&P 500 to finish the year at 1,200. Thomas McManus at Banc of America Securities forecast 1,150. Instead, the index was less than 1,000 in June and plummeted to less than 800 in July. The market was down a lot. Why? We argue that investors have lost confidence in the corporate system and that has affected the stock market.

Investors have not totally lost confidence. Investors do not appear to be moving all of their money out of stocks. Large masses of employees do not appear to be liquidating the equity in their retirement plans. However, investors seem to be holding back new investment money from the market and a few are getting out of the market. For example, in June and July 2002, there was a net $70.9 billion withdrawn from equity mutual funds.[6]

The crisis also seems to be affecting foreigners who invest in the U.S. stock market. Consider what happens when a foreign investor sells his or her U.S. stock. The investor sells the stock in the stock market and receives U.S. dollars. Then, the investor must sell the U.S. dollars and buy the currency of his or her own country. If many people are selling U.S. dollars and buying their own currency, then the U.S. dollar's price will fall. That is, selling of the U.S. dollar will cause its value to decline relative to other currencies. Has this happened? It appears that it has. From February to mid-summer 2002, the U.S. dollar has lost 12 percent of its value against both the euro and the Japanese yen. The lower U.S. dollar will affect your pocketbook. It makes the foreign products you buy more expensive.

LONG-TERM ECONOMIC EFFECTS

The level of the stock market is very important to the economy. Both consumer purchasing and business investment drive the economy. We have already discussed the association between investor confidence and consumer purchasing. When investors lose confidence, they tend to purchase fewer big-ticket items and postpone buying a new car. A prolonged slowdown in consumer purchasing will slow down the economy as well.

However, a depressed stock market also affects business investment. To see this relationship, first consider the effect of a high stock market. Indeed, consider what happens when the market is overvalued, as it was during the bubble of the late 1990s. If a company manager thinks the stock price is overvalued relative to the true fundamentals of the firm, then he or she will be inclined to issue new stock. In other words, the stock can be sold at an inflated value. The company can receive more money for it than it is worth. Thus, it seems easy and cheap to raise capital when the stock is overvalued.[7] Corporations can issue new stock and use the capital to make business investments. Business investments are the equipment needed to conduct and expand business operations. Corporations buy trucks, machines, factories, computers, and other capital items. These purchases improve the economy.

Now consider what happens if the company's stock is perceived by the managers to be undervalued. If the firm wants to raise equity capital, it would have to issue new stock at a low price—a price lower than the managers think it is worth based on the fundamentals of the firm. This seems like a poor deal. Thus, firms tend to issue less stock and, therefore, make fewer business investments when the stock market is low. Or, at least, firms take such actions when managers feel the stock market is undervalued. This relationship between the stock price level and business investment is particularly strong for smaller firms with good growth opportunities.[8] Larger firms have better access to other capital markets (like the bond market), and firms without growth opportunity do not need capital.

An example of the relationship between the stock market level and business investment is illustrated by the real (inflation adjusted) Gross Private Domestic Investment, a measure that the U.S. Department of Commerce uses to track the business investment made in the United States. The record amount of investment was $1.7 and $1.8 trillion in the quarters near the top of the stock market bubble in late 1999 and early 2000. Since then, business has dropped off to less than $1.6 trillion per quarter—a decline of $100 billion per quarter. Consider also how the level of the stock market affects the ability of new firms to raise capital. During the height of the market bubble in 1999, a record 548 companies obtained capital through initial public offerings (IPOs). The first half of 2002 can be characterized by a depressed market with concerned investors. It is no wonder that only 46 IPOs were offered in the first six months of 2002.

Company executives are under attack for being loose with the books. Often, the public's perception is that executives are spending their time rebuilding profits and balance sheets. Executives must certify their financial numbers to the SEC and defend against a sustained media and political attack for misdeeds, and they are not spending as much effort on business expansion activities requiring new capital spending. Companies that sell products that support expansion—like the hardware and software, respectively, of IBM and Siebel Systems—report that they are seeing reduced sales and orders for their products.[9]

If the stock market is only temporarily depressed, it should not create a big problem for the economy. As argued above, the recent market depression is caused more by a lack of investor confidence than poor economic conditions. However, if the stock market remains depressed for long, it may begin to slow down the economy as well. The lack of investor confidence causes consumers to delay their spending. The lower stock market, caused by the confidence crisis, will eventually affect business investment too. With lower consumer purchases and business investment, the economy could sink into another recession. Therefore, it is imperative that investor confidence is restored quickly.

OUR APPROACH

Before remedies can be offered to fix the system, one must understand how the system works. We detail how the American corporate system works in the next chapter. Afterward, we can discuss where and why the failures have occurred in the system. In many instances, the executive leadership of companies failed. In Part 1 of the book, we describe how executive compensation systems can lead to unethical and greedy behavior.

To keep corporate managers working hard for the shareholders and to prevent them from undesirable behavior, several different groups monitor them. This monitoring system is made up of people such as boards of directors, accountants and auditors, analysts, and professionals at investment banks.

Part 2 of this book illustrates how the monitoring system has failed. Were these monitors also greedy? Were they complacent? Indeed, in most cases the corporate system had developed conflicts of interest and incentive problems that distracted monitors from their main duty; we illustrate these problems. The American corporate system also includes regulatory agencies to watch over the system. We discuss the role of these regulatory agencies in the current investor crisis in Part 3. We also discuss how investors themselves have failed to watch over their own companies.

Once the system and its failures are known, we will then be in a position to offer solutions that improve and enhance the system for the long term. Most of the solutions coming from political leaders and regulators are focused on either punishment of offenders or more regulatory oversight. In our view, these proposals are analogous to changing behavior using a stick. Alternatively, we propose solutions in Part 4 that are incentive driven. That is, we offer ways to change behavior by offering the proverbial carrot. It might be useful if corporate leaders avoided wrongdoing because of fear of being caught, but we would rather they work very hard to do the right thing because they want to—because they are rewarded by doing so.

In short, we think that a clear understanding of the interrelated incentives of the many individuals in corporate business will allow for the formulation of targeted policy changes that will both fix and enhance the American corporate system. A complete solution may also convince investors that U.S. companies and the U.S. stock market are the best places to invest for the long term. However, fixing the system may not be enough to restore investor confidence. In Chapter 14, we discuss what it will take to regain investors' trust in the corporate system.

ENDNOTES

1. Carol Loomis, "Lies, Damned Lies, and Managed Earnings," *Fortune*, August 2, 1999, pp. 74–92.
2. Jon Birger, "Glowing Numbers," *Money*, November 2000, pp. 112–122.
3. Thomas Donlan, "Cisco's Bids," *Barron's*, May 8, 2000, pp. 31–34, *www.cbsnews.com/htdocs/cak/bizback.pdf.*
4. U.S. Trust Survey of Affluent Americans; a random sample of 150 affluent Americans was surveyed through a telephone interview, June 2002.
5. CBS News Poll, "The Ethics of Business," July 8–9, 2002.
6. Amy Baldwin, "Investors Cling to Bond Funds," *Associated Press*, September 14, 2002.
7. Stanley Fischer and Robert Merton, "Macroeconomics and Finance: The Role of the Stock Market," *Carnegie Rochester Conference Series on Public Policy* 21 (1984): 57–108; Olivier Blanchard, Changyong Rhee, and Lawrence Summers, "The Stock Market, Profit, and Investment," *Quarterly Journal of Economics* 108 (1993): 115–136.
8. Malcolm Baker, Jeremy Stein, and Jeffrey Wurgler, "When Does the Market Matter? Stock Prices and the Investment of Equity-Dependent Firms," Harvard University working paper, December 2001.
9. Rich Miller, "What's Crippling Capital Spending?" *BusinessWeek*, June 24, 2002, p. 44.

2

THE STRUCTURE
OF CORPORATIONS

Capitalism is the economic system of business. This is a system based on private enterprise. Individuals and businesses own land, farms, factories, and equipment, and they use those assets in the attempt to earn profits. Capitalism is a good economic system because it can provide rewards for those who work hard and are inventive and creative enough to figure out new and better ways of doing things. The capitalistic system provides most of the jobs and creates most of the wealth in our society. One of the potential rewards for creating value in the economy is wealth for you. The wealth incentive provides the fuel for the constant generation of new ideas and fosters economic value that provides jobs and raises the American standard of living.

Selling products and services for a profit creates economic value. The goal of the firm is to create an environment in which it can earn profits over the long term. The creation of long-term profits is based on two main sources. First, a business must provide products and/or services to its customer base. A large portion of the value of the business comes from the profits, now and in the future, of this business activity. Finding ways to increase the profits from these core operations can increase economic value. Second, potential for increasing profits comes from the growth in sales. Sales growth comes from selling more of the existing product and from providing new products to sell.

However, expansion usually requires more money, or capital. Business activities also entail risk. The ability to access capital and control risk is an important aspect in the success or failure of a firm. Access to capital and ability to control risk are influenced by the manner in which a firm is organized. A business can be a sole proprietorship, a partnership, or a corporation. Each of these organizational forms has different advantages and disadvantages in the business world.

BUSINESS FORMS

The first form is the sole proprietorship, which is a business owned by a single person. These businesses are relatively easy to start up, and business tax is computed at the personal level. Due to its simplicity, sole proprietorships are ubiquitous, representing more than 70 percent of all U.S. businesses.[1] However, there are several significant drawbacks to this form of business. In particular, such a firm has a limited life (it dies with the owner's death or retirement), it only has a limited ability to obtain capital (it relies on either the firm's own ability to generate funds or personal borrowings), and the owner bears unlimited personal liability for the firm.

A partnership is similar to a sole proprietorship, but it includes more than one owner. As such, a partnership shares similar advantages and disadvantages as the sole proprietorship business form. While one obvious advantage of a partnership over a sole proprietorship is the pooling together of capital, this advantage may not be as important as the pooling together of service-oriented expertise and skill—especially for larger partnerships. Examples of such partnerships include accounting firms, law firms, investment banks, and advertising firms.

The third business form is the corporation, which is the focus of this book. Less than 20 percent of all U.S. businesses are corporations, but they generate approximately 90 percent of the country's business revenue.[2] The corporation is its own legal entity, as if it were a person. It is an entity that is essentially separate from its owners in the sense that the corporation, in and of itself, can engage in business transactions and other business activities in its own name. The officers of the corporation act like agents for the firm who authorize those activities.

The biggest advantage of the corporate form of business is the access to the capital markets. Public companies can raise money by issuing stocks and bonds to investors. While sole proprietorships and partnerships may access millions of dollars through the business owners' wealth and banks, corporations may eventually access billions of dollars. It is access to this capital that causes entrepreneurs like Bill Gates of Microsoft, Steve Jobs of Apple, and Larry Ellison of Oracle to take their companies public. To raise money for expansion in the capital markets, the business sells stock to investors.

For example, between 1977 and 1980, Apple Computer sold a total of 121,000 computers. In order to meet the potential demand for millions of computers per year, Apple needed to massively expand operations. In 1980, Apple became a public corporation and sold $65 million worth of stock. Steve Jobs, co-founder of Apple, still owned more shares than anyone else. However, he didn't own more than half of the firm. He gave up much ownership in the firm to the new investors for the capital needed to greatly expand the firm. This would later come back to haunt Jobs.

Stockholders, sometimes called shareholders, are the owners of the corporation. These shareholders receive any value that is created by the firm, but they can also lose their investment if the firm goes bankrupt. The process has two benefits. First, ordinary people with some money can invest in business and increase their wealth over the long term. Second, businesses with growth potential can get the capital they need to expand. The expansion creates economic value, jobs, and tax revenue. The corporation has an infinite life unless it is terminated by bankruptcy or merger with another firm. The owners of corporations enjoy limited liability because they can only lose, at most, the value of their ownership shares. Further, corporate ownership is usually quite liquid, which means ownership stakes can be easily bought and sold as stocks in a marketplace, such as the New York Stock Exchange or Nasdaq.

While the advantages of the corporate business form are appealing, there are several major disadvantages. First, corporate profits are subject to business taxes before any income goes to shareholders in the form of dividends. Subsequently, shareholders must also pay personal taxes on their dividend income. Therefore, shareholders are exposed to double-taxation. Second, because corporations typically have many shareholders, running a corporation can be quite expensive. For example, the costs of hiring accountants and legal experts, communicating with all of the shareholders, complying with regulations, and so forth can cost millions of dollars per year. Finally, perhaps the most important disadvantage from our perspective is that corporations suffer from potentially serious governance problems. Because—unlike a sole proprietorship or partnership business—corporations are owned by so many investors, and most investors can only own a small stake of a large public corporation, it is likely that shareholders in a corporation do not feel any true sense of ownership, and especially control, over the firms in which they own stock.

While this book focuses on U.S. corporations, we should point out that one major difference between business forms in the United States and those in other countries is the lack of the government-owned and -operated form of business, known as state-owned enterprises (SOEs). For example, in many countries, television, telephone, oil, airline, utility, and other types of companies are state owned and operated. However, we have witnessed a worldwide trend of privatization recently (including countries in Europe, Latin America, and Asia), during which governments have sold these SOEs to private companies and individuals.

PEOPLE IN BUSINESS

There are four types of people involved in the public corporation: shareholders, directors, officers, and employees. Shareholders literally own the public firm. As owners, they capture the economic value of the firm in the form of stock price increases and dividends. They also suffer the losses when a firm fails. In general, there are two types of shareholders: individuals and institutions (such as pension funds and mutual funds). For now, we will think of shareholders as individuals, since this has direct pertinence to us, but we will also discuss the importance of institutional investors in a later chapter. Directors hire, oversee, evaluate, and fire the officers of the firm. In doing so, they are supposed to represent the interests of the shareholders. (We will dedicate an entire chapter to directors later in the book.) The officers, such as the chief executive officer (CEO) and/or president, represent the firm's top level of management, and they are ultimately responsible for the day-to-day operations of the firm. Employees have a stake in the firm because they dedicate their human capital, i.e., their labor, to the firm. By holding company stock in their retirement plans, they, too, are sometimes owners.

There are others who also have a stake in the firm. Creditors, government officials, suppliers, and customers are stakeholders because they *deal* with the firm.

With so many people involved with the company, who actually controls the corporation? Who makes the big decisions and has the most power? One might think that it is the owners who control the firm. Or the boards of directors who hire the officers might have the control. But, for the most part, it is the officers who control the firm.

SEPARATION OF OWNERSHIP AND CONTROL

A corporation's ownership and control are separated between two parties—shareholders and officers. The shareholders own the firm, and the officers (or executives) control the firm. This situation comes about because public firms are owned by thousands, even hundreds of thousands, of investors. Obviously, thousands of people could not possibly join together to make the daily decisions needed to operate a business. They hire managers to do this.

Besides, most shareholders are not interested in being involved in the firm's business activities. These shareholders act like investors, not owners. The difference is subtle, but important. An owner is focused on the business performance of the firm. An investor is focused on the risk and return of his or her stock portfolio. In other words, investors spread their wealth around rather than have it staked into one or a few investments. Many investment professionals and academics know the mathematics and logic of portfolio diversification, but perhaps the best way to understand it is to think about the old adage that one should not put all of one's eggs in one basket. While diversifying reduces risk for the investor, it also makes participation and influence in that many companies less likely. Therefore, investors tend to prefer to be inactive shareholders of many firms.

There is a problem with this separation of ownership and control, and it exists at a simple level. Why should the managers care about the owners? It is not far-fetched to imagine that managers may do what's best for them if they can get away with it—even if it is at the expense of owners. This idea is usually attributed to Adolph Berle and Gardiner Means in their book *The Modern Corporation*, published in 1932. The argument that they put forward makes just as much sense today as it did when it was first published. In academic jargon, the problem with the separation of ownership and control is known as the principle-agent problem, or the agency problem.

Consider the owner of a nightclub (the principle) who hires a bouncer (the agent) to check IDs at the front door and take a cover charge from the customers who enter. The bouncer may pocket some of the cash if he thinks that no one is looking. That is, he may try to maximize his own wealth at the expense of the owner. If the owner cannot effectively monitor the transactions and the activities of the bouncer, she could lose money. Thus, monitoring is important to help overcome the agency problem.

The shareholders of a corporation are the principals, and the managers who run the company are the agents. If shareholders cannot effectively monitor the managers' behavior, then the managers may be tempted to use the firm's assets to increase their own lifestyle. Or, as James Burnham put it in his 1941 book *The Managerial Revolution*, managers will behave as if they are the owners. Executives may enjoy perks such as liberally charging the corporate expense account, chartering the company jet, ordering top-grain leather office equipment, and so on at the expense of shareholders. Of course, we have recently seen abuses that make these examples seem petty. We discuss the astonishing abuses throughout this book.

Solutions to this problem tend to come in two categories: incentives and monitoring. The incentive solution is to create situations in which the executive's wealth is tied to the wealth of the shareholders. That way, the executives and the shareholders want the same thing. This is called aligning executive incentives with the shareholders. Executives would then act and behave in a way that is also best for the other shareholders. But how can this be done? For most U.S. companies, executives are given stock and/or stock options as a significant component of their pay. The advantages and disadvantages of this form of incentive solution are explored in the next chapter. Suffice it to say, there are problems.

The second type of solution is to set up mechanisms for others to monitor the behavior of managers. Indeed, there are several mechanisms for monitoring executives, which we discuss shortly.

CAN INVESTORS INFLUENCE MANAGERS?

On a theoretical level, managers run the firm. But they are supposed to run it on behalf of their shareholders. In reality, however, we admit that it seems as though the firm actually belongs to management. Most investors view stocks as an investment vehicle rather than as an ownership stake of a firm. Investors don't really feel as though the CEO is working for them. Indeed, management often does not act like they are beholden to the shareholders.

Some active shareholders have tried to exercise their influence as owners in attempts to influence management, but they have often been met with defeat. The recent evidence on the unsuccessful outcomes of shareholder proposals is quite telling. Shareholders have at their disposal the power to make proposals that can get voted on at the annual shareholders meeting. There are generally two types of proposals: those that are governance oriented (e.g., suggesting changes in board structure) and those that are social-reform oriented (e.g., proposing to stop the selling of chemicals to rogue countries). However, only about half of all shareholder-initiated proposals make it far enough in the process to get voted on. When there is a vote, they usually get rejected.[3] A huge factor in whether a proposal is successful depends on management's opinion. Without management approval, proposals have little chance of succeeding. Why? It has generally been the case that shareholders have trusted management to know what is best for the firm (or at least they used to feel this way!). That is, most shareholders will go along with whatever management wants.

For a different illustration of management control and influence, consider the recent merger between Hewlett Packard (HP) and Compaq.[4] Carly Fiorina, the Hewlett Packard CEO, announced on September 4, 2001, that HP would acquire Compaq for $25.5 billion. The stock markets, industry experts, and business media reacted negatively to the news. What is particularly noteworthy is that David W. Packard and Walter Hewlett, both significant shareholders (when including the Packard Foundation, they owned 18 percent of HP's stock) and sons of HP's founders, were also strongly opposed to the acquisition. In fact, they took out newspaper ads asking other HP shareholders to vote against the merger. Fiorina went ahead with her plan, despite the attacks from both Packard and Hewlett, and on March 19, 2002, most of the other shareholders voted in favor of the acquisition—despite the fact that HP's stock price had fallen significantly since Fiorina took over as CEO. The price had also fallen since the merger announcement, indicating that investors were wary of the deal. HP's stock was down 18 percent following the September 4, 2001, announcement, and even Compaq's stock declined by 10 percent following the announcement, which is very rare for a target firm. Nevertheless, shareholders voted with management's wishes and approved the acquisition. Even if some investors want to have an influence on business strategy and direction, it is management that controls the firm.

ARE INVESTORS HELPLESS?

In general, it is pretty safe to say that the investing public does not know what goes on at a given firm's operational level. Of course, that's why there are managers—to handle these day-to-day operations. And, yes, it is also pretty safe to say that managers know that their behavior is mostly unknown to the investors. Therefore, the daunting question that needs to be asked is, do managers have investors right where they want them? It seems so. However, all may not be lost. There are several groups that monitor the actions of corporate management.

Figure 2–1 illustrates the separation of ownership and control between stockholders and managers. In addition, the figure shows that monitors exist inside the corporate structure, outside the structure, and in government.

The monitors inside the public firm are the board of directors who oversee management and are supposed to represent shareholders' interests. The board not only evaluates management, but members can also design compensation contracts to tie the salaries of management members to the firm's perfor-

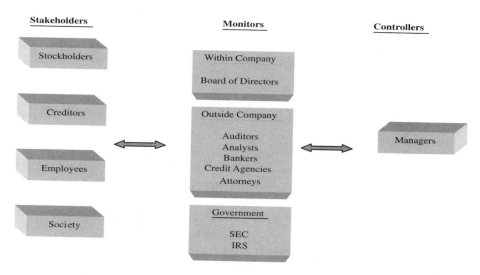

FIGURE 2–1 This figure illustrates the separation of ownership and control by those groups that monitor a firm.

mance. Perhaps most importantly, the board can fire management—even the CEO. Remember that Apple Computer was co-founded by Steve Jobs. When the firm became a public corporation, Jobs was the largest shareholder and also became CEO of the company. However, Apple's board of directors felt that Jobs was not experienced enough to steer the firm through its rapid expansion. Therefore, they hired John Sculley as CEO in 1983. However, in 1985, a power struggle ensued for control of the firm, and the board backed Sculley. In September, Jobs was kicked out of Apple. Even though Jobs was the largest shareholder in Apple and its co-founder, he no longer had a say in its business operations. He later became so disgusted with the company that he sold all his shares. Interestingly, the story has not ended for Steve Jobs. Apple Computer was having difficulties in the late 1990s, so the board hired Jobs back to be CEO. After more then ten years away from the firm, he was back.

There are also outsiders who monitor a firm. Figure 2–1 shows that auditors, analysts, bankers, credit rating agencies, and outside legal counsel all interact with the firm and monitor management activities. The mission of auditors is to examine a firm's accounting systems and comment on whether financial statements are a fair representation of the financial position of the firm. Investors and other stakeholders use the public financial statements to make decisions about the firm's financial health, prospects, performance, and value. Even though investors may not have the ability or opportunity to validate the firm's activities, at least there are accountants and auditors to attest to the firm's financial health and verify its activities for them.

The investment analysts who follow a firm conduct their own independent evaluations of the company's business activities. These analysts report their findings to the investment community. They are supposed to give unbiased and expert assessments. Investment banks also interact with management. They help firms access the capital markets. When obtaining more capital from public investors, firms must register documents with regulators that show the public investors the condition of the firm. Investment banks help firms with this process and advise managers on how to interact with the capital markets.

The government also monitors business activities through the SEC and the Internal Revenue Service (IRS). The SEC's mission is to regulate public firms for the protection of public investors. It has the power to make policy and punish violators in civil court. However, for criminal prosecution, it must turn to the U.S. Justice Department. The IRS enforces the tax rules to ensure corporations pay taxes—just as it ensures that individual Americans pay taxes.

Taken together, this is a pretty impressive set of monitors, isn't it? So, everything is okay, right? With these many and talented monitors, it doesn't matter that ownership and control are separated, does it? Unfortunately, we have seen all of these mechanisms fail in recent times, and we are in the midst of a crisis of investor confidence. One of the main purposes of this book is to outline, in an easy-to-understand way, how these monitors have failed us and what we may be able to do about it. Part 2 examines the failure of auditors, boards, analysts, and banks. Part 3 reviews the role of regulators.

A SYSTEM OF PROBLEMS

Investors are reeling from corporate scandals. Regulators are investigating and promising that they will take action against these white-collar criminals. Politicians appear on TV talk shows. They show their anger over the problems and promise tougher laws and more regulation. President Bush even talks about ethics in corporate America. Certainly, the criminals need to be punished. We also need laws that make it easier to prosecute offenders in the future. Also, some new laws and policies need to be put in place to change the incentives of the people in the business system.

However, the system is integrated and complicated. The incentives for executives, auditors, boards, banks, etc., to misbehave are tied together. By focusing on one part of the system, politicians and regulators are not likely to fix anything in the long run. Consider the diagram of corporate participants in Figure 2–2. The arrows show the relationships that occur between the groups. These relationships are interrelated.

For example, analysts talk to the management members of a firm to try to gauge the prospects of the firm. Managers want to paint a rosy picture so that the analysts will recommend a "buy" rating and the stock price will rise. However, this causes the analysts to predict a high profit forecast for the company, and the managers may struggle to meet the high forecast. If the business activities of the firm do not merit the high profit forecast, managers pressure their accounting department to help. In some cases, consultants are hired who recommend aggressive accounting techniques to give the appearance of increased profits.

The public auditors for the firm have had a long and fruitful relationship with the company. They have audited the books for many years and are proud to have a prestigious corporation as a client. They do not want to end this long relationship and do not press too hard on limiting the aggressive accounting methods used. This is especially true if the con-

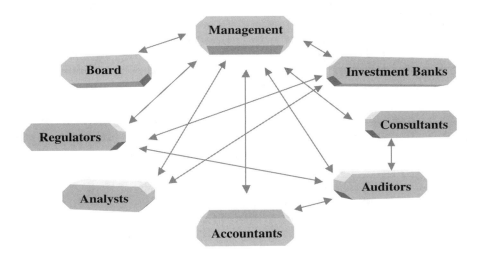

FIGURE 2–2 Corporate participants and the various interlinking relationships.

sultants who recommended those methods are from their own accounting and auditing firm.

Why are managers so obsessed with pushing hard for smooth and increasing profits, and with gaining analysts' favor? It is because they have been awarded stock and stock options by the board. If they can increase the price of the stock, they can cash in their options and stock and become rich. These incentives were awarded by a board that is largely picked by the managers.

We also rely on regulators to monitor corporate behavior. However, regulators often come from this very system. They often have experience as partners in consulting firms, auditing firms, or law firms that are an integral part of the system. By participating in the corporate system, they know how it works. However, they may also have conflicts of interest. The former director of the SEC, Harvey Pitt, has been accused of just this sort of conflict of interest. His career before joining the SEC was in securities law, which means that he had major companies and accounting firms as clients.

INTERNATIONAL MONITORING

The types of monitoring and incentives used in the United States to align the interests of executives and shareholders are also used in other capitalist-oriented countries. However, important differences do occur. Indeed, in many countries, the laws, regulations, and enforcement are considerably more lax than in the United States. For example, Japan's version of the SEC is the Securities and Exchange Surveillance Commission (SESC). The SESC has only one tenth of the employees (364) as the SEC, which is considered grossly understaffed.[5] The SESC does not even have the power to file civil suits or bring administrative action against market participants. The securities regulator in Taiwan, the Securities and Futures Commission, does not have the authority to conduct investigations. Instead, it must rely on local prosecutors who have little experience with the market and with accounting fraud. Even more astounding is that in 2001, Italy reduced the charge of false accounting to a mere misdemeanor.

The tale of Germany's Gerhard Schmid, the former CEO of MobilCom, is telling. As CEO in 2001, Schmid transferred 70.9 million euros ($69.5 million) in new MobilCom stock to a shell company that his wife controlled. The German regulators, the German Financial Supervisory Authority, said that the actions did not fall under its jurisdiction. Therefore, it wouldn't investigate even though Schmid broke the law by not informing other executives or the board. Even though the German securities laws and enforcement are more lax than that of the United States, MobilCom's board of directors did find out about the transfer and investigated. In June 2002, the board fired Schmid and demanded the return of the money. It remains to be seen whether the company will get the money back. While U.S. executives are shown on TV in handcuffs after misdeeds, it appears that the German authorities may not even investigate Schmid.

In most countries, the laws, regulators, and enforcement are so weak that the chances of getting a conviction for corporate fraud are slim. Therefore, the lack of scandalous news in other countries may be the result of a reduced ability to catch criminals and not the result of better governance mechanisms. As a result, some see Asia, Europe, and Latin America as having been in their own confidence crises for quite some time. Consider, for example, that no Asian economy has fully recovered from its stock market bubble-bursts of the early to late 1990s.

SUMMARY

The corporate form of business allows businesses that need capital to get it and expand, thereby helping the economy. It also allows people with money to provide those funds to a business and profit from having ownership in that business. The disadvantage of public corporations is the separation of ownership and control. Managers who control a firm can take advantage of investors who own the firm. To inhibit poor managerial behavior, shareholders try to align the executives' interests with their own through incentive programs involving stock and stock options. In addition, the corporate system has several different groups that monitor managers. Unfortunately, both alignment incentives and monitors have failed recently. The system has interrelated incentives that combine to create an environment in which people might act unethically. We believe that the best solutions are ones that fully recognize the integrated nature of corporate America and alter the present incentives. In the following chapters, this book documents the extent of the failure. Later, we examine solutions to the problem.

ENDNOTES

1. William J. Megginson, *Corporate Finance Theory* (Reading, MA: Addison-Wesley, 1997), p. 40.

2. Ibid.

3. See, for example, Stuart Gillan and Laura Starks, "A Survey of Shareholder Activism: Motivation and Empirical Evidence," *Contemporary Finance Digest* 2, no. 3 (1998): 10–34; Cynthia Campbell, Stuart Gillan, and

Cathy Niden, "Current Perspectives on Shareholder Proposals: Lessons from the 1997 Proxy Season," *Financial Management* 28, no. 1 (1999): 89–98; and Lilli Gordon and John Pound, "Information, Ownership Structure, and Shareholder Voting: Evidence from Shareholder-Sponsored Corporate Governance Proposals," *Journal of Finance* 47, no. 2 (1993): 697–718.

4. Mike Elgan and Susan B. Shor, "Gloves Are Off in Merger Fight," *HP World*, February 2002, *www.interex.org/hpworldnews/hpw202/01news.html*.

5. Almar Latour and Kevin Delaney, "Outside the U.S., Executives Face Little Legal Peril," *Wall Street Journal*, August 16, 2002, p. A1.

1

THE FAILURE OF EXECUTIVES

3 EXECUTIVE COMPENSATION AND INCENTIVES

Corporate executive behavior is the result of many factors. These factors include the relationship between the board and the CEO and between auditors and the firm, regulators, and executive pay structures. Boards, auditors, accountants, analysts, regulators, investors, and others in the corporate system are discussed in other chapters. Here, we focus on the incentives induced by modern executive compensation.

The SEC requires that the pay of the CEO in public firms be disclosed. Therefore, anyone can obtain and know the pay of the top executives of a firm. Many people take an interest—particularly stockholders, employees, labor unions, the media, and even Congress. However, executive pay did not really come into the public debate until the early 1990s. Stories about CEO pay aired on *60 Minutes* and *Nightline* in 1991. Then, Graef Crystal's book *In Search of Excess* was published in October 1991. *Time* came out against the excess pay to executives in 1992.[1] Congress also heard the beat of the drum and (in an election year) proposed bills that limited the tax deductibility of excessive pay. These bills never become law, but the SEC and the IRS enacted policies with similar spirit.

However, this attention did not seem to change the trend of increasing executive pay. The pay of CEOs escalated in the mid-1990s while firms were downsizing. That is, the CEOs were paid more while the rank-and-file employees were laid off. The base pay of CEOs was nearly 100 times greater than that of the average production worker. If incentive awards like stock options were included, CEO pay was more than 200 times higher. Again, the media clamored about the injustice.

In the late 1990s, the bull market increased the value of executive stock and stock options further. The gap between realized CEO pay and the income of average employees grew even more. While the controversy continued, it also seemed to lose some strength. Employees were finding that they, too, could profit by owning the company stock. Instead of anger at CEOs who made millions, the media reported more stories about secretaries at dot-com firms who received stock options and became rich. However, by late 2000 and 2001, the stock market fell and employees no longer felt rich. Instead, it appeared that the executives had cashed in their stocks and options before the stock prices fell. The impression is that the CEOs are still rich, while the employees lost significant portions of their pension money and are now making plans to retire later than previously anticipated. Through the good times and bad times, the pay of executives has continued to increase.

We now examine executive compensation and illustrate how the structure of the compensation provides incentives for specific CEO behavior. Unfortunately, the behavior induced by some compensation plans is not the kind valued by shareholders or society.

TYPES OF EXECUTIVE COMPENSATION

Company executives are compensated in many different ways. They receive a base salary that also includes pension contributions and perquisites (such as a company car, club memberships, etc.). In addition, top executives may receive a bonus that is usually linked to accounting-based performance measures. Lastly, executives may receive additional wealth through long-term incentive programs. These incentives programs are commonly in the form of stock options, which reward managers for an increasing stock price. Stock grants are also a common form of long-term award.

BASE SALARY AND BONUS

The base salary of a company's CEO is often determined through the "benchmarking" method.[2] This method surveys salaries of the CEO's peers for comparison. Salaries that are less than the 50th percentile are considered under market, while salaries in the 50th to 75th percentile are "competitive." Since CEOs always argue for competitive salaries, CEO base pay has continuously drifted upward. Interestingly, this base pay is based more on characteristics of the firm (industry, size, etc.) than on characteristics of the CEO (age, experience, etc.). In recent years, the average base salary has been around $500,000. Pay at large companies can be much higher. Benchmarking also occurs for bonus and option programs.

At the end of every year, the CEO is given a cash bonus payment. The size of the payment is based on the performance of the firm over the past year. The most common ways to examine firm performance are the accounting profit measurements of earnings and earnings before interest and taxes (EBIT). Measures of economic value added (EVA) are also common. These value-added measures are usually a variant on earnings minus the cost of capital. The idea is to measure how much value was added to the firm in relation to the firm's costs of using the different sources of money to conduct the business activities. Whether EBIT or EVA is used, a low threshold needs to be reached in order to qualify the CEO for a bonus. A higher bonus is awarded for higher levels of firm performance up to a specific maximum, or cap.

The use of accounting profits to measure performance has several drawbacks. First, to boost accounting profits, a CEO has an incentive to forego costly research and development that might make the firm more profitable in the future. Second, accounting profits may be manipulated (see the next chapter). Third, a bonus plan is developed each year. Therefore, if the threshold cannot be met one year, the CEO has an incentive to move earnings from the present year to the future. This would lower the expectations during the time next year's bonus plan is created and artificially increase the chance of receiving that bonus. In short, CEOs may place too much focus on manipulating short-term earnings instead of focusing on long-term shareholder wealth. The average bonus payment has been around $250,000 in recent years.

Though not frequent, the annual bonus has been abused. For example, Tyco International paid a $20 million executive bonus in conjunction with its acquisition of CIT Group in 2001.[3] One year later, Tyco was trying to sell CIT Group for half of the $9.5 billion price it paid. Apparently, the purchase wasn't that good after all—certainly not worth a $20 million bonus! Or, consider that Enron's board awarded executives a total bonus of $750 million in 2000—a year in which the firm reported net income of $975 million.[4] That is, executives took three quarters of the firm's profits!

STOCK OPTIONS

Executive stock options are the most common form of market-oriented incentive pay. Stock options are contracts that allow the executive to buy shares of stock at a fixed price, called the exercise or strike price. Therefore, if the price of the stock rises above the strike price, the executive will capture the difference as a profit. For example, if the stock of a company is trading at $50 per share, the CEO may be given options with a strike price at $50. Over the next few years, if the stock price increases to $75 per share, then shareholders would receive a 50 percent return on their stockholdings. The CEO could buy stock for $50 per share with the option and sell it for $75 per share, thus making a $25 profit on each option owned. If the executive has options for one million shares, then he or she could pocket $25 million. If the stock price goes to $100 per share, the executive could cash in for $50 million. If the stock price were to drop to less than $50 per share, the options have no exercisable value and are said to be "underwater." Executives treat stock options as compensation. In other words, they nearly always exercise the options to buy the stock and then sell the stock for the cash. Only rarely will an executive keep the stock.

Stock options give the executives of a firm the incentive to manage the firm in such a way that the stock prices increase. This is also precisely what the stockholders want! Therefore, stock options are believed to align managers' goals with shareholders' goals. This alignment helps to overcome some of the problems with the separation of ownership and control discussed in the previous chapter. The typical executive option contract assigns the strike price of the options to the prevailing stock price at issue. The most common length of the contract is ten years. That is, the CEO has ten years to increase the price of the stock and exercise the options. After ten years, the options expire. Executives cannot sell or transfer the options and are discouraged from hedging the stock price risk. Average incentive awards realized—mostly stock options—jumped from $500,000 in 2000 to more than $800,000 in 2001. Indeed, executive stock options were not common prior to 1980.

Options and Accounting. The popularity of stock options as incentive compensation in the United States partly comes from its very favorable tax treatment for both the executive and company. When options are granted, the company only has to report an accounting cost when the strike price is less than the current stock price. This means that the cost is amortized over the life of the option. Since most options are granted with the strike price equal to the current stock price, the firm never has to report an accounting cost. Of course, there is an economic cost to the firm, but that is not reported in the SEC-required reports that adhere to a set of standards, known as generally accepted accounting principles (GAAP), for public companies. Also, managers are allowed to pick the year in which they will exercise the options, and they can thus determine the year in which the tax liability occurs. In addition, the compensation is treated as a capital gain, not as income. This is an advantage to the CEO because capital gains taxes are lower.

The current use of options and reporting of standards of GAAP usually make the cost of options non-reportable in the income statement. That is, if an executive cashes in his or her shares for $100 million, this cost is not reported on the firm's income statement. The firm does not have to report an accounting cost, but the economic cost to the firm is real. Consider this simple example. A firm has 100 million shares outstanding and has given the executives options for 10 million shares. The firm currently has earnings of $100 million, or $1 per share. If the executives were to exercise their options, they would buy 10 million shares from the firm at the strike price and sell them into the stock market. At that point, there would be 110 million shares outstanding. This means that the $100 million in earnings becomes only $0.91 per share. The earnings per share have fallen by 9 percent! The firm has become less profitable.

The economic cost to shareholders is real. The question being debated recently is whether to change the standards for reporting options, and if so, how. Coca-Cola and the *Washington Post* have not waited. Pushed by board member Warren Buffett, they have decided to report the cost of the options as an expense of the company. This method immediately recognizes the economic cost of executive options, but it could have a dramatic impact on company earnings. For example, a study by Merrill Lynch concludes that expensing options would decrease the earnings of the largest 500 companies by 21 percent.[5] For companies that use options to a larger degree, like technology firms, the drop could be much higher. However, this was a pretty good strategy for Coke. While its earnings may decline a bit, it is signaling to investors that it uses conservative and trustworthy accounting methods. Several more companies decided that they would also expense stock options after the announcements made by Coke and the *Washington Post*. Investors want to see more of these types of signals.

Stock Options and (Mis)Alignment. Despite the tremendous growth in the use of stock options as incentive compensation for executives, very little direct evidence exists that it works. That is, does awarding managers stock options cause the firm and its stock to perform better on average? Financial economists have studied this question for at least two decades. The evidence is mixed. One study identifies a positive relationship between executive stock incentives and firm performance. Another study takes into account other corporate monitoring mechanisms (like capital structure, board structure, and institutional owners) in a different way and finds no relation between stock-based incentives and firm performance.[6] In this way, the academic debate continues. Overall, there remains little direct evidence that a company can expect higher stock returns by introducing aggressive incentive-based compensation programs.

Stock options may not be as effective in aligning managerial incentives with shareholder goals as once thought. Following is a short list of improperly aligned incentives involving options:

1. Shareholder returns are a combination of both stock price appreciation and dividends. The stock option is only affected by price appreciation. Therefore, the CEO might forego increasing dividends in favor of using the cash to try to increase the stock price.

2. The stock price has a better chance of increasing when the CEO accepts risky projects. So, when a firm uses options to compensate the CEO, he or she has a tendency to pick a higher-risk business strategy.

3. Stock options lose some incentive for the CEO if the stock price falls too far below the strike price. In this case, the options would be too far underwater to effectively motivate the CEO and other executives.

4. Stock analysts and investors focus a great deal on a firm's accounting profits. The firm often has some ability to manipulate earnings (see Chapter 5). As a result, the CEO may have an incentive to manipulate earnings to maximize profits in one target year so that the stock price will be high for the option exercising. This manipulation can have the effect of reducing earnings (and consequently lowering the stock price) after the target year.

The very advantage that stock options use to align manager incentives with stockholder goals is also a major problem. Stock options are tied to a firm's stock price, and that helps align incentives. But executives only have partial influence on stock prices. Stock prices are affected by the performance of the company. However, many other factors that executives have no control over influence prices. Stock prices are mostly affected by the strength or weakness of the economy. Consider the graphs from the first chapter that relate the economy and the level of the stock market. When the economy thrives, stock prices rise. Stock prices can also rise and fall with the exuberance or pessimism of investors. The stock of a poorly run company may still rise. It would not rise as far as more successful competitors, but it can still go up. This may richly reward executives through their options when they do not deserve rewards. Alternatively, the stock market may fall because of poor economic conditions or investor pessimism. A company with managers who are able to outperform their competitors may still suffer from falling stock prices. Managers who should be rewarded for such good performance are not because their options become underwater when the overall market falls.

Options lose their effectiveness when the stock price falls far below the strike price. The stock price fall could be either related to a poor performance by the company or to a general stock market decline. To reestablish motivation for the executives, boards sometimes reprice the options. (Repricing is lowering the strike price on previously issued options.) Consider the incentives listed above and how they create interesting dynamics for CEO behavior. CEOs choose risky projects that have a chance of dramatically increasing the stock price. If the projects succeed, the CEO becomes rich and the stockholders experience increased wealth. However, if the projects fail, the stockholders lose wealth. After such a failure, the CEO simply asks the board to reprice the options and he or she can then repeat the strategy. Is this the type of strategy stockholders want the managers of a firm implementing? Proponents of option repricing claim that it is necessary in order to keep executives at the firm. This argument has some truth, but that doesn't change the skewed incentives it causes.

Consider the case of Kmart. Kmart's stock price started 1990 at $17 per share. In 1992, the stock climbed to more than $25 per share. However, the stock price steadily declined over the next three and a half years to nearly $7 per share. In March 1996, Kmart's board repriced the executives' stock options.[7] This seemed to have worked since the stock price slowly climbed to more than $15 per share. This was not to last. The firm's business strategy failed and it experienced financial difficulties. Its stock price deteriorated. The company filed for bankruptcy protection in 2002, and the stock price fell to less than $1 per share.

A similar move is to simply give the executives new options. In 2000, Apple Computer gave Steve Jobs 20 million options with a strike price of $43.59 as a reward for coming back to Apple and turning around the firm. However, one year later, the stock price had fallen substantially. So the board gave him 7.5 million more options with a strike price of $18.30.[8]

Who Gets Options? The executives of most firms receive options. However, in the past, stock options have been a form of compensation that smaller, newer firms use the most. Small, fast-growing firms typically have less access to cash and prefer to pay executives through options, which does not require the firm to give up any cash. Indeed, in the 1990s, the era of the technology and dot-com firms, young companies offered nearly every employee stock or stock options as compensation. The stock market drop starting in 2000 hurt Silicon Valley, whose firms use stock options as an essential part of employee compensation. Many large companies use options to motivate and compensate employees. For example, 24,000 employees (out of 57,000) have stock options at Qwest Communications International. But for most companies, it is the executives of the firm—especially the CEO—who receive stock options.

Some executives should not need stock options to motivate them. Larry Ellison, CEO and founder of Oracle, owns 1.4

billion shares of stock, which represents 24 percent of the company.[9] At $10 per share, that is $14 billion of wealth. Therefore, if the stock rises only 10 percent, he receives $1.4 billion in increased wealth. If the stock price falls 10 percent, he loses $1.4 billion. Shouldn't the potential to make such gains be incentive enough to work hard for the company? Why does he need options to purchase another 104 million shares to motivate him? Other super-rich executives who possess material ownership in their firm, such as Ross Perot, Bill Gates, and Warren Buffet, do not accept options.

CEO PAY AROUND THE WORLD

Paying the top officer in a company with long-term incentive awards is most common in the United States. Figure 3–1 (with data from surveys conducted by Towers Perrin[10]) shows the total compensation of CEOs in the United States for 2000 and 2001 as well as CEO compensation in 17 foreign firms in 2001. The figure shows estimates of average CEO pay in firms with at least $500 million in sales. CEO compensation is reported as incentive awards versus base and bonus pay.

Several things are worth noting from the figure. First, both the base pay and incentive awards for U.S. companies grew substantially between 2000 and 2001. Total compensation for U.S. CEOs grew 38 percent—from $1.4 million to $1.9 million. Both base salary and incentive awards grew. Base salaries in the United States have been growing quickly.

The second item to note is that total compensation for U.S. CEOs is much higher than for the CEOs of foreign firms. After the United States, the next highest total compensation figures for CEOs in 2001 were in Argentina and Mexico, which averaged $879,000 and $866,000 respectively. Note that this is less than half of the U.S. CEO compensation. Other notable countries shown are Canada ($787,000), Hong Kong ($736,500), Germany ($455,000), Japan ($508,000), Spain ($430,000), and the United Kingdom ($668,500). Lastly, note that the United States appears to use incentive awards, like stock options, as compensation

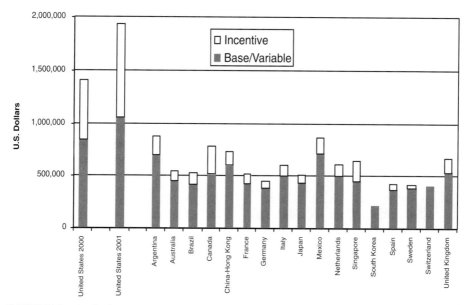

FIGURE 3–1   Levels of 2001 CEO compensation around the world. Compensation is categorized as incentive awards, and base and variable salary.

much more than in other countries. In 2001, 45 percent of total compensation came in the form of incentive awards in the United States. The country with the next highest proportion of incentive pay to total pay is Canada (30 percent). South Korea and Switzerland use no material amounts of incentive awards.

Using stock options can be a powerful way to align the interests of the managers and the shareholders. But is it an effective way? Consider the compensation of Disney CEO Michael Eisner and the value he created at the company. He was given millions of stock options, so if he could add substantial value to Disney, he could cash in for incredible wealth. Consider what he did in the five years starting in 1992. By 1997, Disney was earning three times the profits of 1992. Eisner had added more than $13 billion in value to the firm. The stock price more than doubled from $14.33 to $33.00.[11] Disney's stockholders benefited greatly from this value creation—so did Michael Eisner! His annual salary in 1997 was $750,000. He received a $9.9 million bonus. He also cashed in $565 million in stock options, for a total compensation of $575.7 million.[12]

Unfortunately for Disney shareholders, the story doesn't end there. Over the next four years after 1997, Disney's profits struggled and the stock price suffered. In 2001, Disney lost $158 million, and the stock price ended the year at only $20.72. Eisner received his $1 million salary, but he received no bonuses and did not exercise stock options.[13] Eisner's pay, and that of the other Disney managers, has been closely tied to the performance of Disney's profits and stock price. These executives received much lower pay when Disney declined. However, the shareholders lost more than half of the value that was created between 1992 and 1997. Yet Eisner got to keep the incredible income he received for generating that wealth, even though much of it disappeared. Most of that wealth came from Disney stock options.

This also brings up another question about motivating managers with performance-based compensation. After managers have exercised options and become rich, how much incentive will more options provide? If a CEO's net worth is a couple of million dollars, options that could earn tens or hundreds of millions of dollars are a strong motivator. But if a CEO has a net worth of hundreds of millions of dollars, how much motivation are those options? At some point, people enjoy taking the time to spend their wealth.

HIDDEN COMPENSATION

The stock market has been the engine that has driven executive compensation upward. However, as the stock market stumbles, executives find that their stock options become underwater. They can no longer rely on them for cashing in and experiencing big paydays. You may have heard or read news reports about "off-balance sheet" transactions that have ultimately sunk some companies. Be aware of "non-publicly disclosed" compensation. Executives are stepping up hidden compensation sources to make up some of the lost income. And forget the old-style club membership dues. That is passé compared to modern perks. After being paid millions, executives apparently need the company for which they work to pay for financial advisors, luxury cars and chauffeurs, reimbursement for personal travel, access to Manhattan apartments, and more.

One method of creating stealth-wealth is through compensation agreements after the executive has left the firm. For example, when Terrence Murray, former CEO and current chairman of FleetBoston, retires, he will receive a pension payment of $5.8 million per year. In addition, he gets to use corporate jets (for him and his guests) to travel up to 150 hours per year.[14] Louis Gerstner retired as CEO of IBM (though he continued for a while as chairman) in March 2002. In addition to his $2 million per year pension, he has access to corporate planes, cars, and apartments for 20 years. If IBM wants a little advice from him, it has to pay him $600 per hour.[15] Another way to leave a firm is when another firm acquires yours. Richard Korpan was the CEO of Florida Progress Corp. until Carolina Power & Light purchased it. His severance from the firm was a lump sum of $15.8 million plus $69,070 per month.[16]

Probably the most publicly known CEO pension is that of the former head of General Electric, Jack Welch. The divorce filings of his estranged wife, Jane, have enabled the media to gain access to his retirement perks. He receives a $9 million per year pension. Apparently, that is not enough to live on. Welch also had GE pay for his Manhattan apartment, groceries, flowers, and even dinners at one of Manhattan's finest restaurants. He, and GE's board, received severe criticism when this news became known. Welch decided that it was best for GE shareholders if he no longer received the extra perks.[17] He'll have to tighten his belt and only live on the $9 million he receives each year as a pension.

Another source of perks for executives is obtaining a loan from the company they work for. It is common for executives to borrow hundreds of thousands, or even millions, of dollars at extremely low interest rates—sometimes even interest-free. These loans may be used to purchase expensive homes or luxury items. Wells Fargo CEO Richard Kovacevich borrowed $1 million for a down payment on a house. The savings on low-interest loans can quickly add up to tens or hundreds of thousands of dollars. But the real wealth kicker is that executives frequently do not pay back the loans! Mattel Corp. absolved ousted CEO Jill Barad from repaying a $7.2 million loan and then paid her an additional $3.3 million to cover the cost of the additional taxes that would be incurred.[18] The new CEO, Robert Eckert, received a $5.5 million loan and will not have to repay it if he stays with the firm for two years. A similar arrangement exists with Compaq and its CEO Michael Capellas for his $5 million loan. But these loans are chump-change compared to the $343 million borrowed by WorldCom CEO Bernard Ebbers. Ebbers pays an interest rate of only 2.15 percent per year.

These extra perks and arrangements between CEOs and firms are not illegal. Indeed, the board of directors freely gave them to the executives. In such cases, the board members have simply failed to guard the shareholder assets. The structure and the incentives of board members are discussed in Chapter 6.

SUMMARY

U.S. executive pay is the highest in world. Part of this compensation comes from basic cash salaries and bonuses. While the bonus system can be abused, it is the incentive programs that create real problems. The main security used in the incentive program is the stock option. Stocks and options are used to try to align manager goals with shareholder goals. This is necessary because while the stockholders own the firm, the managers control it. This separation of ownership and control creates opportunities for managers to act in their own interest. Managers, academics, and boards of directors have argued that stock and option incentives reduce this conflict. We demonstrate that stock options also create other incentives that are not aligned with stockholder interests. Indeed, stock options may not even be an effective means of inducing better company performance.

ENDNOTES

1. Thomas McCarroll, "The Shareholders Strike Back: Executive Pay," *Time*, May 5, 1992, pp. 46–49.

2. Much of the compensation description in this section is summarized from Kevin Murphy, "Executive Compensation," in *Handbook of Labor Economics*, vol. 3B, Orley Ashenfelter and David Card, eds. (Amsterdam: North-Holland, 1999).

3. John Byrne, "Restoring Trust in Corporate America," *BusinessWeek*, June 24, 2002, pp. 31–35.

4. John Byrne, "No Excuses for Enron's Board," *Business-Week*, July 29, 2002, pp. 50–51.

5. "Curing What Ails the Market," editorial, *San Francisco Chronicle*, July 21, 2002, p. E4.

6. Hamid Mehran, "Executive Compensation Structure, Ownership, and Firm Performance," *Journal of Financial Economics* 38 (1995): 163–184; Charles Himmelberg, Glenn Hubbard, and Darius Palia, "Understanding the Determinants of Managerial Ownership and the Link Between Ownership and Performance," *Journal of Financial Economics* 53 (1999): 353–384.

7. Kris Maher, "The Price of Doing Poorly," *Wall Street Journal*, April 12, 2001, p. R7.

8. "Apple Gives Jobs New Set of Stock Options," *Houston Chronicle*, March 22, 2002, p. 10.

9. Carol Emert, "Ellison Cashes In Stocks for $895 Million," *San Francisco Chronicle*, February 14, 2001, p. C1.

10. "2000 Worldwide Total Remuneration" and "Worldwide Total Remuneration 2001–2002," studies by Towers Perrin, *www.towers.com/towers_publications/publications.*

11. These are split-adjusted stock-price figures.

12. Tim Smart, "An Eye-Popping Year for Executive Pay," *Washington Post*, March 22, 1998, p. H1.

13. Richard Verrier, "Eisner's Paycheck Humbled in 2001," *Los Angeles Times*, January 5, 2002, p. C1.

14. Joann Lublin, "As CEOs' Reported Salaries and Bonuses Get Pinched, Many Chiefs are Finding Hidden Ways to Increase Their Compensation," *Wall Street Journal*, April 11, 2002, p. B7.

15. Joann Lublin, "How CEOs Retire in Style," *Wall Street Journal*, September 13, 2002, p. B1.

16. Ellen Schultz, "Big Send-Off: As Firms Pare Pensions for Most, They Boost Those for Executives," *Wall Street Journal*, June 20, 2001, p. A1.

17. Matt Murray, "SEC Investigates GE's Retirement Deal with Jack Welch," *Wall Street Journal*, September 17, 2002, p. B1; Deepa Babington, "Welch Renounces Generous Retirement Perks," *Reuters*, September 16, 2002, 5:15 p.m.

18. Gary Strauss, "Many Execs Pocket Perks Aplenty," *USA Today*, May 1, 2001, p. B1.

4 EXECUTIVE BEHAVIOR

In some cases, company leaders have let us down by committing acts of fraud and deception. For example, Tyco CEO Dennis Kozlowski is accused of using company locations to drop
ship personal purchases in order to avoid paying $1 million in
state sales tax. Former ImClone Systems CEO Samuel Waksal
was indicted by federal prosecutors for using inside information about the firm to tip off relatives about upcoming problems in time for them to sell their stock. Family members sold
$10 million in stock just before it became public that the Food
and Drug Administration (FDA) had rejected the firm's primary product. Martha Stewart has also been caught up in the
ImClone scandal because she sold ImClone stock just before
the announcement (Stewart and Waksal shared the same
stockbroker). In other cases, executive behavior has just been
suspicious and even disappointing, but not necessarily illegal.

Corporate executives are greedy—but then, so are most
people. Most people in a capitalistic economy are partially
motivated by greed. It is not greed itself that is a problem; the
problem is how greed motivates some people. Greed may
motivate a person to work hard and create long-term economic value in a firm by expanding into new products or new
locations. These activities create wealth, jobs, taxes, and help
our society. On the other hand, greed may push a person to
take advantage of shareholders, the capital markets, and the

government. Consider modern television shows. A person can become rich on either *Who Wants to Be a Millionaire?* or *Survivor.* The participants in both games are greedy. However, a person can become rich on one show by using his or her knowledge and talents, and a person can become rich on the other by scheming, lying, and being cut-throat. Which kind of greed is exhibited by many corporate leaders? Which kind does society want them to exhibit?

OPTIONS AND FRAUD

While cases like that of Eisner and Disney in the previous chapter may anger shareholders, we must understand that these events are not fraudulent. Boards of directors freely give executives the stock options and, therefore, create the possibility that only short-term value will be created instead of long-term value. However, in other cases, it appears that managers may purposely mislead the public in order to fraudulently enrich themselves. Consider the management actions at Xerox Corporation.

In a civil action by the SEC against Xerox, the SEC claimed that senior management directed a scheme that improperly accelerated revenue from its leasing operations from 1997 to 2000. The accounting maneuvering increased revenue by $3 billion and profits by $1.5 billion over the period. In subsequent financial restatements, Xerox shifted $6.4 billion of revenue in the period. The accounting actions violated generally accepted accounting practices and were not disclosed to shareholders or regulators. The scheme was perpetrated to help Xerox meet ever-increasing internal and analyst earnings expectations. It became common for Xerox executives to assign numerical goals to be produced through accounting gimmickry.[1] Indeed, the CFO/vice chairman of Xerox and the president of Xerox Europe conveyed that excluding accounting actions, the firm had essentially no growth in the 1990s.[2]

The artificial profits helped drive the stock price from a split-adjusted $13 at the end of 1996 to more than $60 in 1999. During this time of inflated stock prices, Xerox CEO Paul Allaire sold stock and profited by $16 million. Xerox executives, in total, sold $79 million worth of stock between 1997 and 1999. Of the total, $48 million was from exercising stock options, and the other $31 million was from stock sales. Figure 4–1 shows the relationship among the fraudulent reporting, the stock price, and the executive sales. In April 2002, Xerox admitted to the SEC that it had improperly recorded the earnings and agreed to pay a $10 million fine. Of course, this fine is paid by the firm, and it is thus a cost to the stockholders who end up getting victimized again.[3] The stock price fell to less than $10 per share, approximately the price ten years earlier. While the firm has lost any value created in the 1990s, the managers received millions of dollars. The SEC has expressed its intent to prosecute those managers.

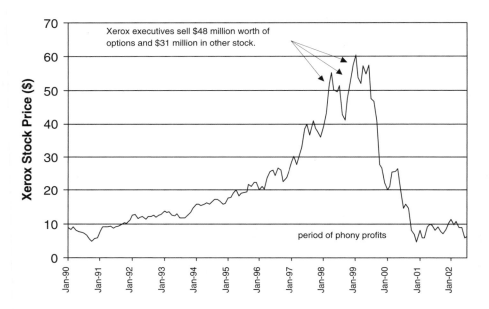

FIGURE 4–1   Xerox stock price from January 1990 to July 2002.

Many cases like this one have occurred recently (Enron, WorldCom, Guess, Global Crossing, Sun Microsystems, Rite Aid, and Tyco, to name a few). These cases suggest that executive options and other stock incentives may not be as effective as previously thought in aligning manager and shareholder incentives.

TIMING OF SALES

Many insiders of a firm own stock in the firm. In some cases, like Microsoft's Bill Gates and Oracle's Larry Ellison, insiders participated in founding the company and own substantial amounts of the firm's stock.

Insiders have material information about the firm that the public does not. Therefore, the SEC regulates trading by these insiders so that they do not take advantage of public investors with this inside information. Insiders are allowed to buy and sell their firm's stock, but they need to convince the regulators that the trades were driven by motives other than profiting from inside knowledge. Common motives for selling are to generate money for consumption or to diversify wealth. However, even with noble motives, the timing of stock sales may look suspicious to investors. This is particularly important now because investor perceptions have an especially strong impact on their confidence.

Consider the stock sales of Bill Gates, co-founder of Microsoft. Gates sells hundreds of millions of dollars of Microsoft stock every quarter. This is actually just a drop in the bucket for Gates, given that he owns tens of billions of dollars in Microsoft stock. No one questions the timing of his stock sales because he sells every quarter—nearly every month—and has been doing so for many years. Gates is dollar-cost averaging his sales over many years—even decades.

On the other hand, Bill Gates' nemesis, Larry Ellison of Oracle, has taken some heat for the timing of his sales. Like Gates, Ellison owns tens of billions of dollars of stock in his company, but Ellison has only sold stock once in recent years. During a week in January 2001, Ellison sold $900 million worth of stock. He had not sold any material amounts of stock for five years before this sale, and he has not sold any stock since. A couple of events have made this sale look suspicious to investors. First, in late 2000, Ellison mocked Microsoft for lowering its earning forecast and blaming the slowdown in the economy. Ellison said that it must be Microsoft products and not the economy because Oracle wasn't seeing any slowdown.[4] These comments helped increase Oracle stock when Microsoft's was falling.

A month later, Ellison made his stock sale. A month after that, Oracle warned that it would not meet earnings forecasts.[5] Figure 4–2 shows Oracle's stock price in relation to these events. When an insider sells substantial amounts of stock over a short period, such as one week, then he or she risks appearing to be trading on inside information. Certainly in Ellison's case, investors have a reason to be suspicious.

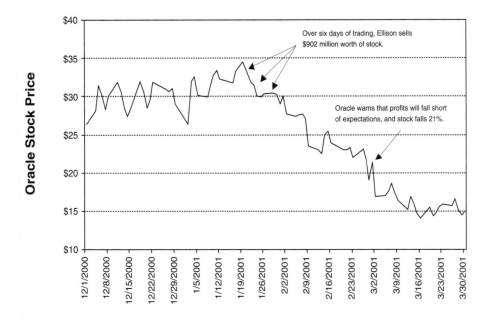

FIGURE 4–2   Oracle stock price in relation to Larry Ellison's selling and earnings warning.

Financial economists have investigated executive stock option exercises and found some evidence of timing. Specifically, Jennifer Carpenter and Barbara Remmers of New York University examined nearly all executive option exercises between 1992 and 1995.[6] They show that the stock price of firms in which managers are exercising options had been steadily increasing. Indeed, during the 12 months before the option exercise, the stock outperformed the market by nearly 20 percent. The stock outperformed the market by 75 percent during the previous 10 years. During the year immediately after the option exercises, the stock stopped outperforming. It didn't collapse, but it just stopped performing better than the general stock market. The study did not examine the stock prices more than one year after option exercise. Managers seem to have some timing ability.

This study ended in 1995. Since then, it appears that some executives have pushed accounting methods and have even lied in order to keep profits climbing when the economy started waning. In many cases, executives have cashed in stock or options when the stock price was high and then restated earnings a few years later. These actions and events make it appear that executives are taking advantage of shareholders with their inside information.

Consider Bristol-Myers Squibb, one of the world's largest pharmaceuticals firms. The SEC is investigating whether the company inflated its revenues by $1 billion in 2001.[7] This was also the year that its CEO, Charles Heimbold, cashed in more than $70 million in stock options. The aggressive accounting used by Bristol may turn out to be perfectly legal, but the timing of the large option sale looks suspicious. In September 2001, Heimbold retired from Bristol and immediately became the U.S. ambassador to Sweden.[8]

Also consider the predicament of the U.S. President. In 1986, George W. Bush sold his failed oil drilling company to Harken Energy Corp. After the sale, Bush owned more than 200,000 shares of Harken stock and was appointed to its board of directors. By 1990, Bush was part owner of the Texas Rangers baseball team and wanted to pay off the $500,000 he had borrowed to purchase his ownership stake. On June 22, 1990, Bush sold 212,140 shares of stock at around $4.00 per share for a total of $848,560.[9] What is suspicious about this event is that Harken announced huge losses for the quarter ending June 30 and the stock price plunged. Over the ensuing six months, the stock price slowly declined to around $1.60 per share, for a loss of 60 percent.

The timing of Bush's sale is suspicious because, as a board member and consultant to the firm, he likely had inside information about the performance of the firm.[10] Did he really desire to pay off his loan at that time? If so, the subsequent stock price plunge was just a coincidence. Or, did he know it was time to sell the stock and just used his loan as an excuse? Records show that the SEC looked into the matter and concluded, "Based upon our investigation, it appears that Bush did not engage in illegal insider trading because it did not appear that he possessed material nonpublic information."[11] Whether Bush sold out because he knew of the upcoming problems or whether he just wanted to pay back his loan, we may never know for certain. However, from the stockholders' perspective, it looks bad. A board of directors member liquidating nearly all of his stock before the stock price plunges shows—at the very least—that he was not looking out for the shareholders. Boards of directors are supposed to be looking out for the shareholders' interests, not their own.

Or consider the lawsuit filed against Martha Stewart and her associates at her company, Martha Stewart Living Omnimedia (MSLO). The suit was filed on behalf of investors who bought stock in early 2002 and claimed that MSLO insiders sold tens of millions of dollars in stock after realizing that the ImClone insider trading scandal could significantly affect the price of the MSLO stock.[12] Insiders to a public company are not allowed to sell stock based on important information that has not yet been made public. The suit alleges that the SEC made inquiries about the ImClone trades in early January 2002, around the time Stewart sold 3 million shares of stock for $45 million. Other insiders sold shares in March 2002. The link between Martha Stewart and ImClone insider trades were publicized in June 2002. Again, when insiders sell around the time of trouble for a firm, it looks suspicious. Martha Stewart didn't exactly sell out—the 3 million shares represent less than 10 percent of her ownership in MSLO.

The suit names other MSLO insiders as defendants, such as President and Chief Operating Officer Sharon Patrick. Patrick sold 150,000 shares (for $2.8 million) in March 2002. This lawsuit will not be resolved by the time this book goes to print, but Patrick will probably be able to show that her sales were not motivated by inside information because she has frequently sold shares. In December 2000, she sold 120,080 shares, and in 2001, she sold 356,400 shares in November, 93,600 shares in August, and 120,000 shares in June. Therefore, Patrick can claim that the $15 million in stock she sold was spread out over one and a half years. This looks much less suspicious than a large, one-time sale.

Whether selling stock options or restricted stock, the timing of many executive sales has been suspicious. Global Crossing Chairman Gary Winnick sold $735 million in shares from 1999 to 2001—the firm is now bankrupt. Another $500 million in shares was sold by other Global Crossing executives. At bankrupt Enron, Chairman Kenneth Lay cashed in for more than $100 million. At troubled Tyco, the CEO and CFO sold $500 million in stock back to the company. Galesi Francesco of WorldCom sold more than $25 million worth of stock six months before the firm filed for bankruptcy. The list goes on.

COMPANY LOANS—A POTENTIAL ABUSE

One area of recent abuse by executives is borrowing money from the company they work for. Not all borrowing is bad. When recruiting a new executive who needs to relocate, a company may offer that person a loan to purchase a new house. The company may offer to lend several hundred thousand or even a million dollars as a mortgage. After all, a relocating executive must sell one house and buy another. The loan makes this process easier and quicker. This is a perk that most new employees don't get, but it is a relatively harmless one.

The problem occurs when executives start borrowing much larger sums of money for other purchases. Consider the predicament Bernard Ebbers, former CEO of WorldCom, found himself in. In the late 1990s, Ebbers borrowed $61.5 million from WorldCom to buy WorldCom stock for himself. He also borrowed another $100 million that WorldCom guaranteed in order to buy more stock.[13] WorldCom stock sold in the $40 and $50 range in the late 1990s, so, to illustrate the problem, let's say that Ebbers bought $160 million of stock at $40 per share. By late 2000, the stock was trading at only $20 per share. Ebbers owned stock worth $80 million, but owed $160 million in loans. He was down $80 million. That kind of personal trouble can cause someone to do things he or she would not ordinarily do. In total, Ebbers borrowed more than $400 million from WorldCom, and much of this was to purchase WorldCom stock.

As the economy started slowing in 2000 and 2001, WorldCom's business also slowed. The stock price also slowly declined to $15 per share. As the stock price fell further, Ebbers' personal financial problems deepened. He became desperate. The following events appear suspicious. On April 29, 2002, Ebbers resigned from WorldCom, and the stock price was just $2.50. Two months later, WorldCom announced that it had inflated earnings over the past five quarters by nearly $4 billion. The Justice Department and SEC are investigating.

As another example, consider how Enron CEO Kenneth Lay abused a loan arrangement with Enron. The Enron board approved a credit line of $7.5 million for Lay. In the twelve months before the Enron scandal broke, Lay repeatedly drew out $7.5 million in cash from the credit line and immediately paid off the loans using some of his Enron stock. In this way, he was able to sell $77 million in stock back to Enron without having to report the stock sales for more than a year.[14] By then, the stock price had plummeted and the firm was in bankruptcy court. All the while he was secretly selling stock, he was publicly encouraging Enron employees to buy stock. This particular scheme could not have succeeded without the company line of credit and an agreement that the loans could be repaid with stock.

But even the home loan can be abused. Tyco's former CEO, Dennis Kozlowski, received a zero-interest loan of $19 million from Tyco to purchase a new home in Boca Raton, Florida, in 1998. Two years later, the firm forgave the loan as a "special bonus." Tyco also kicked in another $13 million to help Kozlowski pay the taxes on the bonus. Neither the loan forgiveness nor the cash were disclosed to shareholders as executive compensation.

Allowing executives to borrow substantial amounts from the company they run creates an environment in which the executives are tempted to break the trust between themselves and shareholders. Not all executives would break this trust. But high levels of debt and personal financial problems can cause desperation.

GRAND THEFT

Some of these examples are suspicious, and they are disappointing to shareholders, but other instances are just plain criminal. One of the biggest examples of corporate grand theft may be the plunder of the TV cable company Adelphia Communications Corp.

ADELPHIA

John Rigas and his brother Gus founded Adelphia in 1952 (*adelphia* is the Greek word for brothers). John bought out Gus in 1982, and by the mid-1980s, John Rigas was running the firm with his three sons, Michael, Tim, and James. The firm had some trouble competing with larger competitors in the cable market, like Comcast and AT&T, in the late 1990s. So Adelphia embarked in an ambitious acquisition program that effectively doubled the company by 2001. The larger Adelphia had reached 5 million customers, but it paid a high price to get there. The firm had gone from a debt of $3.5 billion to $12.6 billion. The interest payments on the loans quickly started to deplete Adelphia's cash. Credit-rating agencies and analysts pushed Adelphia to reduce this crushing debt load.

It now appears that the Rigas family was stealing from the firm and hiding even more debt. All the while, they were claiming to be helping the firm clean up its financial status. On Wednesday, July 24, 2002, company founder and former CEO John Rigas and two of his sons—former CFO Tim Rigas and former director of internal reporting Michael Rigas— were arrested for perpetrating massive financial fraud and looting the firm.[15] Investigations by the U.S. Justice Department, the SEC, and U.S. Postal Inspectors claim that the Rigas family was involved in rampant self-dealing in using the public company's money and assets. They are also accused of falsifying transactions and accounting reports to hide their misdeeds and the true financial condition of the firm.

The SEC accused the Rigas family of falsifying the public accounting records in many ways. For example, even though Adelphia significantly increased its debt in acquiring smaller, local cable firms, it really had even more debt that was hidden. The family had borrowed $2.3 billion in personal loans in which Adelphia guaranteed. Thus, these loans were a liability for Adelphia, but they were not approved by the board or disclosed to shareholders. The information was finally disclosed in March 2002 as a footnote in the firm's accounting statement. The complaint also alleges that the Rigases would create fictitious transactions between Adelphia and private firms they owned to boost earnings of the public company in order to meet both its own profit forecasts and those of Wall Street.[16] Some of these phony transactions were even backdated so as to occur in the targeted fiscal quarter.

Publicly, the Rigas family was trying to calm investor concerns by explaining how they were buying stock from Adelphia so that the firm could use the cash to lower its level of debt. Privately, the $400 million used to buy stock was actually borrowed from Adelphia. This was not disclosed and would, in fact, increase Adelphia's debt, not reduce it. Tim

Rigas had Adelphia create sham receipts showing payment by the family for the stock to hide the truth.

In addition to the falsified accounting and reporting, the Rigases are accused of using Adelphia as their own "personal piggy bank." In a case like this one, you expect to see abuses such as cars, jets, and vacation homes bought with company assets. These abuses appear to have occurred here, too, but the fraud went much further. For example, while Adelphia reported that John Rigas' compensation was $1.9 million per year, he withdrew much more than this. In fact, his son, Tim, had to step in and limit his father's withdrawals of cash to only $1 million per month. For the year, John Rigas transferred $12 million from Adelphia into his personal bank account. Getting access to Adelphia's cash was easy because the Rigases co-mingled the money from their other businesses with Adelphia's money into one central account.[17] The Rigas family also used their other businesses to extract wealth from Adelphia. For example, John Rigas owned a car dealership that leased cars to Adelphia. His wife, Doris, owned a decorating shop that sold furniture and design services to the company. Adelphia also bought hundreds of tickets every year to the Rigases' hockey team, the Buffalo Sabres. Then, there is the golf course that Tim Rigas was building on 169 acres of land owned by Adelphia. He used $13 million of Adelphia's money for building it. The course remains only partially completed—needing another $40 million to finish it. The board did not approve the project, and it was not disclosed to shareholders.

Apparently, the Rigases also borrowed money from their brokerage firm by using their stock in Adelphia as collateral. However, as these scandals started coming to light in the spring of 2002, Adelphia's stock price plummeted. The problems forced the outsiders on the firm's board to take over the company. The Rigas family members resigned, but not before they diverted $252 million from corporate accounts to their broker to cover 65 separate margin calls associated with the falling stock price. On June 25, 2002, Adelphia was forced to file for chapter 11 bankruptcy. The very public arrest of the three Rigas family members would occur one month later.

ENRON

There are many ways that the executives at Enron bilked shareholders. While we describe many specific abuses throughout this book, we focus this section on how Enron CFO Andrew Fastow and his chief lieutenant Michael Kopper used offshore partnerships to enrich themselves. Enron used these partnerships to hide billions of dollars in debt and generate phony profits. In later chapters we describe how these partnerships were created and used for accounting fraud.

Fastow and Kopper set up many of the partnerships in such a way that one or the other of them was the general partner. As executives of Enron, they would negotiate deals and transactions with the partnership on behalf of Enron's interests. They negotiated with attorneys they had also hired to represent the partnerships. Obviously, that is an extreme conflict of interest. As Enron representatives, they "gave away the farm," in that the deals were very sweet for the partnerships. The deals paid the general partners millions of dollars in fees for structuring the deals. Of course, Fastow and Kopper were the general partners. Using these schemes, they were able to siphon tens of millions of dollars of Enron's money to themselves.[18] Kopper pleaded guilty to money laundering and fraud charges in August 2002 and agreed to forfeit $12 million in restitution. To minimize his sentence, Kopper cooperated with federal prosecutors in their attempt to bring charges against higher-level Enron executives.

TYCO

It also appears that Dennis Kozlowski used his position as CEO of Tyco to extract wealth from its shareholders. Kozlowski's condo in New York cost Tyco $18 million in 2000 and another $11 million to furnish it. The *Wall Street Journal* estimated that Kozlowski enriched himself with $135 million in Tyco money that was spent on real estate, charitable donations, personal expenses, and loan forgiveness.[19] Just the loan forgiveness amounts to $75 million. Indeed, the tax evasion charges that we mentioned at the beginning of this chapter are for the purchase of $13 million of art that Tyco partially paid for. Investigations by the SEC, Manhattan prosecutors, and Tyco itself accuse Kozlowski of working with CFO Mark Swartz and Tyco's former general counsel Mark Belnick to loot the firm of more than $600 million.[20] One of Kozlowski's schemes was to take money from the company's employee loan program and then forgive the loan. He took $270 million from this program and bought himself yachts, art, jewelry, and vacation estates. He also billed Tyco for extravagant personal expenses such as a $17,100 traveling toilette box, a $445 pin cushion, and a $15,000 umbrella in the shape of a dog. Prosecutors have indicted the three former executives. Tyco is also suing Kozlowski in an attempt to recover some of the money.

WHY DO SOME EXECUTIVES MISBEHAVE?

We do not want to give the impression that all corporate executives are untrustworthy, greedy scoundrels. Quite the contrary, we believe the great majority to be highly educated, intelligent, hardworking, ethical people. Indeed, many of the executives who have committed crimes probably started their business careers on a more ethical footing than they are finishing them. That is, people don't say, "I want to steal millions of dollars, so I think I will become a business executive!" Somewhere along the way, some of these people become thieves. How does this happen?

An ethical and moral person usually does not become unethical and immoral overnight. It is usually a slow and gradual process. The big theft often begins with a small one. For example, a manager may get a reimbursement for an airline ticket that was cancelled. He or she may decide to keep the cash as compensation for the hassle the cancelled trip caused. Or, consider managers who use a corporate plane to fly their family to a vacation spot. They may intend to reimburse the company, but they never quite get around to it. After a while, they notice that no one seems to care. Next time, they not only use the plane but also the company's apartment in Manhattan.

We've picked airline examples because it is a real temptation. The temptation was too much for a former manager at the investment bank Lehman Brothers. Douglas Spainer was fired in July 2001 for submitting 12 bogus flight invoices between November 2000 and May 2001.[21] The fraudulent behavior cost the firm $371,000, though Spainer is repaying the money.

It doesn't take long before someone convinces himself or herself that he or she deserves the extra perks. One small indiscretion leads to another—sometimes bigger—one. This is why monitors of executives need to be diligent in watching the little things as well as the big things. If a manager is reprimanded for a small indiscretion, he or she probably will never make a big one.

People have a way of rationalizing to themselves that what they are doing is not that bad. So, for example, a manager might think, "Other people are doing it" or "I work hard and deserve it" or "I have earned this firm a lot of money, I should get some of it." The celebrity-type status that many CEOs attained during the 1990s certainly didn't help their attitudes. When everyone is treating a CEO like royalty, he or she might start acting like it. Even though most executives held fast to their ethical footing, we desire an incentive system and monitoring mechanisms that are able to catch the few scoundrels before they can wreck too much havoc.

SUMMARY

The behavior of many corporate executives has been atrocious. While criminal activity is disappointing, we believe those committing crimes will be punished. We are disappointed that the monitoring mechanisms put in place failed to deter and even detect the misdeeds. What were the boards of directors doing? How did the auditors and analysts miss the problems? How were the bankers involved? We explore these questions in the chapters of the next section, Part 2, "The Failure of Monitoring Systems."

Other behavior can only be classified as suspicious. We suspect that those who have acted suspiciously will not be held accountable. There may never be enough evidence to prove criminal actions. There is also simply too much ambiguity in the policies dealing with insiders. In addition to strengthening monitoring mechanisms, there clearly needs to be some better policies and rules that apply to corporate insiders to prevent activities that appear to be suspicious. We offer ideas in Chapter 13.

ENDNOTES

1. James Bandler and Mark Maremont, "Seeing Red: How Ex-Accountant Added Up to Trouble for Humbled Xerox," *Wall Street Journal*, June 28, 2001, p. A1.

2. Civil Action No. 02-272789, *SEC vs. Xerox Corporation,* Southern District of New York, United States District Court, April 11, 2002.

3. Andrew Countryman, "Focus of Xerox Probe Shifts to Stock Sales," *Chicago Tribune*, July 2, 2002, p. 1.

4. David Leonhardt, "Tell the Good News: Then Cash In," *New York Times*, April 7, 2002, p. C1; Carol Emert, "Ellison Cashes In Stocks for $895 Million," *San Francisco Chronicle*, February 14, 2002, p. C1.

5. David Leonhardt, "Oracle Says Earnings Won't Meet Forecasts," *New York Times*, March 2, 2002, p. C5.

6. Jennifer Carpenter and Barbara Remmers, "Executive Stock Option Exercises and Inside Information," *Journal of Business* 74, no. 4 (2001): 513–534.

7. Ransdell Pierson, "Bristol-Myers Under SEC Probe for Sales," *Reuters Business Report*, July 11, 2002, 6:04 p.m. EST.

8. "Bristol Has New Chairman," *New York Times*, September 14, 2001, p. C2.

9. Mike Allen and George Lardner, Jr., "Harken Papers Offer Details on Bush Knowledge; Motive for Stock Sale in '90 Remains Unclear," *Washington Post*, July 14, 2002, p. A1.

10. Mike Allen, "Bush Uncooperative at First in '90 Probe, SEC Memo Suggests," *Washington Post*, July 12, 2002, p. A7.

11. Ibid.

12. Tom Hamburger and Jerry Markon, "Martha Stewart Faces New Suit Alleging She Sold Before News," *Wall Street Journal*, August 22, 2002, p. A6.

13. Bruce Meyerson, "Ebbers' Woes Mounted with World-Com," *Associated Press*, July 26, 2002, 2:24 p.m. EST.

14. John Byrne, "No Excuses for Enron's Board," *Business-Week*, July 29, 2002, pp. 50–51.

15. Devlin Barrett, "3 Former Adelphia Execs Arrested," *Associated Press*, July 24, 2002, 11:08 a.m. EST.

16. Jerry Markon and Robert Frank, "Five Adelphia Officials Arrested on Fraud Charges," *Wall Street Journal*, July 25, 2002, p. A3.

17. Sallie Hofmeister, "Low View of Adelphia's High Life," *Los Angeles Times*, July 26, 2002, p. A1.

18. Kathryn Kranhald and Alexei Barrionuevo, "Enron's Fastow Took Kopper Under His Wing," *Wall Street Journal*, August 23, 2002, p. C1.

19. Mark Maremont and Laurie Cohen, "How Tyco's CEO Enriched Himself," *Wall Street Journal*, August 7, 2002, p. A1.

20. Jeanne King and Tim McLaughlin, "3 Former Tyco Execs Charged with Fraud," *Reuters Business Report*, September 12, 2002, 2:10 p.m. EST.

21. "NYSE: Bogus Flights for Ex-Lehman Manager," *Reuters Business Report*, August 28, 2002, 3:48 p.m. EST.

2 THE FAILURE OF MONITORING SYSTEMS

5 Accountants and Auditors

Accountants and auditors are an important part of the monitoring system. We rely on them to provide us with an accurate picture of a firm's business activities. However, to be effective monitors, they have to be credible. Unfortunately, public opinion of the accounting profession is at an all-time low. It's no wonder that Arthur Andersen's shredding important Enron documents was front-page news. Its eventual conviction on obstructing justice charges brings the "Big 5" accounting firms down to only four. Since then, news of one accounting scandal after another has dominated the media.

In response, the government has proposed many solutions for bringing ethics to the profession and trust back to investors. The proposals are full of new laws and regulating authorities. In looking at these possible solutions (which we do in Chapter 12), we find that they seem to be targeted at specific, perceived problems in the industry or at individual accountants. However, we feel that the accounting profession is a system of interlinked monitors, advisors, and evaluators. Designing solutions to fix any problems in the industry can only be effectively accomplished through the full understanding of this system.

ACCOUNTING FUNCTIONS

Historically, accounting has been the function of gathering, compiling, reporting, and storing a firm's business activities. The purpose of this accounting information is to help individuals make decisions. Many different kinds of people depend on the information. For convenience, we categorize those who need accounting information as insiders or outsiders of a firm.

Management accounting is the development of information for the insiders (i.e., company managers). Managers use this information to measure the progress toward their goals and highlight any potential problems in advance. For example, managers want to know which products are selling the best and which are selling poorly, which products tend to sell together, and how inventory is being managed. Managers also want to know about cash—will the firm have enough cash to pay its upcoming debt payments?

Accountants answer these questions with budgets, variance reports, revenue reports, cost projections, and even competitor analysis. When firms are considering how to expand products and services, managerial accountants help formulate profit projections from revenue and cost projections. In short, managerial accounting has historically played a big part in the control and evaluation of a business and its performance.

Outsiders of the firm also use accounting information. Investors, banks, the government, and other stakeholders have a keen interest in the financial health of a firm. Banks and other creditors want to know if the firm will be able to pay its debts. Investors want to know how much profit the firm is making—both now and in the future. Employees have a double interest because they have both their career/employment at stake as well as possibly being investors through their retirement plans.

Providing information for outsiders is the purpose of *financial accounting*. Whereas managerial accounting reports may break down performance for managers by individual products or regions of the country, financial accounting reports summarize the business as a whole, though they can be broken into business segments and regions. These reports are the quarterly and annual financial statements that public firms must file with the SEC.

The three main statements (income statement, balance sheet, and statement of cash flows) are used by outsiders to determine a firm's value, profits, safety—among other pieces of important information. Outsiders want to be able to easily compare among firms. So, the SEC requires these reports to adhere to generally accepted accounting principles (GAAP). These statements are prepared by the accountants of a firm and reviewed by independent accountants from an auditing firm. (More on auditors later in the chapter.)

Another outsider that requires accounting information is the IRS. The accountants of the firm report the profits to the IRS and determine the tax bill. Interestingly, the accounting methods and record keeping of a business can be very different for reporting to managers (for financial statements) and to the IRS. For example, there are ambiguities for how to record some transactions in GAAP. When reporting the business activities in the annual report, choices are made to maximize earnings. When the IRS forms are being completed, choices are made to minimize earnings in order to minimize taxes.[1] A private-sector body, Financial Accounting Standards Board (FASB), sets the rules for financial statements.

The first accounting standard-setting body was the Committee on Accounting Procedure, and it existed from 1939 to 1959. It was replaced by the Accounting Principles Board (APB) in 1959. The SEC recognized the APB as authoritative until 1973, when it was replaced by FASB. The SEC recognizes FASB as authoritative, which means that the SEC recognizes FASB's decisions on creating and amending GAAP. However, the SEC and the U.S. Congress have been able to influence FASB's accounting policies. FASB is sponsored by associations in the accounting profession. To promote independence, its seven board members are required to serve full time and divest their interest in the firms they once worked for. Even non-CPAs serve on the FASB board.

AUDITING

Auditors are accountants from outside a firm who review the financial statements and a firm's procedure for producing them. Their job is to attest that the statements are fair and that they materially represent the condition of a firm. While banks and other creditors have always wanted independent verification of a firm's financial health, the role of monitoring the firm was cemented by the Securities Act of 1933 and the Securities Exchange Act of 1934. In the Great Depression, after the excess of the late 1920s, the country was reeling from business scandals. The U.S. Congress reacted with stronger oversight, regulation, and punishment. Does this reaction seem familiar?

This legislation required annual independent audits of all public companies. Therefore, in the late 1930s and the 1940s, accounting firms flourished with the increased demand for auditing services. Initially, the high demand for auditing was due to the new laws that required independent verification of a firm's books. Later, the demand for auditing services continued to grow because the economy eventually picked up, increasing the number of public firms. This environment was such that auditing firms could play an effective role of independent monitor—even becoming adversarial with a firm if necessary. For example, Al Bows was one of the first partners at Arthur Andersen and recalls the days when auditors were very credible and influential. At that time, while auditing a fruit juice company, Bows discovered that the CEO was starting another juice company on the side for his own benefit. Bows was concerned about the conflict of interest and told the CEO to dissolve the other company. The CEO did.[2] In another audit of a real estate firm, the CEO complained that Bows was imposing tougher standards on his company than on other companies in the industry. Bows responded that Arthur Andersen didn't care what other firms did—it was going to do what is right. Being confrontational with firms was not very risky at that time. Firms rarely switched auditors and auditing firms were too busy with existing clients and new companies to poach the clients of other auditing firms. Indeed, competitive marketing of auditing services was originally banned by the code of ethics.

In the 1970s and 1980s, the auditing business began to change. The number of new companies that needed auditing services was no longer expanding. If auditing firms wanted to grow, they would have to steal the clients from other auditing firms. The code of ethics was changed to permit advertising and other competitive practices. Auditing firms began to advertise and cut auditing prices to lure new clients. The relationship between the auditing firm and the audited company also began to change. With other audit firms courting them, corporate managers no longer tolerated adversarial auditors. Auditors became friendlier in order to keep their clients, especially the larger companies. It is prestigious to have Fortune 500 companies as clients, so auditing firms changed from Doberman watchdogs to poodle lapdogs in order to keep them as clients. During this period, auditing firms also developed consulting services to advise companies on how to improve their accounting methods and business activities. This provided both another source of income for auditing firms and solidified their relationship with company management.

THE CHANGING ROLE OF ACCOUNTING

Over the past couple of decades, the role of accounting within a company has changed. Instead of just providing information to insiders and outsiders of a firm, the accounting department began to transition into its own profit center. Instead of simply reporting the quarterly profits of the firm, the accounting department was asked how to increase profits through application of accounting methods. In some areas, the ambiguity in GAAP and the subjectivity of business activities provide for different ways of accounting for the same transaction. Different methods often lead to different levels of reportable profits.

One example is the desire of companies to exhibit a steady and continuous growth in profits. If the profits generated from business activities grow, but at an erratic pace, accountants are asked to smooth out the earnings over time. This is referred to as managing earnings. GE has been accused of using accounting manipulations to manage its earnings.[3] In Figure 5–1, notice how steady the growth in GE's earnings has been—especially since 1995.

Money magazine wrote in 2000 that GE employs a number of confusing—but apparently legal—gimmicks to achieve its consistent growth. For example, GE's financing division, GE Capital, can reduce current earnings for the firm by being pessimistic in its estimates of losses from problem loans. If those loans eventually end up getting repaid, this will increase future profits. The maneuver effectively shifts some earnings into the future. If the firm is in need of more earnings in the present, it can conduct a real estate sale and leaseback. This transaction could work in the following way. GE sells a factory to a group of investors for $100 million, but GE signs a long-term lease with the group so that it still uses the factory. How-

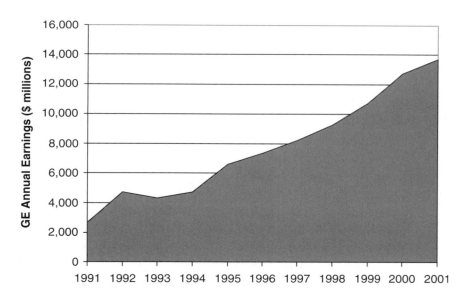

FIGURE 5–1 Annual earnings of General Electric in millions of dollars.

ever, since the factory had been depreciated to $50 million, GE could claim the difference as a capital gain and increase pre-tax profits by $50 million. The profit could have been amortized over the life of the lease. This method would not have affected profits. Due to GAAP ambiguities and loopholes, firms can choose methods that benefit them the most.

Both taking reserves for bad loans and the real estate sale/ leaseback are perfectly legal. However, the accounting treatment of them assumes that these transactions occur as normal business activities. Some firms use them as accounting gimmicks to manage earnings over time. There are other firms that can be used as an example for managing earnings. For example, IBM has also been accused of using financial steps in the 1990s to create double-digit earnings growth when revenue grew at only 5 percent.[4] However, GE holds a special place in the investment industry because it is the only company in the Dow Jones Industrial Average that was an original Dow firm when the index was created more than 100 years ago. If GE is using accounting methods to manage earnings, many other companies are likely to do so as well.

U.S. Vice President Dick Cheney has taken heat over his five-year tenure as CEO of Halliburton Company.[5] The SEC investigated Halliburton over accounting practices that occurred during the years when Cheney ran the firm. The issue appears to be why Halliburton accounted for projected overrun reimbursements as revenue while work was still to be completed on projects. By changing its method of booking these revenues in 1998, Halliburton was able to substantially increase revenue. Additionally, the SEC wants to know whether Halliburton adequately disclosed the change and its impact on financial statements. Whether Halliburton or Cheney did anything wrong, we don't know. However, this is just one more instance that illustrates a CEO walking off rich while the shareholders suffer. Cheney pocketed $45 million in compensation over the five years of his tenure while investors have since seen the stock price drop from $54 per share to $13 per share.

The accounting gimmicks that are used can be either simple or quite complex. Indeed, modern consulting by accounting and auditing firms concerns structuring deals that may not have any value in conducting business, but it spins off either profits or losses now that can be reversed in the future to manage earnings.

FROM MANAGEMENT TO FRAUD

How much can companies manipulate accounting figures before they cross the line and managed earnings become fraud? Where is the line?

Enron was certainly pushing the envelope at every chance. The firm used sophisticated and very complicated methods to generate earnings out of thin air. Paul Krugman of the *New York Times* describes one type of technique called the fictitious asset sale. For example, Enron could sell an asset, like a truck, to its own subsidiary (technically a special-purpose entity) for an outrageously high price. The book value of the truck is low, so Enron books a huge capital gain and profits go up. The subsidiary capitalizes the cost of the truck. This means that the subsidiary will have to report a little lower earnings in each of the future years as the truck cost is depreciated. In effect, Enron is taking a profit now that it will have to offset as expenses in the future over the sale of a truck that it still owns! This kind of accounting trickery is just the tip of the iceberg for Enron. While these types of maneuvers help to manage earnings, their effect is limited unless the company crosses the line and uses them fraudulently.

As another example, Enron would enter into a contract to sell energy to a customer for 30 years. Then they would deliberately underestimate the cost of providing that energy, thereby overestimating the annual profit of the contract.[6] Lastly, Enron would book all 30 years of inflated profits in the current year. This practice made Enron appear incredibly profitable over the short term, but it was detrimental to its longer-term financial health.

It appears that Enron went over the line and committed fraud. Indeed, the examples given here are only the simplest of the gimmicks that can be used. Enron created complex partnership arrangements and foreign subsidiaries to perpetrate the worst of its accounting offenses. These partnerships are mostly created and used with the help of investment banks, which we discuss in Chapter 7.

FRAUD, PLAIN AND SIMPLE

The pressure on accounting departments to smooth earnings or even produce earnings can be intense when the firm is not meeting investor (analyst) expectations. Since the role of accounting has changed and accounting departments are viewed as profit centers, they are pressed to make up shortfalls created by the business operations of the firm. Sometimes, firms cross way over the line to fraudulent practices.

Consider the case of Rite Aid Corp. On June 21, 2002, a federal grand jury indicted four former and current executives of the firm for conducting a wide-ranging scheme to overstate income.[7] The SEC noted in its investigation that Rite Aid reported false and misleading information in ten different areas—ranging from reducing its costs to accelerating revenue to manipulating numbers between quarterly and annual reports.[8] Indeed, Rite Aid restated earnings for its fiscal year 1998 that caused $305 million in net income to become $186 million in net losses. The restatement in fiscal year 1999 changed from a $143 million profit to a $422.5 million loss. That is more than $1 billion in earnings that disappeared!

Figure 5–2 shows the price of Rite Aid's stock from 1997 to 2000 and its relationship to the stated and restated earnings. Rite Aid stated that it earned $116.7 million in fiscal year 1997 (which ended February 28, 1997). The stock price at this time was $21 per share. As indicated earlier, Rite Aid then stated that it earned $305 million in 1998, and the stock price rose to $34.25. The stock price reached its maximum of $50.94 on January 8, 1999. A few months later the firm

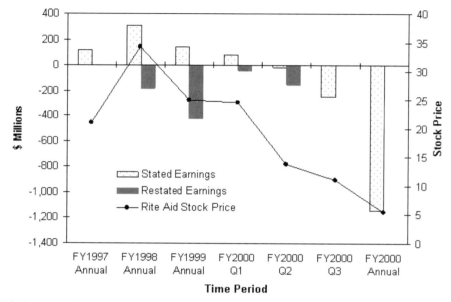

FIGURE 5–2 The statement and restatement of Rite Aid's earnings and associated stock price.

reported fiscal year 1999 earnings of $143 million. However, investors started to figure out that something was wrong. By July 10, 2000, the stock had slowly fallen to $7.85 per share. The stock price fell to $5 per share the next day when Rite Aid restated its earnings from 1998 to 2000. The stock spent the summer of 2002 at under $2.50 per share.

Rite Aid's stock price was artificially inflated in the late 1990s because of fraud in financial reporting. Those investors who purchased Rite Aid's stock in 1999 because they thought the firm was a profitable and growing company were lied to and lost a lot of money. Even the existing investors would have been better off knowing the extent of the firm's loss so that they could have made an informed decision to stick with it or sell out. After the truth finally came out, it was too late—they had lost most of their investment in the company.

Whereas Rite Aid's fraud was hidden in at least ten different types of accounting manipulations, WorldCom Inc.'s gaffe was one of the oldest and simplest tricks in the book. On June 25, 2002, WorldCom disclosed that roughly $3.8 billion had been improperly booked as capital investments instead of operating expenses over the previous five quarters. This is especially distressing because WorldCom is such a large and well-known company. Twenty million Americans were MCI customers, and superstar Michael Jordan was the company's pitchman.[9]

Specifically, WorldCom had to pay fees to other phone companies in order for them to transfer WorldCom customers' calls right away.[10] By capitalizing these fees, contrary to GAAP, WorldCom pushed current expenses into the future, thereby boosting current earnings (at the expense of future earnings). For example, by inappropriately capitalizing the $3.8 billion and depreciating it over, say, five years, the firm did not report the $3.8 billion as an expense, which would have lowered its pre-tax earnings by $3.8 billion.[11] Instead, it only had to claim one fifth of the cost as depreciation, which would have lowered its pre-tax earnings by only $0.76 billion. In this case, WorldCom would have fraudulently increased its pre-tax earnings by $3 billion. As a comparison, WorldCom's income before taxes was only $3.6 billion in the previous five quarters. In other words, nearly all of it was fictional.

While this was simply a case of cooking the books, the scheme seems to be especially effective considering that as a telecom firm, WorldCom needed to make many capital investments in phone lines, satellites, and equipment. Therefore, hiding expenses as capital investments was easy. WorldCom's deception is even more problematic when considering that many analysts and investors follow an accounting measure other than earnings for firms with high capital investment needs. They follow the measure EBITDA (earnings before interest, taxes, depreciation, and amortization). One of the things this measure excludes is depreciation expense. In the example above, EBITDA would not have the $0.76 billion in depreciation expenses deducted and therefore would be higher by the full $3.8 billion (in the scheme). Thus, this scheme is especially misleading for investors who follow EBITDA instead of earnings.

CONSULTANTS

Business consultants are often the people who recommend these complex partnership and off-balance sheet arrangements to companies. Consulting firms typically advise firms on tactical issues, like how to enter a new market, and strategic issues, like acquiring or spinning off other firms. When it comes to consulting, the king is McKinsey & Co. McKinsey is a consultant for more than half of the Fortune 500 firms. In 2001, McKinsey had 7,700 consultants based out of 84 locations worldwide and generated $3.4 billion in revenue.[12] This represents more than a 40 percent market share of the consulting business.

McKinsey has not been implicated in the Enron mess the way Arthur Andersen was. However, McKinsey was a long-term consultant of Enron, recently earning more than $10 million per year in consulting fees from the troubled firm. In fact, former Enron CEO Jeffrey Skilling was a McKinsey partner and consultant before joining Enron. McKinsey promoted many of the business strategies used by Enron. One example is the "asset-light" strategy. McKinsey advised that a company in a normally capital-intensive industry could get an advantage by divesting itself of the physical assets required to do business. Instead of owning and operating oil pipes, the firm contracts the use of another firm's oil pipes. Rather than being a firm based on physical assets, it became based on a myriad of contracts. Enron became very good at negotiating, contracting, and financing. This experience may have also helped Enron move to another strategy promoted by McKinsey—off-balance sheet financing.

One common area for consultants is advising on tax reduction strategies. Consider the shenanigans that Tyco International Ltd. goes through to reduce its U.S. taxes. Tyco is an electrical manufacturing and services firm, and in 1996, it moved to the tax haven of Bermuda.[13] It has also created more than 150 subsidiaries in other tax-friendly places like Barbados and the Cayman Islands. The purpose of these entities is not, for the most part, to conduct business. The purpose is to shelter income from the United States so that it does not have to pay taxes. Tyco is very successful at this. Tyco's CFO claimed that these strategies cut the 2001 tax bill by $600 million. Most of the taxes Tyco pays are to foreign countries. All of this happens beyond the eyes of an investor. The annual report does not provide information about its mysterious subsidiaries—with names like Driftwood, Bunga Bevaru, and Silver Avenue Holdings. Congress seems to have finally noticed that it is losing tens of billions of dollars in tax revenue from companies using these strategies. It is exploring some ways to crack down on corporate tax avoidance. It is about time—the increased revenue to the government can help all Americans. Maybe the executives and consultants can use their immense brainpower to increase business and shareholder value instead of just avoiding taxes.

WHEN THE AUDITOR IS ALSO A CONSULTANT

The advice of consultants can be very beneficial to a firm. However, it can also be very detrimental. One potential problem for a firm's shareholders occurs when a consulting firm also conducts the auditing services for the company. Some advice might be too aggressive in terms of accounting methods. Other advice might just be dubious. However, the income to an accounting firm for conducting an audit is far lower than the fees earned by consulting. Therefore, the auditors may get pressure from their own firm to overlook borderline practices. This is a serious conflict of interest for the auditors. Their duty should be one of effective monitoring for the shareholders. Instead, their bonuses are often dependent on how much money the consulting group earns for the firm. Upsetting the consulting group risks earning a lower bonus. In fact, this conflict may have played a significant role in Enron's demise, as Arthur Andersen was a significant Enron consultant.

FEAR OF ALL SUMS

Investors do not trust the financial statements of public companies. The restatements of large, well-known firms (like WorldCom and Xerox) come right on the heels of the collapse of hundreds of Internet-related firms. The average investor who reads the annual reports could not have predicted these events. These accounting issues may be too complex for the average investor to find. Yet, the letters from the auditors in these reports do not speak of the possible trouble ahead. Surely the auditors understand the financial health of a firm. Investors have also relied on financial analysts to interpret financial statements and comment on the financial health and prospects of a firm. Analysts have also failed the investor (see Chapter 8). Investors need to reestablish faith in the financial statement of a firm in order to restore their confidence in public companies and the stock market.

This will be difficult in the near-term. The collapse of Arthur Andersen has forced many companies to switch auditors from Arthur Andersen to one of the other accounting firms. Consider the motivation of the new auditing firm. Since it must certify that the financial statements it audits are fair, it has an incentive to find any problems with past accounting while it can still blame the previous auditor. Thus, the change from Arthur Andersen to a new auditor may foster many more restatements. Indeed, the pace of earnings restatement seems to be dramatically picking up. A study by the Huron Consulting Group reports that 116 firms restated in 1997. This number has grown to 233 in 2000 and 270 in 2001.[14] As the public focus on accounting increased in 2002, so did the number of restatements and their magnitude. While the 233 firms in 2000 represent less than 3 percent of all listed firms, the 503 restatements in 2000 and 2001 together represent nearly 7 percent of all firms. With many more firms restating in 2002, investors could easily be looking at a minimum of 10 percent or 15 percent of their firms restating over the three-year period.

We want to point out that if aggressive (or even fraudulent) practices occur in 10 percent of the exchange-listed firms, that leaves 90 percent of the firms that did the right thing. It is too bad that the 10 percent will affect the investing industry and the financial environment so much for the 90 percent. It is too bad that the few problems have shaken investor trust so much. However, a typical investor's perspective is that the risk caused by this 10 percent is considerable.

The risk might be growing. Because of the public outrage and the political rush to make changes, it is likely that GAAP will be changed so that firms must disclose "off-balance" sheet transactions with subsidiaries, partnerships, and "special purpose entities." Auditors seemed to have lost the emphasis on "economic substance" for the emphasis on "form." This will probably change. Changes will also be made to close loopholes that foster some of the accounting gimmicks. These changes will make many companies look less profitable than before. As they miss earnings targets and expectations, their stock prices could decline further.

AN INTERNATIONAL PERSPECTIVE

The bankruptcy of major companies and the ensuing media attention and political rhetoric make it seem like the U.S. system of accounting has been a total failure. However, this is simply not true. Compared to the accounting systems used internationally, the United States is quite tough. Characteristics of a high-quality system would have many shareholder rights and strong protection of those rights. This protection comes from strong laws that are enforced and accounting standards that have little ambiguity.

In comparison with the environment in other countries, the United States already has tough laws and a high degree of enforcement. In a recent study of 31 countries, three accounting researchers found that the United States has the best legal environment to discourage earnings manipulations and smoothing.[15] Australia, Ireland, Canada, and the United Kingdom also have good investor protection and enforcement histories. Earnings manipulations are more common in Austria, Italy, Germany, South Korea, and Taiwan. While investors currently lack confidence in the financial numbers reported by U.S. firms, the numbers of some foreign firms could be of lower quality. The scandals in some U.S. firms parallel some recent international scandals. International examples of scandal include embezzlement at the Bank of Credit and Commerce International and at Polly Peck, accounting fraud at Lernout and Hauspie, cash diversions at Daewoo Motors, and numerous shenanigans in Robert Maxwell's firms.

There is work being done to create a high-quality set of international accounting standards. The International Accounting Standards Committee (IASC) was founded in June 1973 by the accounting bodies of ten countries. Effective April 1, 2001, the International Accounting Standards Board (IASB) assumed accounting standard-setting responsibilities from its predecessor body, the IASC. This board is developing a single set of global accounting standards that are high quality, understandable, and enforceable, and that require transparent and comparable information in general-purpose financial statements. In addition, the board wants to encourage convergence in accounting standards of individual countries around the world.

Summary

The incentive system of the accounting and auditing function has two problems that have the potential to decrease the effectiveness of auditors as monitors. The first problem is that auditing firms want to keep the public company as a client over the long term. This makes it less aggressive in rooting out problems because management can easily threaten the firing of the auditing firm. Indeed, accounting firms have become more like the hired guns of management instead of the sheriffs they are supposed to be. The second problem is that auditors are frequently asked to sign off on the dubious gimmicks that their own accounting firm recommended through its consulting group. The government seems to be attempting to rectify this second problem by not allowing accounting firms to provide both consulting and auditing services for the same public company. As explained in Chapter 12, we do not believe that this solution is the best remedy. We offer an alternative in Chapter 13.

ENDNOTES

1. There are limitations on how different the public reporting and IRS reporting can be.

2. Al Bows' tale is detailed in the article by Lanthe Jeanne Dugan, "Auditing Old-Timers Recall When Prestige Was the Bottom Line," *Wall Street Journal*, July 15, 2002, pp. A1, A7.

3. Jon Birger, "Glowing Numbers," *Money*, November 2000, pp. 112–122.

4. Spencer Ante and David Henry, "Can IBM Keep Earnings Hot?" *BusinessWeek*, April 15, 2002, pp. 58–60.

5. Allan Sloan and Johnnie Roberts, "Sticky Business," *Newsweek*, July 22, 2002, pp. 26–30.

6. Paul Krugman, "Flavors of Fraud," *New York Times*, June 28, 2002, p. A27; Paul Krugman, "Everyone Is Outraged," *New York Times*, July 2, 2002, p. A21.

7. "SEC Charges Ex–Rite Aid Execs with Fraud," *Reuters Business Report*, June 21, 2002, 11:05 a.m. EST.

8. Rite Aid Corporation, Accounting and Auditing Enforcement Release No. 1579, Securities and Exchange Commission, June 21, 2002, *http://www.sec.gov/litigation/admin/34-46099.htm.*

9. Howard Gold, "The Graft Next Door," *Barron's*, July 1, 2002, p. T8.

10. Jesse Drucker and Henny Sender, "Sorry, Wrong Number: Strategy Behind Accounting Scheme," *Wall Street Journal,* June 27, 2002, p. A9.

11. WorldCom had not released details of its accounting problem at the time of publication, so we don't know the number of years the expenses were capitalized over. Other information that has leaked out of World-Com hints that accounting problems might go further back than originally feared.

12. John Byrne, "Inside McKinsey," *BusinessWeek*, July 8, 2002, pp. 66–76.

13. William Symonds, "The Tax Games Tyco Played," *BusinessWeek*, July 1, 2002, pp. 40–41.

14. Jonathan Glater, "Recomputing Earnings with Law-book and Eraser," *New York Times*, July 2, 2002, p. C8.

15. Christian Leuz, Dhananjay Nanda, and Peter Wysocki, "Investor Protection and Earnings Management: An International Comparison," Wharton School working paper, May 2002.

6 THE BOARD OF DIRECTORS

"Where Was the Board?" "Pointing Fingers at the Board." "Enron Board Asleep at the Wheel." "What's Wrong with our Boards?" These are the types of headlines that appeared regularly in the nation's newspapers and business magazines following the business scandals. At first, it was the company officials allegedly guilty of various fraudulent acts who were being lambasted in our nation's headlines. Then, people naturally started wondering how these perpetrators were even able to get away with their acts in the first place. Why weren't the perpetrators, and their questionable acts and shifty maneuverings, better monitored? Of course, some of the monitoring responsibility belongs to a firm's auditors, which we discussed in the last chapter. However, even good, objective, independent auditors are limited in their ability to monitor company officials because their main job is to evaluate the accounting numbers. So, whose job is it to monitor the executives? This responsibility belongs to the company's board of directors. The question is, why didn't the boards do a better job to prevent these scandals from taking place in the first place? So, indeed, "Where was the board?"

Many investors do not really know how a typical firm's board of directors is structured, who makes up the group, or even what it does. When you think of a boardroom meeting, you might imagine a large penthouse conference room and a large oval table in the center—the board chairman at the head of the table rubbing shoulders with other distinguished-looking, gray-haired corporate giants, politicians, and even university presidents. While they sit in their large plush black leather chairs and enjoy a professionally catered spread and perhaps a cigar, are they going over the numbers, heatedly debating strategy, and making important decisions? Or are they just looking upon the meeting as a social gathering and cozying up to one another while catching up with their friend, the firm's CEO? The former is the effective, engaged board we want. The latter may be the actual board of many firms. It is hard to know which kind of board a firm has because the vast majority of us have never stepped inside the boardroom.

In 1934, William O. Douglas, a law professor who would later serve as the SEC chairman for 36 years, claimed that directors do not direct.[1] For the most part, it remained this way for quite some time. One director boasted, in 1962, "If you have five directorships, it is total heaven, like having a permanent hot bath.... No effort of any kind is called for. You go to a meeting once a month in a car supplied by the company, you look grave and sage, and on two occasions say, 'I agree.'"[2] By all reports, however, things have changed dramatically for the better, but this is primarily a recent trend. For the past 15 years or so, shareholders have become ever more demanding of directors, and as a result, directors have been working longer hours, taking more stock ownership in the firm to ensure a vested interest, challenging the CEO more often, and taking their duties more seriously. But now board members are asking themselves, is this worth it? After all, think about the humiliation suffered (albeit perhaps deserved) by the Enron directors. Who would want to put himself or herself in a position to be embarrassed like that? According to recruiters Christian & Timbers, 60 percent of nominated directors are turning down the appointments.[3] Nonetheless, with director compensation that averages more than $40,000 per year, along with perks, travel, stocks, and stock options, all for working about 150 hours and attending eight meetings a year, a directorship is still a nice gig.[4] But now, given the recent avalanche of one scandal after another, are board members going to respond to the cry from angry shareholders for even better and stronger boards? Also, how much of our current crisis can we really pin on them?

The main purpose of this chapter is to give some basic background and information regarding boards so that we can better understand them and learn more about their effectiveness (or ineffectiveness).

CURRENT BOARD REGULATIONS

There is really no explicit federal law that dictates that public corporations must have a board of directors. Instead, corporations must follow the state statute in which they are incorporated. This, in and of itself, may cause potential problems. For example, states may try to establish lax corporate laws to encourage incorporation in the state to receive more taxes. This explains why more than 300,000 firms are incorporated in the state of Delaware. Fortunately, every state requires a corporation to have a board of directors, voted on by shareholders.[5] Thus, every corporation has a board.

A type of guideline is set forth by the Model Business Corporation Act, which states, "All corporate powers shall be exercised by or under authority of, and the business affairs of a corporation shall be managed under the direction of, a board of directors."[6] Further, "the fundamental *responsibility of the individual corporate director is to represent the interest of the shareholders as a group,* as the owners of the enterprise, in dealing with the business and affairs of the corporation with the law" [italics is our emphasis]. As such, the board's fiduciary responsibility is clearly to the shareholders. This is pretty much the extent of the law governing boards. The SEC, for example, does not impose specific board regulations with regard to structure and composition, and to be able to list on the New York Stock Exchange (NYSE) and Nasdaq—which, as self regulatory organizations (SROs), can impose their own set of regulations—the only major additional board requirement is that the firm has to have an audit committee primarily consisting of independent directors, but even the definition of independence is quite general (however, dramatic proposals are on the table in this regard, which we will discuss in later chapters). As far as the rest goes, the regulations have generally been lax. For example, firms are not required to have specific director responsibility guidelines, they are not required to have a formal procedure to evaluate the CEO, they are not required to have independent board members, there is no director accountability requirement, and directors are not even required to own stock in the firm. Even rules regarding director elections are weak.

For a while, though, having relaxed and non-uniform regulations seemed optimal in our society. After all, we should let the firms operate in the manner that suits them best. Of course, shareholders didn't like the way a firm was being managed by its board, then they could simply sell their stocks (i.e., doing the "Wall Street walk"), which is as good a reason as any for why firms try to have acceptable boards. Following the recent scandals, there is a push to more strictly regulate boards of directors—both composition and structure. We discuss some of these recommendations and offer our own thoughts and suggestions in Chapters 12 and 13. We next illustrate how modern boards work.

MORE ATTENTION ON DIRECTORS

Even before the recent corporate meltdowns and scandals, the general public was starting to pay more and more attention to directors and their activities. Prior to the mid-1980s, the public paid little heed to directors. For the most part, they were merely ornamental features of corporations. So, what changed? Why were people starting to scrutinize directors even before these scandals proliferated our nation's headlines? There are actually several reasons. First, the demand for better corporate governance occurred partly as a response to the tidal wave of mergers and acquisitions (M&A) activities of the

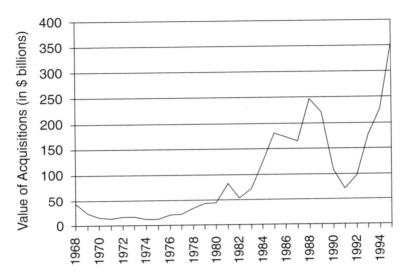

FIGURE 6-1   Yearly value of mergers and acquisitions.

1980s. Figure 6–1 shows the deal value (in billions of dollars) of all acquisitions that took place in the United States from 1968 to 1995.[7]

As we can easily see from the figure, M&A activity really picked up during the 1980s. But why? There are several reasons for this, including a more favorable tax environment, the gaining popularity and availability of junk bonds to finance acquisitions, increasing foreign competition, and the deregulations that were occurring in some industries. A recession and the collapse of the junk bond market lead to a temporary decline in M&A activity during the late 1980s, but one can see that M&A activity has been strong since then.

There are a variety of reasons that companies acquire one another, but the most commonly stated reason is to generate more profits through synergies, be it operational or financial. For example, because HP and Compaq both make computers, they may be able to do a better job as a combined company rather than as two separate firms. In other words, two plus two equals five. A combination could help both firms. In fact, it was this very logic that HP CEO Carly Fiorina used to argue for the HP acquisition of Compaq—cost savings, and the sharing of customers and technology.

Why would an increase in M&A activity lead to more scrutiny of the boards? First, when a firm acquires another firm, the company making the purchase usually has to pay significantly more than the going market price for the company being purchased. This is great for the target firm's shareholders, but it's not so great for the acquiring firm's shareholders. This being the case, the shareholders of both the potential acquirers and targets will wish to keep a close eye on their respective boards. These boards must approve the acquisition before it goes to a shareholder vote. For the acquirer, the shareholders may not wish to pay too much for a target, or they may not wish to acquire the target at all. For the target firm, the shareholders may want to make sure that management does not adopt anti-takeover amendments, such as poison pills (a move by a takeover target to make its stock less attractive to an acquirer), that would make it difficult for the firm to be acquired for a nice price. Thus, the takeover wave that occurred in the 1980s brought more attention to boards.

Other reasons why the board of directors started to get more scrutiny from shareholders have to do with two rules adopted by the SEC in 1992. First, the SEC required much more disclosure from corporations with regard to executive compensation, which included the reporting of granted stock option values. When the values of these compensation contracts were disclosed, there was some shock. As we discussed in Chapter 3, CEOs were receiving millions of dollars per year in salary, bonuses, and stock options. In many cases, the lavish compensations were being granted even if their firms were not doing that well. As such, shareholders began applying pressure on directors to exercise more oversight to make sure that the executives deserved what they were making. Second, the SEC made it easier for shareholders to communicate with one another. It was primarily the institutional investors, such as the pension funds CalPERS and TIAA-CREF, who took advantage of this rule. As a result, they were now able to create stronger shareholder coalitions that made it easier to put pressure on boards to challenge management. We will discuss institutional shareholder activism in more detail in Chapter 11. Given the new environment created by the SEC rules, it may not be surprising that some well-known CEOs, such as John Akers of IBM, Kay Whitmore of Eastman Kodak, Paul Lego of Westinghouse Electric, and John Scully of Apple Computers, all lost their jobs only one year later in 1993.

All in all, with the increased takeover market and the new regulatory environment, shareholders and the general public put more pressure on directors to do their jobs. However, because these changes occurred or took shape only recently, the avid attention being paid to boards is a recent phenomenon. For example, it was only in 1996 that *BusinessWeek* started rating corporate boards. Are the boards ready for their next challenge in the wake of the shareholder confidence crisis?

WHO ARE DIRECTORS?

S&P 500 firms have about 11 directors each. So who occupies these 5,500 or so board seats? Virtually anyone can be a board member, but to believe that this is the reality is being very idealistic. Those nominated by a firm's management or board's nominating committee are the ones who eventually become directors. Therefore, if you don't personally know the firm's CEO or a current board member, it is extremely difficult for you to become a director. According to the 2001 Korn/Ferry Annual Board of Directors Study, about two thirds of current directors say that the CEO/chairman has the most influence in identifying new directors.[8] Of course, there are other ways to get a board seat. If you are a university dean/president or a politician, you could be viewed as a respectable figurehead. A board may therefore solicit your candidacy. If you are not figurehead material, you would probably need to be identified by an executive finder, such as

Korn/Ferry or Heidrick & Struggles, as a viable director candidate. However, getting a recommendation from these finders is tough. For example, Korn/Ferry states that a person would have to possess 10 to 20 years of experience in a business leadership role, be a current COO or CFO of a large company, or be one of the top 15 executives at a very large corporation in order to be considered a viable director.[9] Finally, a shareholder could submit a proposal to obtain a board seat, but unless he or she is well known or wealthy enough to launch an expensive campaign, this route may actually be the most difficult. We'll discuss shareholder proposals in more detail in Chapter 11, where we discuss shareholder activism.

You may think that a person getting a director nomination means that there is only a good chance that he or she will eventually get the directorship, but it's actually more like a sure thing. In the annual elections for board seats, an overwhelming majority of board-nominated directors win—generally going uncontested. Why is this? Usually, shareholders don't show up to vote or return their proxy votes by mail. When shareholders do vote, they often follow the suggestions of management or the board.[10] This being the case, it's not surprising that boards end up being comprised of current and former business leaders—often CEOs from other firms. They also include current or former employees, academics, bankers, university presidents, and even politicians. According to the 2001 Korn/Ferry Study, 91 percent of *Fortune*-listed firms have a retired executive serving as a director, 83 percent have an executive from another firm, 56 percent have an academic, and 52 percent have a former government official.[11] With regard to gender and race representation, the data seems somewhat promising. Seventy-four percent of the boards have a woman director and 65 percent of them have an ethnic minority, with African Americans sitting on 41 percent of our nation's boards. However, with a cynical viewpoint, compensation expert Graef Crystal once stated that a board could be generalized as "ten friends of management, a woman and a black."[12]

THE BOARD'S FUNCTIONS

What are directors supposed to do? In general, the board of directors is charged with four broad functions:

1. Board members hire, evaluate, and perhaps even fire top management, with the CEO being the most important. While they are evaluating management, they must also monitor the firm's performance.

2. Members vote on major operating proposals (e.g., large capital expenditures, acquisitions, etc.).

3. Members vote on major financial decisions (e.g., issuance of stocks and bonds, dividend payments, stock repurchases, etc.).

4. Members offer their expert advice to management. In executing these functions, they are supposed to represent the interests of the shareholders. Given the immense importance of the responsibilities that the board members bear, it would seem that the shareholders have powerful agents working on their behalf.

Further, the board has subcommittees. In fact, a lot of the important board work gets done at the subcommittee level, which subsequently goes to the full board for approval. Some boards have an executive committee, a finance committee, a community relations committee, and so forth. Perhaps the subcommittees most common to all boards are the audit committee (according to the Korn/Ferry study, 100 percent of all boards have this subcommittee), the compensation committee (99 percent of all boards have this), and the nomination committee (73 percent of all boards have this).[13]

The audit committee is charged with the responsibility of finding an outside independent auditor for a firm's accounting statements. It must make sure that the auditor will do its job objectively. The compensation committee is supposed to design the executives' compensation package. The most common procedure used by a compensation committee to design compensation contracts is to benchmark its firm and its CEO against other firms and CEOs, and offer a comparable or slightly better compensation package for its own CEO. The nomination committee is charged with the task of searching for and nominating potential directors to run for an impending vacant board seat in the annual shareholder elections. Finally, we should also mention that a separate stock options subcommittee has gained popularity with boards in recent years, probably due to the controversy surrounding the incentive.

While a board's roles in a corporation seem ideal, especially to ensure that shareholder interests are being met, there are some potentially serious problems with boards. Some reasons include a lack of board independence from the CEO, directors who don't have the time or expertise to adequately serve their roles, and even members who do not have a real vested interest in the firm.

PROBLEMS WITH BOARDS

One of the main functions of a board is to evaluate top management, especially the CEO. For many firms, however, the board's chairman is also the firm's CEO! For example, Philip M. Condit is both the board chairman and CEO of Boeing and C. Michael Armstrong is the chairman and CEO of AT&T. Furthermore, these examples do not represent the exception. Among the 30 firms that belong to the Dow Jones Industrial Average, which consists of our country's major corporations, only eight firms have a separate CEO and board chair. For the *Fortune*-listed firms, only 10 percent have a non-executive chairman.[14] Therefore, the person who manages the firm is the same person who runs the board meetings and its agenda; thus, he or she is the person who controls the information that is given to the board. This being the case, is it really likely that the board is capable of seriously evaluating or challenging the CEO? It can happen, but usually not without significant shareholder pressure. For example, the telecommunications firm Qwest, facing an SEC investigation over accounting procedures, recently fired chairman and

CEO Joseph Nacchio. However, it took a bit of scandal and a large number of business problems to bring it about.

Even if a CEO were not the board chair, it doesn't necessarily mean that he or she is under a more careful watch. While it is true that most boards have more outsiders than insiders (according to the Korn/Ferry study, the average board has three times as many outside directors as insider directors—insiders being defined as company employees), many of these so-called outside board members have some sort of business or personal tie to the CEO, which is how they became members of the board in the first place. For example, Disney's CEO is Michael Eisner, but Disney, which has been criticized by *BusinessWeek* as having one of the worst boards in corporate America, has a board comprised of numerous current Disney managers such as the chief corporate officer and heads of various Disney operations. But Disney claims that 13 of the 16 board members are independent directors. These "outsiders," however, include Reveta Bowers, headmaster of the school that Eisner's children attended; George Mitchell, a paid consultant to Disney and an attorney whose law firm represents Disney; Stanley Gold, president of Shamrock Holdings, which manages investments for the Disney family; Leo O'Donovan, president of Georgetown University, where one of the Eisner children attended school and the recipient of donations from Eisner; Irwin Russell, Eisner's personal attorney; and Robert Stern, architect for several of Disney's projects.[15]

In response to the business scandals and plummeting investor confidence in corporate America, the NYSE adopted new guidelines on board structure for its listed firms. We discuss these new policies in Chapter 12. However, one of the new rules disqualifies board directors from being considered independent if they have relatives working at the company. It turns out that board members Stanley Gold, Raymond Watson, and Reveta Bowers have children working at Disney.[16] They must now be categorized as management-aligned directors.

Will Disney's board challenge Eisner? Not only do some of these directors work for Eisner, but there are also others who benefit from not angering him. In other words, this board has too many insiders, and those insiders have business or other vested interests with the CEO. Among the firms that have been reeling from scandal, Tyco, Global Crossings, and Adelphia have boards that are filled with former or current executives. Furthermore, one of Tyco's outside directors was paid $10 million for helping to arrange the acquisition of CIT Group. Adelphia CEO John Rigas, along with his three sons, held four out of the nine board seats. Should shareholders believe that John Rigas was ever going to hear, "Dad, you're fired?" Eisner also contends that if he started to do irresponsible things and the firm started to fail, the board would get rid of him.[17] However, after a controversial $75 million payout to former Disney President Michael Ovitz and a lucrative contract penned for Eisner a few years ago (he has made more than $700 million as CEO in the last five years), Disney's market value fell to less than half of what it was during the nice run-up of the 1990s. Should anyone be surprised that Eisner is still at the helm? This isn't to say that Eisner should be fired, but no one should be surprised that he hasn't been.

Another problem with some boards is that the directors do not have a significant vested interest in the firm. For example, most of Disney's outside directors own little or no stock.[18] In 1997, *BusinessWeek* reported that Occidental Petroleum's board had approved a $95 million payout to its CEO, but two of its board members, George O. Nolley and Aziz D. Syriani, only owned 2,280 and 1,450 shares of the firm's stocks, respectively—despite the fact that they had sat on the board for 14 years.[19] The article also reported that AMD director Charles M. Blalack and Microsoft director Richard Hackborn owned no shares in the company for which they served as director. Can these board members sympathize with their shareholders? Probably not.

However, things have been changing. For example, some firms, like Ashland Inc., are setting stock ownership targets for their directors.[20] To Eisner's credit, he has asked his directors to own more stock.[21] For General Electric, the outside directors are clearly aligned with shareholders, as they each own (at the beginning of 2000) an average of $6.6 million of GE stock.[22] According to the 2001 Korn/Ferry study, 53 percent of the directors were required to own some of the company's stock.

In general, should investors really worry about the lack of independence and lack of stock ownership of some directors? Eisner has argued that we should not. But according to academic studies, we should. It is pretty well documented in these academic papers that CEOs primarily get fired if the stock price has been declining dramatically or if earnings have been significantly down. According to these same studies, however, it is often the case that those boards that fired a CEO were boards that were comprised of directors who did not have a strong tie to the CEO and held a large portion of the firm's stock.[23] In other words, boards that were more objective and had more personal wealth at stake were more willing to make the dramatic decision to fire the CEO. This may help explain why the CEOs of Coca-Cola, Ford, and Mattel have been fired recently, while Eisner labors on as CEO of Disney. Interestingly enough, when CEOs do get fired, some of those directors who were somehow aligned with the CEO were also let go—perhaps as a way of getting rid of the whole lot.[24] Therefore, directors can serve a meaningful, rather than symbolic, monitoring role for the corporation, but there may have to be enough of them who are independent of the CEO. That is, it seems that directors are fully capable of getting rid of poorly performing CEOs on the behalf of shareholders, but they must be willing and motivated. The next question is, what about their other responsibilities as directors?

Even if a director is someone who really cares about the firm, is independent, and is a significant stockholder, is he or she capable of providing the time and expertise required to fully understand and approve the major operating and financial decisions of the firm? Some directors, especially those who are potentially good at it, may be overextended. For example, many directors serve on multiple boards. According to a 1997 *BusinessWeek* article, Ann D. McLaughlin, Raymond S. Troubh, Frank C. Carlucci, Allen F. Jacobson, John L. Clendenin, Willie B. Davis, and Vernon E. Jordan all held directorships in ten or more firms.[25] Coca-Cola has five directors (out of 13) who serve on at least five boards. Most directors also hold their own highly demanding full-time jobs. According to the same *BusinessWeek* article, Gareth C. Chang served on the board of Mallinckrodt Group, but he had to miss 49 percent of the board meetings because he was busy as the senior vice president of Hughes Electronics. Similarly, the vice chairman of Chase Manhattan, William B. Harrison, missed 29 percent of the board and committee meetings at Dilliards, where he serves as a director. Finally, Vernon Jordon is a senior partner of a law firm, but recall that he also sits on ten boards. Therefore, it should not be surprising that he missed 40 percent of Dow Chemical's board meetings in 1996.

In addition, some directors simply do not have the expertise to be a board member. This means that independence, in and of itself, is not a sufficient quality for being an effective director. Some boards like to have a few figureheads, such as a celebrity or a former army general. O.J. Simpson, for example, was once on the audit committee of Infinity Broadcasting. It is certainly possible that celebrities or figureheads may be able to offer some expertise, but there are probably others who could offer much more. For example, it would be useful for Coca-Cola to have an outside director with experience in consumer marketing, but according to a 1996 *BusinessWeek* article, it doesn't.[26] Further, according to one academic study, having bank executives on boards, even those whose own bank is not linked to the firm, turns out to be very useful because they are able to provide their expertise on the credit markets.[27]

Finally, some boards are simply too big. With large boards, it is unlikely that anything can really get done, and it is unlikely that every director will be actively involved. When there are many directors, it is too convenient for any one of them to believe that the others are doing the monitoring job. Therefore, they do not have to work so hard. In a small board, each director knows that he or she must do more work because there are few others to do it. Kenneth Roman, who chaired Compaq's governance committee, believed that 11 directors allowed for an informal and interactive grappling of the issues. Disney's board has 16 members, and Enron had 15 members. Are such boards too big? Is size part of the problem? Academic researchers believe so. According to some studies, firms with fewer directors have higher market values, indicating the effectiveness of smaller boards.[28] Interestingly, Tyco International, the troubled firm detailed in previous chapters, proposed in 2002 to increase its board size from 11 to 15.[29] The company eventually cancelled the shareholder vote on the matter under heavy criticism that it would move its board in the wrong direction and further decrease investor confidence in the firm.

There are many potential problems that plague boards today. Many directors may not be truly independent, they may be too busy, or they may not have the expertise to carry out their obligations. These problems seem to explain why some of the current scandals occurred.

Is Enron's Board Partially to Blame?

It is alleged that members of Enron's management perpetrated a crime and that the company's auditors, Arthur Andersen, let them get away with it. But what about members of Enron's board? They swear that they had no part in it and that they should not be held responsible.[30] However, in scrutinizing Enron's board, which was comprised of 15 members, it is obvious that the board epitomized the notion of being captive to their CEO, which in and of itself suggests one possible problem. Indeed, in many instances of dependence on the CEO, one wonders if a quid pro quo didn't occur.

Board member John Wakeham is a Conservative Party politician from Britain. He had approved the building of an Enron power plant in Britain in 1990, and four years later he was on Enron's board. Director Herbert Winokur is chairman and CEO of Capricorn Holdings. He also sat on the board of National

Tank Co., which sold equipment and services to Enron divisions for millions of dollars. Former Enron directors Charles LeMaistre and John Mendelsohn were the former president and current president, respectively, of the M.D. Anderson Cancer Center, which received more than $500 million from Enron and its chairman, Kenneth Lay, during a five-year period. Director Wendy Gramm is a former chairwoman of the Commodity Futures Trading Commission. Before she joined the Enron board, she backed several policies that benefited Enron and other energy trading companies. She also heads a program at George Mason University, which received a total of $50,000 from Enron since 1996. Her husband, Senator Phil Gramm, is a major recipient of Enron campaign donations. Board member Robert Belfer is founder and former chairman and CEO of Belco Oil and Gas Corp. Belco and Enron had numerous financial arrangements. Director Charles Walker is a tax lobbyist. Firms partly owned by Walker were paid more than $70,000 for consulting services from Enron. In addition, Enron also made donations to a nonprofit corporation chaired by Walker.

Would a board like Enron's really challenge management? A Senate report argues that the board failed in its fiduciary duties to represent shareholders, and its failure was partly due to the lack of independence.[31] In other words, Enron directors knew enough of what was going on, but they did nothing about it. However, as one Enron director put it, this was only a "part-time job," and the directors did the best they could, so they shouldn't be "criticized for failing to address or remedy problems that have been concealed...." The Senate report finds otherwise. Even in 1999, Enron board members were told by the company's auditors that they were using accounting practices that "push limits" and were "at the edge" of what was acceptable. One of the directors, Robert Jaedicke, used to be an accounting professor at Stanford University. Also, the board knowingly allowed Enron to move more than half of its assets off the balance sheet. Governance experts used by the Senate investigation state that this activity is unheard of, yet only one Enron board member expressed any concern with it when it was occurring. The board even waived a code of conduct stipulation for Chief Financial Officer Andrew Fastow, allowing him to create private offshore partnerships that would transact with Enron. These partnerships are detailed in the next chapter. Under the Enron code of conduct, no employee is allowed to obtain financial gain from an entity that did business with Enron. Under Fastow's watch, these entities profited at Enron's expense, but the board idly sat by—despite Fastow's obvious conflict of interest.

The Senate report concludes that the board missed a dozen red flags that should have warned it about possible shenanigans at the firm. For example, it was told that in a six-month period, Fastow's partnerships had generated $2 billion in funds for Enron. While it doesn't appear that Enron's board was involved in any of the fraud, it should have put a stop to it.[32] After all, board members were being paid more than $350,000 a year in salary, stocks, and stock options by Enron to be its directors. The Senate report's conclusion states that "much that was wrong with Enron was known to the Board.... By failing to provide sufficient oversight and restraint to stop management excess, the Enron Board contributed to the company's collapse and bears a share of the responsibility for it." It could be that the board members were too well paid by Enron. That is, they might not have wanted the gravy train to end. Their $350,000 a year salary was more than twice the average board compensation in the 200 largest public firms. In addition, some members received additional pay as "consultants" to the firm. Board member John Wakeham was paid an additional $6,000 per month as a retainer for consulting. In 2000, John Urquhart received $494,914 for consulting.[33] Such high compensation probably made the board members less likely to challenge Kenneth Lay and other Enron executives.

SUMMARY

We've only recently started paying attention to the activities of the board of directors. It appears that there is little regulation with regard to its composition, structure, and obligations.

Also, there are many potential problems with the way many corporations' boards are set up. For example, it seems that directors lack the independence, the vested interest, the time, and sometimes the expertise to carry out their fiduciary obligations to shareholders. Enron's board is a telling example. Does this mean that there is something wrong with the system? Many suggestions regarding board regulation have been proposed. Will they fix the problem? We will discuss this further in Chapters 12 and 13.

ENDNOTES

1. Ralph Nader, Mark Green, and Joel Seligman, *Taming the Corporate Giant* (New York: W. W. Norton & Company, 1976), p. 95.

2. Katrina Brooker, "Trouble in the Boardroom," *Fortune*, May 13, 2002, pp. 113–116.

3. Ibid.

4. These statistics are based on averages reported in the 28th Annual Board of Directors Study, Korn/Ferry International, 2001, *http://www.kornferry.com/Library/Process.asp?P=PUB_001*.

5. For example, the Delaware General Corporate Law 141.

6. Nasser Arshadi and Thomas H. Eyssell, *The Law and Finance of Corporate Insider Trading* (New York: Kluwer Academic Publishers, 1993), p. 7.

7. "M&A Activity Report," Mergerstat, LP, November 2002, *www.mergerstat.com/newfree_reports_m_and_a_activity.asp*.

8. 28th Annual Board of Directors Study, Korn/Ferry International, 2001, *http://www.kornferry.com/Library/Process.asp?P=PUB_001*.

9. Korn Ferry International recommendations, *www.kornferry.com*.

10. Ralph Nader, Mark Green, and Joel Seligman, *Taming the Corporate Giant* (New York: W. W. Norton & Company, 1976).

11. 28th Annual Board of Directors Study, Korn/Ferry International, 2001, *http://www.kornferry.com/Library/Process.asp?P=PUB_001*.

12. This quote is found in Robert Monk and Nell Minow, *Power and Accountability*, 2001, *http://www.thecorporatelibrary.com/power/*.

13. 28th Annual Board of Directors Study, Korn/Ferry International, 2001, *http://www.kornferry.com/Library/Process.asp?P=PUB_001*.

14. Ibid.

15. John A. Byrne, "The Best and Worst Boards," *BusinessWeek*, December 8, 1997, pp. 90–98.

16. Bruce Orwall, "Disney Board Braces for Impact of New Independence Rules," *Wall Street Journal*, August 12, 2002, p. B1.

17. John A. Byrne, "The Best and Worst Boards," *BusinessWeek*, December 8, 1997, pp. 90–98.

18. Ibid.

19. John A. Byrne, "Directors in the Hot Seat," *BusinessWeek*, December 8, 1997, pp. 100–104.

20. Ibid.

21. John A. Byrne, "The Best and Worst Boards," *BusinessWeek*, December 8, 1997, pp. 90–98.

22. John A. Byrne, "The Best and Worst Corporate Boards," *BusinessWeek*, January 24, 2000, pp. 142–152.

23. Jerold B. Warner, Ross L. Watts, and Karen H. Wruck, "Stock Prices and Top Management Changes," *Journal of Financial Economics* 20 (1989): 461–492; Michael S. Weisback, "Outside Directors and CEO Turnover," *Journal of Financial Economics* 20 (1988): 431–460; Kenneth A. Borokhovich, Robert Parrino, and Teresa Trapani, "Outside Directors and CEO Selection," *Journal of Financial and Quantitative Analysis* 31, no. 3 (1996): 337–355; and Kathleen A. Farrell and David A. Whidbee, "The Consequences of Forced CEO Succession for Outside Directors," *Journal of Business* 73, no. 4 (2000): 597–627.

24. Kathy Farrell and David Whidbee, "The Consequences of Forced CEO Succession for Outside Directors," *Journal of Business* 73 (2000): 597–627.

25. John A. Byrne, "Directors in the Hot Seat," *BusinessWeek*, December 8, 1997, pp. 100–104.

26. John A. Byrne, "The Best and Worst Boards," *BusinessWeek*, November 25, 1996, pp. 82–91.

27. James R. Booth and Daniel N. Deli, "On Executives of Financial Institutions as Outside Directors," *Journal of Corporate Finance* 5, no. 3 (1999): 227–250.

28. Jeff Huther, "An Empirical Test of the Effect of Board Size on Firm Efficiency," *Economics Letters* 54, no. 3 (1996): 259–264; David Yermack, "Higher Market Valuation of Companies with a Small Board of Directors," *Journal of Financial Economics* 40, no. 2 (1996): 185–211.

29. "Tyco Cancels Vote on Expanding Board," *Reuters Business Report*, August 6, 2002, 9:32 a.m.

30. "The Role of the Board of Directors in Enron's Collapse," U.S. Senate Report 107–70, July 8, 2002.

31. Ibid.

32. John Byrne, "Commentary: No Excuses for Enron's Board," *BusinessWeek*, July 29, 2002, p. 50.

33. Pete Yost, "Enron Board Knew of Financial Abuses, Senate Report Says," *Seattle Times*, July 7, 2002, p. A14.

7 INVESTMENT BANKS

Most people are familiar with the activities of *commercial* banks because of the role they play in every day life. Commercial banks take deposits in the form of certificates of deposits, passbook savings accounts, and money market accounts. They use this money to provide loans. You have your checking account at a commercial bank. These borrowing and lending activities are much different from the primary activities of *investment* banks.

The primary role of investment banks is to help companies raise capital by issuing securities. Company managers are experts in the business activities of their particular industry. They know how to build, market, sell, and service their products. These managers are not experts in obtaining the capital they may need to develop new products or expand operations. Should the company sell more stock or conduct a bond issue? What about more complex securities like preferred stock or convertible shares? Financial engineering over the past decade has created some very complicated securities. Should a firm sell the securities to public investors or to deep-pocket private investors like state pension funds? Indeed, even the process of registering new securities with the SEC is complicated. Investment banks specialize in steering firms through this maze of questions and helping them obtain the needed capital with the best security issue.

Both commercial and investment banks find capital for those who need it. Commercial banks are mostly compensated by the difference in interest rates that they receive from lending and paying depositors. Long after money initially changes hands, these banks continue to service both the depositors and lenders. Alternatively, investment banks are compensated by a fee that is charged to the company for selling the new securities. After the firm gets the capital and the investors get their security, the investment bank no longer is involved. That is, investment banks put together deals and then move on. They are an important and integral part of the corporate system.

SOME HISTORICAL PERSPECTIVE

Modern U.S. investment banks are descendents from the merchant bank. Merchant banks used their own capital to stake traders in their various risky endeavors. This was particularly the case for foreign trade in the 1600s and 1700s. In those days, conducting trade over long distances meant taking the risk of losing cargo to weather or piracy, and the normal risks of business, like competition and product substitutes. Merchant banks helped to fund the trade expeditions in exchange for a stake in the profits.

The merchant banks were especially active in the United States when it was still the American British Colonies. Trade ships brought natural resources from America to Europe and returned with goods supplied from all over the world. These voyages were funded through merchant banks. After the Revolutionary War, a fledgling United States found that it had an abundance of natural resources and capitalistic spirit, but very little capital. The merchant banks set up private banks in the United States to help businesses obtain capital. These banks had contacts in Europe, the source of most capital at that time. They became intermediaries between the sources of capital and the American businesses.[1] Junius Spencer Morgan founded one of the best-known firms, J.S. Morgan and Company. Junius, his son, and his grandson were particularly adept at funneling foreign capital to the United States. His son, John Pierpont Morgan, ran the activities in America and eventually named that operation J.P. Morgan. Today, the firm is called JPMorgan Chase & Co. Of course, many things have changed. Now, the United States is the greatest source of capital in the world. Foreign firms and even foreign countries issue securities in the United States to obtain capital.

In the early 1800s, most of the investment banking activities were in treasury, municipal, and railroad bonds. These early investment banks also helped to set up new markets in the United States. For example, Marcus Goldman established Goldman Sachs and Company in 1869 and created the U.S. commercial paper market. Commercial paper is a security similar to U.S. Treasury Bills except that financially strong companies issue them, not the government.

The differences between commercial-bank and investment-bank activities began to vanish in the mid-1920s. The go-go excesses of the 1920s were similar to those of the late 1990s. The economy was strong and the stock market continuously advanced. The government inadvertently contributed to the exuberance in 1927 by allowing commercial banks to participate in the stock issuance process. From 1926 to 1928, the number of new stock issues increased eight-fold. Many new companies were coming to market.

As described later in this chapter, there are different methods for a bank to help issue stock. One process is called underwriting. Underwriting involves the bank taking some risk. The bank guarantees that the company issuing the security will receive a specific amount of capital. If the stock doesn't sell well, the bank can lose money. This had a large impact on commercial banks in the stock market crash of 1929. They were stuck with stock they could not sell. The losses of the banks impacted the depositors. Indeed, worried people with bank deposits demanded their money back. The panicked rush to the banks forced them to close and caused runs on other banks. Soon, the whole banking system was in shambles. This contributed to the severity and duration of the Great Depression that followed.

After the stock market crash of 1929 and the following economic slowdown, the U.S. Congress held hearings and conducted investigations. Investors demanded reform. In the spring of 1933, a bill known as the Glass-Steagall Act of 1933 was introduced and passed relatively quickly. The law had two main components. The first part of the law was to create deposit insurance so that people would have confidence in the banking system and faith in the safety of commercial banks. The second part of the law was the separation of commercial banking and investment banking. Investment banks could not receive deposits from the public and commercial banks could not conduct underwriting activities.

History tends to repeat itself. By the early 1980s, the U.S. commercial banks were lobbying Congress to allow them into investment banking activities. The Federal Reserve Board finally allowed commercial banks to underwrite commercial paper, municipal bonds, and asset-backed securities (like mortgage-backed bonds).[2] This decision went to the U.S. Supreme Court in 1988, which let it stand. At the same time, investment banks were moving into areas of retail banking. For example, the money-market mutual fund plays a similar role as a bank deposit. Finally, much of the Glass-Steagall Act of 1933 was torn away in the Financial Services Modernization Act of 1999 (also known as the Gramm-Leach-Bliley Act). The passage of this act allowed investment banks and commercial banks to affiliate with each other under one holding company structure. Several banks quickly merged into this structure. For example, JPMorgan Chase & Co. is the financial holding company for two main banking entities, JPMorgan and Chase Manhattan Bank USA. JPMorgan is an investment bank while Chase Manhattan is a commercial bank.

It is hard not to notice that investment banking and commercial banking were allowed to merge in both 1927 and 1999. Both convergences occurred during the run-up of a stock market bubble and preceded a severe market decline.

INVESTMENT BANKING ACTIVITIES

The basic investment banking service is to help companies issue new debt and equity securities. There are several different kinds of securities that a firm can issue. The bank advises the company on which security is optimal for the amount of capital being raised and the situation of the company. For this service, investment banks charge the company a fee. The size of the fee depends on how much risk the investment bank is taking to issue the securities. There are two methods that banks take to issue stock and bonds: underwriting and best-efforts.

Think about the case of issuing stock. When underwriting an issue, the bank will guarantee that a company will receive a specific amount of capital. That is, the bank assures the company that a certain number of shares will sell at a target price. If too few shares sell at that price, the investment bank must buy those shares. To illustrate the risk that the bank is taking, consider what would have happened if an issue were being sold when the September 11, 2001, terrorist attacks occurred. Afterward, stock prices plummeted and investors were not interested in buying stock. If the bank guaranteed the company would get $100 million in capital, and only $70 million were raised, the bank would have to buy $30 million worth of stock. The fee for underwriting a $100 million issue is typically around $7 million for a new issue and $5 million for an existing company's issue.

If the investment bank did not want to take risk on a security issue, it could use the best-efforts method. Here, there is no guarantee of raising the desired amount of capital. The bank does its best to sell as much of the security as possible for the company. In this case, it is the company that is taking the risk of not receiving enough capital. Since the risk is low for the investment bank, the fee it charges is much lower for the best-efforts method than for underwriting.

The process of selling securities to public investors involves registration at the SEC. The document submitted to the SEC includes a preliminary prospectus that contains information about the security issue and the company. For example, the prospectus details the company's financial condition, business activities, management experience, and how the funds raised will be used. The final prospectus is distributed to investors who are interested in the stock issue. This information helps investors make decisions about the condition of the company and about buying the issue. In other words, investment bankers provide information and monitor public companies.

That is why bond investors are angry with Citigroup and JPMorgan's underwriting of $11 billion in bonds for WorldCom. The two investment banks are being sued by investors for a lack of due diligence in the underwriting. The bonds were sold in May 2002. The next month, WorldCom announced that it had improperly capitalized $3.8 billion in expenses. The financial health of WorldCom came into question, and the $11 billion in bonds plummeted in price.[3] The lawsuit argues that the banks should have known something was wrong at the firm, but they conducted the bond offering anyway.

The prospectus and the banker's "road show" relay information about the company to investors. The road show is the marketing campaign done by the bankers to pre-sell the issue. They travel the country visiting the large institutional investors, like public pension funds and mutual funds. To sell to individual investors, investment banks use their brokerage operations. For a hot issue, investors call the brokers to order shares of the issue. In a less popular issue, the brokers call them.

The information about the issuing company is especially important to investors when the firm is new. When a firm offers stock to the public for the very first time, it is called an initial public offering (IPO). When a firm comes to market in an IPO, it is typically young, small, and mostly unknown to investors. The information gathered by an investment bank and presented to the SEC may be the only independent data available on the firm. Therefore, investors expect the bank to fully disclose all relevant information so that they can make a good decision.

Investment banks have increased risk when underwriting an IPO because of the uncertainty involved with new firms. To mitigate some of the risk, banks tend to underprice IPO offerings. That is, they offer the new shares of stock at a lower price than the demand for the stock would suggest. For example, on July 25, 2002, the newly public firm LeapFrog Enterprises conducted an IPO to raise $130 million. The company produces technology-enhanced toys and is considered a business of Michael Milken, the junk bond king of the 1980s. Those investors who purchased the stock from the investment banks bought it at $13 per share. There was a syndicate of banks that conducted the underwriting services for this deal. However, there were not enough shares for all the investors who wanted them. Therefore, the investors who were left out of the deal had to buy shares on the New York Stock Exchange later that day. The price opened on the exchange at $15.50 per share and closed the day at $15.85. The first day return for the stock was 22 percent. The investment banks were probably well aware that the first day trading price would be greater than $13 per share, but they underpriced the stock offer anyway to ensure that they would sell all of the stock and reduce their liability to LeapFrog.

Underpricing IPOs lowers the risk to the underwriters and makes the new issues highly desirable to investors. After all, who wouldn't want a 22 percent return in one day? Figure 7–1 shows the number of IPOs offered in each year from 1980 to 2001.[4] The line represents the average first day return for the offerings each year. Note that the average first day return is positive in every year. That doesn't mean that every IPO experiences an increase in price on the first day. Some IPOs are in high demand and earn a positive return— others are in low demand and decline in price the first day. Investors want to get those hot IPO firms and avoid the lemons. The average initial return for IPOs in the late 1990s and 2000 was extraordinarily high. The average in 1999 was more than 70 percent! The average underpricing in the

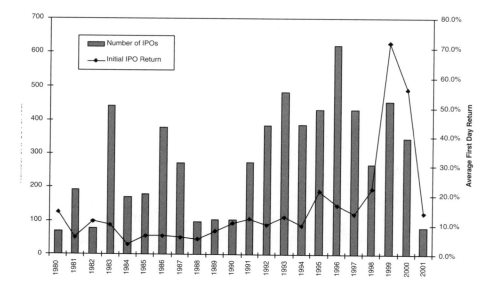

FIGURE 7–1 The columns show the number of IPOs issued each year. The line reports the average return for those issues measured from the issue price to the closing price on the first day of trading.

United States was just over 20 percent in the 1990s. This compares to 16.5 percent in France, 40.2 percent in Germany, and 39.6 percent in the United Kingdom.[5]

The number of IPOs offered is highly correlated with a bull market. Stocks were in a strong bull market in the mid-1980s until the crash of October 1987. After the crash, the number of IPOs declined to around 100 per year. This number increased dramatically in the bull market of the 1990s. Then, after the bear market arrived in 2000, the number of IPOs again declined for 2001. The first six months of 2002 saw only 46 IPOs. In July 2002, during the lows of investor confidence, there were only five IPOs.

IPO PROBLEMS

Investment banks take small, private firms public in IPOs. These small firms want the capital to expand that the stock issue provides. However, every small-business owner would like to get tens or hundreds of millions of dollars to spend. Yet, very few small businesses would make good public companies. That is, the business model of many small firms would not work effectively as large, national firms. The small-business owners may not be capable of running a large business.

Typically, only a small fraction (less than 1 percent) of firms that want to conduct an IPO ever get to. Who decides which firms go public? Investment banks make this decision. After all, they are taking the risk as the underwriters. The banks thoroughly examine potential IPO firms. Traditionally, the policy of many banks has been to only bring a firm public if it has put together a good management team, developed a quality business plan, and perfected its business model enough so that it has earned profits in the past three quarters. The diligence of the banks had been successful. The companies brought public from 1986 to 1995 experienced only a 1 percent failure rate.[6] This rate is defined as a firm's stock price falling to less than $1 (or delisted from the exchanges) within the first three years after the IPO. Investment banks had done a good job of offering quality companies to investors.

Things began to change in the middle to late 1990s. The stock prices of technology firms dramatically increased, and this stock was enormously popular with investors. The demand from investors for more technology stocks seemed insatiable. Hundreds of millions of dollars were to be made by taking tech firms public. The investment banking industry would rake in more than $2 billion in banking fees. However, there were not enough new firms that met the traditionally high-quality standards of the banks. But investors did not seem to care. They seemed to want any new tech stock and at any price. Recall how high the average first-day returns of IPOs were in 1999 and 2000. The risk of underwriting these firms did not seem very high with such strong demand.

So investment banks lowered their standards to offer more firms. The standards seemed to get quite low indeed. Consider the IPO of Pets.com. In 1999, the firm had only $5.8 million in revenue and reported an operating loss of $61.8 million. Yet

Merrill Lynch launched the Pets.com IPO in February 2000. The firm raised $66 million in capital and Merrill Lynch received more than $4 million in fees.[7] Ten months later, Pets.com folded. The firms that offered IPOs in the period 1998 to 2000 experienced a 12 percent failure rate. This is much higher than the 1 percent historical rate. The investment banks apparently lost their desire to be gatekeepers of quality firms and monitors for investors.

Investors probably measure success differently. They measure it by their investment return. Of the 367 Internet firms that went public since 1997, only 15 percent have made money compared to their offer prices. More than 200 firms have lost more than 75 percent of their value. What makes this even worse for average individual investors is that they rarely get the good IPOs at the offer price. They are usually forced to buy the stock when it starts trading on the stock exchange. By then, it has typically already increased in price. Therefore, the poor returns are even worse for individual investors.

In other words, investment banks consider an offering to be a success if they sell all the securities offered, raise the amount of capital needed for the firm, and receive their fees for the service. However, investors consider the offering a success if the security meets or exceeds the expected rate of return over the next month, year, and longer. The investment bank's focus ends when the securities are sold, but this is when the investor's focus begins. Therefore, banks and investors do not have the same interests at heart in this particular securities issue.

IPOS AND FRAUD

The euphoria over the wealth that investment banks were generating from taking technology firms public caused some investment banks to bend—even break—the rules. The banks wanted to keep the exuberance over IPOs going and also get more of the wealth being created. Investment banks controlled a scarce commodity—IPO shares. They used their control of the shares in several dubious ways.

Since the IPO shares were earning such high rates of return on the first day of trading, many institutional investors wanted them. Because those shares were scarce, the investment banks were in a position to allocate them in ways that allowed themselves to get kickbacks. One way to receive a kickback was to charge an institutional investor an unusually large commission rate for trading stock. Normally, the commission that investment banks charge institutional investors is around five cents per share. In order to secure IPO shares, these institutions agreed to pay commissions of more than $2 per share. In other words, the banks wanted to get some of the big returns the investors were getting on the first trading day of a hot IPO. This practice, a form of "tie-in," is not allowed by either the SEC or the National Association of Securities Dealers (NASD), a private regulator of securities firms.

In 1999, Steve Kris ran a small investment firm in Denver called Ascent Capital. His investment fund was known to be a "flipper." That is, it tries to get shares of hot IPOs at issue and then immediately sell (or flip) them during the first day or two that the new company trades. Kris wanted to get a lot of shares of one company going public, VA Linux Systems. The investment banking firm Credit Suisse First Boston (CSFB) underwrote the issue. Kris was not happy with the modest 2,500 shares he was allocated and so pressed for more. After agreeing to be a good CSFB customer on commissions and to buying more Linux shares in the open market, Kris received 17,950 shares of the IPO.[8]

On the first day of trading, Linux stock soared an incredible 698 percent. Kris had made $3.8 million on the IPO shares. That same day, he traded many shares in other companies that were so large that no one would have noticed the extra volume. For example, he traded 50,000 shares of Citigroup using CSFB as the broker and paid a commission of $2.70 per share, for a $135,000 bill. He also traded in Compaq, Kmart, Kroger, and AT&T for a total commission bill of more than $500,000. These trades would normally have cost less then $20,000. Another flipper firm, Back Bay Management, also received 17,950 shares of Linux. On that day, Back Bay traded in the likes of American International, Anheuser-Busch, Champion International, IBM, and Merck. Back Bay paid nearly $400,000 in commissions to CSFB. Institutional investors that did not agree to kick back some of the IPO profits found themselves with very few shares of the firms going public.

The other concession that CSFB wanted from investors was to purchase additional shares of the IPO in the stock market on the first day of trading. This buying would create the kind of high demand that would guarantee a very high first day return. Both the high commission and the agreement to buy additional shares in the open market must be construed as a quid pro quo by the investment bank—an arrangement that is illegal. Indeed, CSFB agreed to pay a $100 million fine to resolve SEC and NASD investigations.[9]

Giving shares to investors based on quid pro quo arrangements reduces the number of IPO shares available for average individual investors. This is one reason individual investors commonly failed to get the shares of hot IPO issues they wanted. During the height of the tech bubble in 1999 and 2000, 75 percent of the shares of an IPO went to institutional investors, leaving only 25 percent for individual investors. Since individuals had to buy the shares in the stock market and because many institutions were flipping the shares, the ownership quickly shifted to 25 percent institutions and 75 percent individuals.[10] The institutions had bought low and sold high. The individuals had bought high. The quality of these firms was also suspect. The stock prices eventually collapsed and individuals were resigned to selling low. It seems clear that the actions of these banks were not in the best interest of the public investor.

It also appears that some investment banks allocated shares of hot IPOs to corporate executives and venture capitalists. By currying favor with executives, the investment banks hoped to get investment banking services from their companies in the future. The venture capitalists were in a position to steer more IPO business their way. This practice is called "spinning" because its purpose is to give the executives a chance to sell, or spin, the shares for a quick profit. The investment bank hopes that the executives will be grateful for the cash and use the bank to help it obtain capital in the future.

Spinning is not allowed. Not only are investment banks prohibited from allocating IPO shares this way, but executives are prohibited from accepting this type of deal. Nevertheless, in 1998, the Manhattan U.S. attorney's office, the SEC, and the NASD were investigating spinning. In one example, the investment bank Robertson Stephens allocated 100,000 shares of the IPO firm Pixar Animation to Joseph Cayre. Cayre was the executive of another firm that would soon go public. He turned a quick profit of $2 million with those shares and subsequently chose Robertson Stephens to conduct its own IPO.[11] While Robertson Stephens claimed that it did nothing wrong, it also changed its internal policy on such matters. Though these kinds of quid pro quo arrangements are not allowed, they are very difficult to prove in court. However, the investigations themselves in 1998 seemed to change the behavior of the banks for a while.

Unfortunately, it appears that spinning might be back. A former (disgruntled) broker from Citibank's investment banking business, Salomon Smith Barney, claims that the firm curried favor with executives by allocating them shares of hot IPO issues. Executives who allegedly received shares are Bernard Ebbers (former CEO of WorldCom) and Joseph Nacchio (former chairman of Qwest). The broker, David Chacon, says that Ebbers received 350,000 shares of the firm Rhythms Net-Connections at the IPO price of $21 in 1999. When the stock priced jumped more than 600 percent after starting to trade on the stock exchange, Ebbers quickly sold for a $16 million profit.[12] The investment banking firm later participated in lucrative offers by WorldCom, including the $11 billion bond offering in May 2002. It appears that banking firm Credit Suisse First Boston also allocated hot IPO shares through a $100 million fund created for wealthy clients.[13] Typical clients just happened to be CEOs and CFOs of companies that had hired the investment bank to underwrite large issues.

STRUCTURED DEALS

When companies need more capital, or even just more cash, they turn to investment banks. It is very difficult to help some firms. As an extreme example, consider a firm that is likely to go bankrupt. In bankruptcy, the equity of the firm is taken from the stockholders, who get nothing, and given to some of the creditors. Therefore, investors are not likely to buy additional shares of stock of a firm in financial trouble. The firm would also have trouble borrowing money from banks or from bond investors because these creditors typically do not get all of their money back in bankruptcy. They often get a small fraction of what they are owed and then receive some stock to become the new owners of the firm. Since lenders do not get their money back in bankruptcy court, they are unlikely to lend money to a financially troubled firm.

There are many times when a firm would have trouble raising capital even if it was not on the brink of bankruptcy. For example, the current creditors of a firm may have stipulated in their loan that the firm cannot borrow more money unless they are repaid first. Also, hardly any firms can issue additional stock when investor confidence is low, like in the summer of 2002.

Unfortunately, it appears that investment banks have been active participants in helping some companies secretly raise capital and even fraudulently prop up profits. Enron's strategy was to launch structured deals using special purpose entities (SPE) created in tax havens like the Cayman Islands. The SPEs are formed as partnerships and are used to create the appearance of third-party companies doing business with Enron. The "business" actually turns out to be loans that were recorded as revenue instead of debt. For the structured deals to work, Enron needed complicated structures to fool auditors and regulators. To help create and fund the deals, Enron turned to investment banks.

The use of offshore partnerships to prop up Enron's financial status was greatly accelerated in the summer of 1999. Enron had heavily invested in an Internet start-up called

Rhythms NetConnections. Rhythms stock had jumped and the investment of $10 million grew to $300 million—a $290 million profit! Due to restrictions on selling ownership in the recent IPO, Enron could not sell this stock. Because of its mark-to-market method of accounting, it could book the gain. The mark-to-market method allowed Enron to report its assets at market value instead of the traditional method of using purchase price less depreciation. However, Enron worried that a big decline in price later would require booking a large loss.[14] Enron could not get the investment banks to hedge the price risk because of the huge position and the high risk of the start-up. So Enron created the partnership called LJM in the Cayman Islands that would guarantee the profit.[15] Enron's CFO Andrew Fastow would run the partnership. In fact, the SPE name LJM comes from the names of his wife and children. The new partnership was funded by Enron stock. Therefore, Enron was really insuring itself. This profit would represent 30 percent of Enron's total profit for the year. However, if both Rhythms' stock and Enron's stock price fell, LJM would not have enough capital to make the guaranteed payment. Enron would then have to reverse the profit and record a loss of $290 million. The large loss would further depress the Enron stock. It created LJM anyway and completed the deal. Enron considered LJM a big success and entered into similar arrangements to hedge other risky tech stock holdings. These arrangements were called Raptor partnerships.

Fastow's position as CFO of Enron and general partner of the SPE in the Caymans presented a serious conflict of interest. He made the deals between Enron and the partnerships that made him rich at the expense of Enron. Fastow made $45 million from running the structured deals.[16] The conflict of interest violated Enron's ethics code. But, inexplicably, Enron's board ignored the code and approved the arrangement.

The myriad partnerships created were actually a sophisticated Ponzi scheme. Enron would create fictitious profits to meet earnings expectations. Those profits would have to be offset in the future as losses. As the losses came due, Enron had to continue the process again and create new structured deals to hide (or delay) the losses and generate additional profits. In this way, the deals quickly mushroomed in number and in size. Eventually, the scheme collapsed as Enron's stock price fell in 2001. Many of the partnerships funded with the stock were unable to complete their transactions. Enron was forced to disclose $1 billion in losses that it had previously booked as profits, and the company was forced into bankruptcy.

Consider a simple example of the use of offshore partnerships that Enron used to prop itself up financially. Enron owned three barges located in Nigeria that generated electricity. They were trying to sell the barges, but they had no takers. According to the U.S. Senate investigation, Enron convinced Merrill Lynch to buy the barges for $28 million. Enron assured Merrill Lynch that it would get its money back with profit in six months because Enron would repurchase the barges at that time. Enron wanted to record the sale and capture a $12 million profit in order to meet its earnings expectations. However, the sale of an asset with an agreement to repurchase it is not really a sale. Instead, it is simply a loan with the asset as collateral for the loan. Enron did not want a loan. In fact, it already had too much debt on its books. It wanted the money and the recorded profit without creating more debt.

The solution was for Enron and Merrill Lynch to create another SPE in the Cayman Islands, which they named Ebarge. Ebarge was set up with $7 million in equity from Merrill Lynch and $21 million in debt from Enron.[17] In 1999, Ebarge used this capital to purchase the three barges. Six months later, Ebarge was purchased from Merrill Lynch for $7.5 million by another SPE controlled by Fastow called LJM2.[18] The $500,000 profit in six months is equivalent to a 15 percent annualized return—a pretty high interest rate for 1999 and 2000. Including these third-party partnerships made the deal look like a real sale, not a loan. However, Ebarge was controlled by Merrill Lynch and LJM2 by Enron, so the transaction was really a loan. LJM2 finally sold the barges to another company. LJM2 was created after the perceived success of LJM and was capitalized with 20 times more money, mostly from investment banks that wanted to continue doing business with Enron. In the meantime, Enron made its earnings forecast and Merrill Lynch made its profit.

This barge example is only the tip of the iceberg. The Senate subcommittee on investigations charges JPMorgan Chase and Citigroup with partnership arrangements that effectively hid $5 billion worth of debt in the first half of 2001 alone.[19] Most of these arrangements are alleged to be in the form of "prepaid" deals. It is not uncommon for energy companies to contract to sell oil, gas, or electricity in advance. An energy user may want to lock in a supply of energy for the future. The energy firm may even offer a customer a discount if he or she pays in advance. This is known as a prepaid arrangement. The energy firm books the revenue.

Congressional investigators claim that the investment banks used prepaid deals to funnel cash to Enron. The cash would fraudulently appear on Enron's financial statements as revenue when it was really debt. The offshore SPEs conducted deals with Enron from 1992 to 2001 that brought $8.5 billion in loans that Enron kept off the books.[20] If properly reported, Enron's debt in 2000 would have been 40 percent higher than actually reported and its operations revenue would have been 50 percent lower. However, the investment banks didn't want the oil and gas. JPMorgan Chase and Citigroup are banks, not energy firms or energy traders. They expected to get back the money with interest. These prepay deals also had to take place through offshore partnerships to keep the appearance that the transactions were legitimate business activities. JPMorgan Chase used the entity called Mahonia, while Citigroup backed one named Delta. The banks funded the partnerships with their own capital and also by marketing ownership to institutional investors.

The ongoing charade continued to allow Enron to financially survive and even boosted Enron's stock price. Enron dealt with nearly 700 SPEs in all, many of them with colorful names like Chewco, JEDI, Kenobe Inc., Obi-1 Holdings, Raptor, Southampton, Talon, and Zephyrus. Since many of the partnerships were interlinked, they were at risk of a domino effect if one or two failed. JPMorgan Chase and Citigroup made more than $200 million in fees for their part.[21] The longer the charade continued, the more money investors and employees would invest in the company. As the stock price tripled between 1998 and 2000, more investors flocked to the firm. Finally, in the fall of 2001, the dominos fell.

Merrill Lynch has denied that it has done anything wrong and claims that it is not responsible for Enron fraudulently booking loans as revenue. However, that misses the point. Even if Merrill Lynch did nothing illegal, it broke the trust of its clients and the public investor by participating in a scheme that was designed to hide a firm's financial troubles. The bankers had to know that Enron's financial statements were misleading—at the least. The Senate seems to have some compelling evidence against the banks. It has an e-mail from a JPMorgan Chase banker stating that Enron loves the deals because they are able to hide debt.[22] It also has a tape of a phone conversation between two JPMorgan Chase bankers during which one realizes the transactions are just debt and the other banker confirms it.[23] As a monitor of the corporation, the investment banks failed. This is of particular concern because JPMorgan Chase and Citigroup are the nation's two largest financial institutions. The banks have tried to soften some of the criticism by enacting their own rules to not finance a company unless the firm publicly discloses the debt.[24] Of course, this new policy also implies that the banks weren't concerned about this issue before the pressure from investors and the media.

While we have only detailed the role of investment banks in Enron's structured deals, there is evidence that they have helped other firms create SPEs. JPMorgan Chase pitched these financing vehicles to other firms and entered into arrangements with seven companies. Citigroup discussed the deals with 14 companies and developed them with three.[25] JPMorgan Chase and Citigroup may not be the only banks pitching these deals. Smaller deals were structured between Enron and the bankers of Credit Suisse Group, Barclays PLC, FleetBoston Financial Corp, Royal Bank of Scotland Group PLC, and Toronto-Dominion Bank. Indeed, Credit Suisse First Boston has been helping the energy company El Paso Corporation to create complex Enron-style deals in the year after Enron imploded.[26] It appears that El Paso is hiding debt in partnerships and booking future revenue as current profits just like Enron.

SUMMARY

Investment banks play a vital role in the American corporate system. They help firms acquire the capital they need to expand business operations. This expansion contributes to the growth in economic activity, wealth, and job creation in a capitalistic economy. However, capital is a scarce commodity. Not every person or firm that wants more money deserves to get it. Investment banks are the gatekeepers. They must be sure to conduct due diligence activities and only bring quality firms and security issues to the public. They have failed in recent years. While this chapter has detailed those failures, the next chapter discusses security analysts' failure. These issues are related, as analysts are frequently part of an investment bank.

ENDNOTES

1. This history is adapted from Charles Geisst, *Wall Street* (New York: Oxford University Press, 1997).
2. David S. Kidwell, Richard Peterson, David W. Blackwell, and David Whidbee, *Financial Institutions, Markets, and Money*, 8th ed. (Hoboken, NJ: John Wiley & Sons, 2002).
3. Heather Timmons, "Citi's Sleepless Nights," *BusinessWeek*, August 5, 2002, pp. 42–43.
4. Jay Ritter and Ivo Welch, "A Review of IPO Activity, Pricing, and Allocations," *Journal of Finance* 57, no. 4 (2002): 1795–1828.

5. Alexander Ljungqvist and William Wilhelm, "IPO Allocations: Discriminatory or Discretionary?" *Journal of Financial Economics* 65, no. 2 (2002): 167–201.

6. Andrew Ross Sorkin, "Just Who Brought Those Duds to Market?" *New York Times*, April 15, 2001, p. C1.

7. Peter Elstrom, "The Great Internet Money Game," *BusinessWeek*, April 26, 2001, p. 16.

8. Susan Pulliam and Randall Smith, "Sharing the Wealth: At CSFB, Lush Profit Earned on IPOs Found Its Way Back to Firm," *Wall Street Journal*, November 30, 2001, p. A1.

9. Susan Pulliam, Randall Smith, Anita Raghavan, and Gregory Zuckerman, "Coming to Terms: CSFB to Pay $100 Million to Settle Twin IPO Investigations," *Wall Street Journal*, December 11, 2001, p. A1.

10. Daniel Quin Mills, *Buy, Lie, and Sell High* (Upper Saddle River, NJ: Financial Times Prentice Hall, 2002).

11. Michael Siconolfi, "'Spinning' of Hot IPOs Is Probed," *Wall Street Journal*, April 16, 1998, p. C1.

12. Susanne Craig and Charles Gasparino, "Salomon IPO Suit Claims Special Accounts Were Used," *Wall Street Journal*, July 19, 2002, p. C1.

13. Tom Hamburger, Susan Pulliam, and Susanne Craig, "Salomon IPO Deals Provoke Congress," *Wall Street Journal*, August 29, 2002, p. C1.

14. Peter Fusaro and Ross Miller, *What Went Wrong at Enron* (Hoboken, NJ: John Wiley & Sons, 2002).

15. Peter Behr and April Witt, "Visionary's Dream Led to Risky Business," *Washington Post*, July 28, 2002, p. A1.

16. April Witt and Peter Behr, "Losses, Conflicts Threaten Survival," *Washington Post*, July 31, 2002, p. A1.

17. Randall Smith and Anita Raghavan, "Congress Probes Merrill-Enron Deal," *Wall Street Journal*, July 30, 2002, p. C1.

18. Charles Gasparino and Randall Smith, "Merrill Lynch Puts Energy Official on Leave," *Wall Street Journal*, July 29, 2002, p. C1.

19. Peter Behr and April Witt, "Hidden Debts, Deals Scuttle Last Chance," *Washington Post*, August 1, 2002, p. A1.

20. Kevin Drawbaugh, "Congress Grills Chase, Citi on Enron Prepay Deals," *Reuters Business Report*, July 23, 2002, 8:47 p.m.

21. Paul Beckett and Jathon Sapsford, "Energy Deals Made $200 Million in Fees for Citigroup, J.P. Morgan," *Dow Jones Newswire*, July 24, 2002, 1:06 a.m. EST.

22. Edward Iwata, "Did Banks Play Role in Enron Scandal?" *USA Today*, July 23, 2002, p. 1B.

23. Campion Walsh, "Chase, Citigroup Defend 'Prepaid' Deals with Enron," *Dow Jones Newswire*, July 23, 2002, 7:44 p.m. EST.

24. Kathleen Day, "2 Big Banks to Insist on Debt Disclosure," *Washington Post*, August 8, 2002, p. E1.

25. Jathon Sapsford and Paul Beckett, "Citigroup, J.P. Morgan Marketed Enron-Type Deals to Other Firms," *Wall Street Journal*, July 23, 2002, p. C13.

26. David Barboza, "Complex El Paso Partnerships Puzzle Analysts," *New York Times*, July 23, 2002, p. C1.

8 ANALYSTS

When Salomon Smith Barney's former star analyst Jack B. Grubman finally downgraded his assessment of WorldCom stocks to "neutral," the stock had already lost 90 percent of its value and was trading at $4 per share.[1] Merrill Lynch's former star analyst Henry Blodget never recommended selling Internet Capital, even though its stock price fell from $143 a share to 31 cents a share.[2] In fact, less than one month before Enron filed for bankruptcy, 11 out of 16 analysts had "buy" or "strong buy" ratings for Enron stocks.[3] Imagine! Are analysts terrible at analyzing? If so, why did Grubman make about $20 million a year?

Basically, analysts are paid to generate revenue for their firms. This, in and of itself, should not be surprising. However, you may think that they do this by providing their clients with unbiased analysis that is more often right than wrong, but this generally may *not* be the case. Instead, many analysts do more than just follow stocks. For example, Grubman attended board meetings and helped plan strategy for some of the firms that he analyzed. In fact, he helped Qwest recruit Joseph P. Nacchio as its CEO, and he provided assistance to Global Crossings in its acquisition of Frontier Communications.[4] These are not the normal duties of an analyst—at least, they didn't used to be.

Perhaps the most significant divergence from the traditional function of analyzing is that more and more analysts became involved in the investment banking arm of their firms. On the surface, it may not seem troubling that analysts go beyond their explicit job descriptions. However, there is a serious conflict of interest problem. Consider this: Those same firms that Grubman analyzes are also investment banking clients of Grubman's employer, Salomon Smith Barney. Investment banking generates huge fees. Given this, would Grubman ever issue a non-glowing assessment of a firm that is also an investment banking client? What if Grubman also helped out with the investment banking deal? What are analysts really being paid to do? Are their recommendations for investors or for banking clients?

This chapter discusses securities analysts. We first consider their traditional roles in our capital markets—to conduct research and recommend securities to clients. Then we look at their overall stock-picking abilities. They seem to be okay at it, but a recent SEC regulation may make their job a bit tougher. We go on to explore how analysts get compensated, which is important to understand when you consider the major conflict of interest that analysts face. Specifically, many analysts work for an investment bank, so they end up analyzing the same firms that their bank may wish to obtain as clients. Regulations to address this conflict of interest have passed. Will they work?

THE TRADITIONAL ROLE OF THE ANALYST

Analysts are supposed to analyze. This is their traditional role. For the firms that they are supposed to evaluate, they look at the operating and financial conditions, the immediate and long-term future prospects, the effectiveness of management teams, and the general industry outlook in order to make a useful assessment. Most analysts follow a specific industry so that they can gain expertise in a particular sector. For example, Grubman follows telecom stocks and Blodget used to cover Internet stocks. Based on their evaluations, analysts will make earnings predictions. Usually, they will try to predict the quarterly earnings per share (EPS) numbers. These predictions are useful to investors who rely on these estimates to determine the health of the companies in which they may or may not own stock. For example, many investors use P/E ratios (stock price divided by EPS) as an important gauge of a stock's attractiveness as an investment. Some investors like to examine forward-looking P/E ratios. That is, they use a P/E ratio in which the earnings are the estimate for the next year. Therefore, these earnings estimates of analysts are important and useful to investors.

Perhaps more importantly, the analyst is also supposed to make a recommendation to investors. For example, an analyst may recommend the buying or selling of a particular stock. These recommendations usually boil down to one-word or two-word recommendations such as "accumulate" or "buy." Unfortunately, these one-word recommendations are not standardized in the brokerage industry, which may lead to some confusion. Table 8–1 illustrates this point.[5]

TABLE 8–1   Three Examples of Analyst Recommendations

A	B	C
Buy	Strong Buy	Recommended List
Outperform	Buy	Trading Buy
Neutral	Hold	Market Outperformer
Underperform	Sell	Market Perform
Avoid		Market Underperformer

The table shows the stock rating system used by three different analysts' firms. A quick glance at the table reveals some potential problems. One analyst may use a five-category scale while another may use a four-category scale. Further, while both analysts A and C use a five-category scale, analyst A has two categories below average, but analyst C has only one category below average. Note also that a "buy" recommendation from analyst A is his highest recommendation, but for analyst B, it is only his second-highest rating. Lastly, each firm's definition of a market outperformer may be different. Is it for the upcoming one-year or two-year period? Is 5 percent or 10 percent considered outperformance? The answers depend on the analyst's firm.

However, given the recent scrutiny that is being placed on the analyst recommendations, there has been a trend toward making analysts' ratings uncomplicated. For example, analysts at Goldman Sachs, Lehman Brothers, Merrill Lynch, Morgan Stanley, and Prudential will all be using a three-tier rating system to eliminate the ambiguity between ratings such as "strong buy" versus "buy."[6]

With regard to these recommendations, perhaps the most important point is that they are supposed to be timely. For example, if on a particular day an interested investor finds that the analyst's recommendation for a given stock is a "buy," then that recommendation should reflect the analyst's most updated opinion. This means the recommendation should be updated quite frequently. If a news item breaks that could potentially affect an analyst's recommendation, he or she has to revise and disseminate an updated recommendation immediately. For his or her largest customers, an analyst may even make a phone call. However, a revision to a recommendation may sometimes have to go through an approval process, which may take a couple of days. Lengthy research reports that are mailed out or personally presented to potential investors may also be a bit less than timely. Nonetheless, analysts are generally relied upon for *timely* advice.

The traditional role of analysts is to conduct thorough analyses of the firms that they are assigned to cover in order to make earnings estimates and trading recommendations. Further, they should also make timely stock recommendations. Are analysts good at these functions?

CAN ANALYSTS PREDICT?

With regard to predicting earnings, analysts have actually been consistently, but slightly, conservative. That is, they make earnings predictions that end up being slightly lower than the eventual actual earnings. Sort of surprising, isn't it? It is especially surprising given their known penchant for over-optimism. These "conservative" earnings predictions are a well-known phenomena, and it is *not* difficult to explain. There are two factors involved. First, companies like to meet or beat the earnings expectations. Members of management will be viewed as being good at their jobs, and the company will be viewed as being as good as, or better than, expected. Second, for analysts to do a good job predicting earnings, they need information. If analysts can get full access to the firms that they follow, such as having personal meetings with the CEO or with other top executives, it really helps their task. However, will a CEO be 100 percent cooperative with an analyst who will not make an estimate that is either makeable or beatable? Probably not. In fact, Bill Gates and sales chief Steve Ballmer of Microsoft once purposely criticized *their own firm* to analysts in order to depress their expectations. Later, upon being told by one analyst that they had succeeded in painting a grim picture, Gates and Ballmer gave each other a high-five![7] What is the general outcome of these two factors? The answer is that analysts make slightly conservative estimates because this is what the management of the firm they are analyzing wants.[8] This makes the CEO happy and willing to grant further and future access. Analysts end up being "off" on their estimates by only a very tiny margin, so they are still considered good analysts. The company will either make or beat the estimate, so it will be considered a good company. Everyone wins. "Under-promise, over-deliver" is the name of this game.

So, analysts may be able to predict rather accurately, but they have far more superior information than the rest of us. With the private information that they have, they can probably make more precise earnings estimates than anyone else.

However, despite their ability to be very accurate, they will publicly and knowingly come out with slightly conservative estimates to keep the firms that they follow happy. While analysts are going to end up being systematically wrong by a small amount, their behavior is rational.

However, the ability of analysts to predict earnings accurately may suffer in the future. Since October 2000, the SEC has prevented firms from divulging privileged information to any analyst. Any information that the firm wishes to convey to an analyst must simultaneously be conveyed to the public. The SEC thought it was unfair that some investors, through analysts, were getting private information that other investors were not getting. The SEC policy creates a level playing field for all investors. Without privileged access to information, it is likely that analysts' forecasting accuracy will go downhill. However, John Coffee, securities law professor at Columbia University, suggests that forecasts will now become more honest assessments of future earnings.[9] It's too early to tell what kind of effect this SEC regulation is going to have on analysts' forecasts, but one academic study finds that analysts' forecasts since the passing of the SEC regulation have become less accurate.[10]

What about analysts' ability to recommend stocks? It is unclear whether analysts are any good at picking stocks. Older academic studies from the 1970s contended that analysts did *not* have good stock-picking abilities.[11] However, the more recent studies suggest that analysts may have some marginal ability as stock pickers.[12] If you were to have bought the stocks recommended as a "strong buy" during 1985 to 1996 and held them until the rating was downgraded, you would have outperformed the market by 4.3 percent per year if transactions costs were not considered. Analysts did indeed pick good stocks! However, if transaction costs were considered, you would have underperformed the market by 3.6 percent. While the picks were good, they were not good enough to implement a successful trading strategy.

Probably the most well-known evidence of analyst stock-picking abilities is from the *Wall Street Journal*'s "Dartboard

Competition," which is no longer printed. Throughout the 1990s, the *Wall Street Journal* pitted the stock picks of buy-side analysts against stocks picked by a random throw at a stock dartboard.[13] Out of 146 contests, the pros beat the dartboard 62 percent of the time. When pitted against the Dow Jones Industrial Average, the pros beat it 55 percent of the time. This evidence indicates that analysts can pick stocks, but, at the same time, it also shows that they're not that great at it.

But what about Blodget and Grubman, whom we mentioned earlier, and the famous Mary Meeker? Meeker is the star Internet analyst at Morgan Stanley who was once dubbed Queen of the Net by *Barron's*. Before and during the 85 to 97 percent price decline of Priceline, Amazon, Yahoo!, and FreeMarkets, Meeker never downgraded them.[14] Why were all three analysts so terribly off on many of their recommendations? Why were they being so well compensated at the same time? To understand this, you should know how analysts' compensation has been structured.

ANALYST COMPENSATION

We explore two questions here. If analysts are often wrong, why do they make so much money? Aren't they being rewarded for their stock-picking ability? For the most part, the answer to the first question may surprise you, and the answer to the last question is "sort of." Analysts are trying to help their brokerage firms or banks get trading commissions in the securities that they cover. That is, an analyst is hoping that his or her research will generate enough interest in a security that it will spur an investor to trade in it. This partially explains why so many analysts are trying to "sell" the stocks that they cover. As such, brokerage and investment bank analysts are commonly known as "sell-side" analysts, and they often appear like salespeople for the stocks that they cover. In a commentary that appeared in *Money* magazine, Blodget was even coined as a cheerleader for Amazon stock.[15] This need for analysts to root for the stocks that they cover may explain why Meeker was hesitant to downgrade Internet stocks even while the Internet bubble was bursting. Perhaps even more revealing is the fact that during the first part of 2002, only 2 percent of all stocks carried a "sell" recommendation[16] despite the unambiguous bearishness of the markets! Most savvy investors, however, know that a "neutral" or "hold" recommendation is a euphemism for getting the heck out of a stock, but this optimistic lingo used by analysts still promotes a bullish attitude. After all, not all investors are savvy.

Investors are not even obligated to transact in securities with the firm from which they obtained research. Large investors, especially, will simply search for the best execution prices regardless of the recommendation source. Shopping around for best execution prices is an outcome of the elimination of fixed commission fees back in 1975—previous to which time every brokerage firm was making large commissions off trades without having to compete in price. Without knowing how much analysts really contributed to commission revenue, how do they get compensated fairly for what they do? Indeed, quantifying an analyst's contribution to his or her firm's profits is difficult. One way around this may be to have analysts sell their research directly. Today, sell-side analysts' ratings and earnings estimates are widely and freely available, but this option may not be the most attractive one. The research reports that are the basis for those ratings and estimates still generally require a relationship with the analysts' brokerage or bank to obtain. Therefore, it is generally difficult to determine the fair compensation for analysts.

Given the difficulties associated with merit-based compensation for analysts, a significant portion of analyst compensation is now based on their reputations. For example, money managers and institutions participate in annual surveys, such as those conducted by Institutional Investor, asking them to rate and evaluate analysts along various dimensions. For each industry, analysts are ranked. A high ranking implies that the analyst is highly visible and is winning over customers. As such, he or she is likely to be well compensated. This form of compensation may encourage analysts to spend more time promoting themselves rather than working on their analyses. Henry J. Herrmann, chief investment officer at Waddell & Reed, claims that analysts get focused on saying what they think the client wants to hear in order to win the client.[17]

How much money do analysts make? The answer is a little tricky because it depends on whom the analysts work for. Senior analysts working for companies with no investment banking services earn an average of about $500,000 per year. The average rises to $1.5 million per year for senior analysts working for investment banks.[18] The top few analysts in the industry have earned closer to $10 or $20 million, depending on the particular year. Even relative rookies in the field often earn more than $100,000. Jack Grubman earned about $20 million per year. He left Salomon Brothers in August 2002 while he and the firm were under investigation from regulators. His severance package included forgiveness of a $19 million loan and $12 million in Citigroup stock.[19]

Why do analysts make so much money? Especially curious are those analysts working for investment banking firms who don't earn commission revenue. However, there is another way for analysts to get compensated. A part of their compensation has increasingly been dependent on the amount of investment banking business that they can bring in. For example, some star analysts have been getting 75 percent of their compensation from the investment banking side of the firm for which they work.[20] As such, equity research departments seem more like a support function for investment banking. In 2000, Grubman even boldly stated that, as a banking-intensive analyst, he represented the new model of analysts.[21] This trend bucks the traditional view of what analysts do for a living. This, in and of itself, may not seem so bad. However, this partnership between traditionally separate arms of an investment banking firm leads to a very serious conflict of interest problem.

POTENTIAL CONFLICTS OF INTEREST

Analysts need access. Analysts may be better than the rest of us at assessing the quality of a firm, but they also need to be better than the next analyst. To do this, analysts will try to get their hands on as much information as possible. Of course, the best source of a firm's information is from the firm itself. As mentioned earlier, analysts want to be able to have frank discussions with a firm's management. This represents an obvious conflict of interest. How can an analyst who needs to be chummy with management turn around and give it a bad rating, and then expect to be able to get access again? One analyst said that without access, it becomes difficult to make quality stock assessments, akin to playing basketball with one hand tied behind your back.[22] In addition, since analysts typically specialize in a particular industry or two, they get to know the managers in the field. That is, they may even develop friendships.

Specializing in a particular industry or sector allows the analyst to become an expert in the different influences and nuances of the industry. However, it is human nature for analysts to be optimistic about the firms they follow so closely. This makes it hard to be objective about the industry in general. Consider the predicament of an analyst following the airlines industry after the September 11, 2001, terrorist attacks. It would be hard for an analyst to recommend selling all the firms in the industry. Yet, it was clear that the airlines were going to experience both lower passenger demand and higher costs due to new regulations. Analysts rarely recommend selling stock in all firms in an industry. Instead, they recommend buying stock in the few companies that they think will hold up the best in a problematic industry. Therefore, investors may misinterpret a "buy" rating on a firm in a troubled industry.

These conflicts of interest certainly jeopardize an analyst's ability to be completely honest when he or she is pessimistic. For example, analyst Daniel Peris was bearish on AOL Time Warner. As a result, he charges that his attempts to gain more access to AOL Time Warner were met with roadblocks from management.[23] Incidentally, how is it that Peris feels free to be bearish on AOL Time Warner while other analysts are hesitant to be? Perhaps it's because Peris works for an independent research firm that doesn't trade and isn't involved in investment banking. In other words, he doesn't have to be a salesperson, and he doesn't have to worry about angering investment banking clients. This latter fact touches on an important issue with regard to a potential conflict of interest. Would an analyst who works for an investment bank be objective?

ANALYSTS AT INVESTMENT BANKS

Analysts can work for an independent research firm, for a brokerage firm, or for the brokerage operation of an investment bank. Most of the high-profile analysts who many investors follow are analysts who work for investment banks. Why is this? The cost of collecting, analyzing, and disseminating information is enormous. The high cost is less burdensome for an investment bank.

Consider that investment banks have corporate clients with firms that one of their analysts follows. The fees for investment banking services can easily run into the tens of millions of dollars. Do you think that these analysts will feel free to publicly make honest assessments if they would jeopardize those banking fees? If analysts came out with a negative rating, wouldn't the investment bankers get mad? Also, if a non-client firm received a negative assessment from an analyst, do you think it would ever give the analyst's firm any investment banking business? This conflict of interest is similar to the one that occurs when a firm is both a consultant and an auditor to a public company, as described in Chapter 5. No matter how you cut it, analysts who work at investment banks may feel the need to compromise their integrity for the good of their employer.

According to an article in *Time* magazine, when brokerage firm Smith Barney merged with Salomon Brothers in 1997, there was a cultural shift among the Smith Barney analysts.[24] There was now big money to be made. Before, analysts had primarily relied on brokerage commissions, but now they were trying to help lure investment banking clients by promising to "cover" (i.e., promote) the stock to investors. One academic study provides evidence that is consistent with this allegation.[25] The study finds that stocks of firms that are *promoted* by analysts at investment banks (in cases in which the bank recently provided services for the firms) performed worse than stocks that are promoted by unaffiliated analysts. Also, according to a commentary in *BusinessWeek*, the stock-picking performance of independent shops such as Callard Asset Management and Alpha Equity Research outperformed the stock-picking performance of powerhouse investment banks such as Goldman Sachs, Salomon Smith Barney, Morgan Stanley, and Merrill Lynch.[26] Is this because independent analysts are harder working and smarter? Or is it because their assessments are uncompromised?

Some analysts go so far as to become actively and directly involved in the investment banking side of their employer. For example, telecom analyst Jack Grubman calls himself "banking-intensive."[27] He claims that being active in both the analyst function and the banking function leads to a synergy. He has a good point. By working on investment banking deals, one can become better acquainted with the health of the firm, which, in turn, could lead to superior insights into making assessments and assigning ratings. However, despite his intimate relationships with telecom firms, he did not publicly come out against them as their stocks were plummeting in value. Since the summer of 2002, he has been under investigation by New York State Attorney General Eliot Spitzer for his role in WorldCom's fall. Whether or not he compromised his stock recommendations because of his banking ties is also a question. This may not be the worst of it. According to one lawsuit, Grubman may have allocated hot IPOs to telecom executives as bribes to win investment banking business. (Recall that these types of activities were discussed in detail in the prior chapter.) If true, it is an explicit violation of securities regulation and an explicit portrayal of how a conflict of interest may play itself out.

It became common in the late 1990s for analysts to be a part of an investment banking team. When bankers were pitching their services to a firm that wanted to issue securities, an analyst would be there. After the bankers were hired to underwrite the security, they took the analyst on the road show to help market the issue to institutional investors. In this capacity, analysts become salespeople and promoters of a firm instead of objective analyzers of financial performance.

The name Spitzer may also ring a bell. Eliot Spitzer is the person who went after Blodget and his employer Merrill Lynch. Blodget was accused of misleading investors by promoting the stocks of Merrill Lynch's investment banking clients—even though he knew that they were bad stocks. Normally, this would be hard to prove. However, in subpoenaed e-mails, it was discovered that Blodget had criticized stocks to his colleagues that he was publicly trumpeting. For example, he called some stocks "junk" and "crap," but he was still recommending a "buy" because these firms had investment banking business with Merrill Lynch. Blodget also had a direct vested interest in seeing happy investment banking clients instead of happy investors who followed his recommendations. Apparently, he spent 85 percent of his time on banking and only 15 percent on stock research.[28] From December, 1999 to November, 2000—less than one year—he worked on 52 investment banking transactions that generated $115 million in fees for Merrill Lynch.[29] Blodget subsequently received a raise—from $3 million to $12 million.

Merrill Lynch has also been criticized for two apparent incidents in which one analyst with a bearish recommendation on a firm was replaced with another analyst who was bullish in order to obtain investment-banking business from the firm. In one incident, an analyst covering Enron was replaced with a more optimistic analyst in order to gain favor with Enron executives. Early in 1998, analyst John Olson recommended Enron stock with a "neutral" rating. Olson's negative rating and his personal style rubbed Enron executives Skilling and Lay the wrong way. So Merrill Lynch bankers complained to their CEO about the analyst. The complaint was that Merrill Lynch could not gain any investment banking business with Enron while Olson rated the firm so poorly. The investment banking business kept going to banks that employed analysts who rated Enron as a "buy" or better. In August 1998, Olson left Merrill Lynch for another company. Merrill Lynch then hired Donato Eassey to be its analyst covering Enron. Eassey quickly upgraded Enron to "accumulate." By the end of 1998, Merrill Lynch was participating in investment banking services with Enron that would generate $45 million in fees.[30] Olson, Eassey, and Merrill Lynch all deny that anything inappropriate occurred. Indeed, Eassey was one of the few analysts to downgrade Enron when its troubles began to become public. Regardless, the story illustrates the strong power companies have over analysts who work at investment banks and the motivation of banks to be optimistic in order to gain business.

In 1999, Merrill Lynch replaced analyst Jeanne Terrile (who covered Tyco International) after Tyco CEO Dennis Kozlowski complained to Merrill Lynch CEO David Komansky about her.[31] The new analyst, Phua Young, promptly upgraded Tyco to a "buy" rating. The next year, Merrill Lynch underwrote Tyco's $3 billion stock issue.

Internet stock analyst Mary Meeker may be viewed as more of an investment banker than as an analyst. One former banker at Deutsche Morgan Grenfell stated that Meeker (an analyst) was talked about as being one of the best investment bankers on the planet.[32] When going after investment banking clients, one rival banker considered that he was not competing with Morgan Stanley at all. He was competing with Mary Meeker.[33] Eventually, Internet firms started chasing after Morgan Stanley to take their firms public, instead of the other way around, because it would mean, they felt, having Meeker give their stock her seal of approval. It appears that Meeker started to feel more loyalty to the stocks that she helped take public than to the investors who relied on her advice. She was being protective. She even privately referred to Netscape as "her baby," so that when one analyst downgraded Netscape stock, she quickly responded by upgrading her rating on it. Now, however, investors are hopping mad. The betrayal has been exposed.

JUST WHO IS THE CLIENT?

From the point of view of the sell-side analyst, the public investor is not the client. The analyst's clients are those institutional or individual investors who trade through the brokerage arm of a firm or buy new security issues from the banking arm. In addition, analysts don't really consider the published ratings and earnings estimates to be the whole of their research product either. Indeed, analysts don't just write a report and consider themselves done. They constantly reevaluate their opinions and advise their biggest institutional clients. The public investor is not included in this process.

While this is the traditional role and duty of the analyst, we believe that things have substantially changed. If analysts just kept to their paying clients, the public investor would not know about their recommendations. But this is not the case. Analysts market themselves and their firms precisely where the public investor is tuned in. Analysts commonly appear on TV networks like CNBC and CNNfn and on TV shows with Lou Dobbs and Louis Rukeyser. When they make changes in their ratings, they alert the media. They also promote themselves and their ratings through numerous financial websites. Since analysts use the public to promote their own agendas, they must also be responsible to those investors. For an analogy, consider that a private company does not have to jump through all the hoops of the SEC regulations because public investors are not the owners and, thus, do not need to be protected. Alternatively, if a private company wants the benefits of accessing the capital of public investors, it must become a public company and succumb to being fully regulated. Likewise, if analysts want the benefits of interacting with the public, they must also take on the duty of protecting the public.

CHANGING ROLES

The days of analysts aspiring for a piece of the investment banking action may be over. Merrill Lynch settled its case with Spitzer for $100 million, and its chairman and CEO David H. Komansky publicly apologized to clients, shareholders, and employees by saying that the firm had failed to live up to its traditionally high standards.[34] Merrill Lynch has adopted a new policy that will not compensate analysts for generating investment banking business.

In fact, the NASD and the NYSE both put forth new or amended rules that would address the conflict of interest problem. The SEC approved these new regulations on May 10, 2002. Under the new rules, sell-side research analysts cannot (1) be subject to supervision from investment banking operations, (2) have their compensation tied to investment banking deals, or (3) promise favorable ratings to lure investment banking deals. Time will tell whether the new rules will help.

There are also different kinds of analysts other than the sell-side analysts who work for brokers or bankers. Institutional investors like pension funds and mutual funds hire analysts to help decide which stocks the funds should buy. Therefore, they are referred to as buy-side analysts. The recommendations of these analysts are not public. Indeed, they are only used within the institution. According to one survey of buy-side professionals, the new rules are not likely to help resolve sell-side analyst problems. Survey respondents doubted that regulations aimed at separating research activities from banking activities could be credibly enforced.[35]

They may have a point. The SEC told analysts to simplify their ratings to just three categories (like "buy," "hold," and "sell") in May 2002. By September, the rating system hadn't changed much. Sure, the ratings were in only three categories. However, only 7.5 percent were listed as "sell." Not only that, analysts from investment banking firms were still not giving "sell" ratings on firms that were also investment banking clients. For example, for every 25 firms that Merrill Lynch had listed as a "sell," only one was a Merrill Lynch client.[36] On the other hand, 60 percent of the companies that received a "buy" rating were clients. It doesn't appear that a separation between analysts and banking had effectively occurred by this time.

SUMMARY

Analysts are supposed to analyze firms and make stock recommendations. For the most part, they seem to be okay at it. However, there is more money to be made in investment banking, and many analysts work for investment banks. Has this compromised their objectivity? It seems so. Analysts were getting rewarded for luring investment banking businesses. They were encouraged to be bullish to keep firms—both potential and current investment banking clients—happy. This loyalty to the investment banking side of the business comes at the expense of analysts' loyalties to the investors who depend on their recommendations. Rules aimed at eliminating conflicts of interest have been passed. It may take some time before we know if they will work.

While we have focused on the problems in the analyst industry, there are many analysts who are trying to rectify some of these problems. The Association of Investment Management Research (AIMR), a professional association of analysts, has already been working with the SEC, Congress, and others to improve the integrity of analyst recommendations. Many of the new rules enacted by the SEC have been advocated by AIMR. As with the other governance monitors that we have discussed, the misbehavior of a minority has tarnished the reputation of the majority.

ENDNOTES

1. Steven Rosenbush, Heather Timmons, Roger O. Crockett, Christopher Palmeri, and Charles Haddad, "Inside the Telecom Game," *BusinessWeek*, August 5, 2002, pp. 34–40.

2. Susan Harrigan, "Merrill's Internal Workings," *Newsday*, May 21, 2002, p. A53.

3. Marcia Vickers and Mike France, "How Corrupt Is Wall Street?" *BusinessWeek*, May 13, 2002, pp. 37–42.

4. Steven Rosenbush, Heather Timmons, Roger O. Crockett, Christopher Palmeri, and Charles Haddad, "Inside the Telecom Game," *BusinessWeek*, August 5, 2002, pp. 34–40.

5. The source of these analysts recommendation examples comes from the NASD website, *http://www.nasdr.com/pdf-text/0239ntm.pdf*, July 2002.

6. Stephanie Smith, "How Are Analysts Changing?" *Money*, September 2002, p. 89.

7. Justin Fox, "Learn to Manage Your Earnings and Wall Street Will Love You," *Fortune*, March 31, 1997, pp. 77–80.

8. Many academic articles have cited this phenomenon. For example, see Francois Degeorge, Jayendu Patel, and Richard J. Zeckhauser, "Earnings Management to Exceed Thresholds," *Journal of Business* 72 (1999): 1–34.

9. Paul Sloan, "Blame the Pundits," *U.S. News & World Report*, October 9, 2000, p. 44.

10. Anup Agrawal and Sahiba Chadha, "Who Is Afraid of Reg FD? The Behavior and Performance of Sell-Side Analysts Following the SEC's Fair Disclosure Rules," University of Alabama working paper, February 2002.

11. Examples of earlier academic studies that cast doubt on analysts' abilities to pick stocks are many, so we have cited just two: R. E. Diefenbach, "How Good Is Institutional Research?" *Financial Analysts Journal* 28 (1972): 54–60; Dennis Logue and Donald Tuttle, "Brokerage House Investment Advice," *Financial Review* 8 (1973): 38–54.

12. Brad Barber, Reuven Lehavey, Maureen McNichols, and Brett Trueman, "Can Investors Profit from the Prophets? Security Analyst Recommendations and Stock Returns," *Journal of Finance* 56 (2001): 531–563.

13. Georgette Jasen, "Investment Dartboard: Readers Easily Beat Pros and Darts," *Wall Street Journal*, August 9, 2002, p. C10.

14. Peter Elkind, "Where Mary Meeker Went Wrong," *Fortune*, May 14, 2001, pp. 68–82.

15. Joseph Nocera, "The Big Picture: The Cheerleader, It Wasn't Analysis That Made Merrill's Internet Stock Analyst a Star," *Money*, June 1, 1999, p. 71.

16. Marcia Vickers and Mike France, "How Corrupt Is Wall Street?" *BusinessWeek*, May 13, 2002, pp. 37–42.

17. Ibid.

18. Mara De Hovanesian, "How Analysts' Pay Packets Got So Fat," *BusinessWeek*, May 13, 2002, pp. 40–41.

19. Gretchen Morgenson, "Bullish Analyst of Tech Stocks Quits Salomon," *New York Times*, August 16, 2002, p. A1.

20. Daniel Kadlec, "Buy (I Need the Bonus)," *Time*, May 20, 2002, p. 55.

21. Steven Rosenbush, Heather Timmons, Roger O. Crockett, Christopher Palmeri, and Charles Haddad, "Inside the Telecom Game," *BusinessWeek*, August 5, 2002, pp. 34–40.

22. Marcia Vickers and Mike France, "How Corrupt Is Wall Street?" *BusinessWeek*, May 13, 2002, pp. 37–42.

23. Mara De Hovanesian, "How Analysts' Pay Packets Got So Fat," *BusinessWeek*, May 13, 2002, pp. 40–41.

24. Daniel Kadlec, "Buy (I Need the Bonus)," *Time*, May 20, 2002, p. 55.

25. Roni Michaely and Kent L. Womack, "Conflict of Interest and the Credibility of Underwriter Analyst Recommendations," *Review of Financial Studies* 12 (1999): 653–686.

26. Emily Thornton, "Research Should Pay Its Own Way," *BusinessWeek*, June 3, 2002, p. 72.

27. Steven Rosenbush, Heather Timmons, Roger O. Crockett, Christopher Palmeri, and Charles Haddad, "Inside the Telecom Game," *BusinessWeek*, August 5, 2002, pp. 34–40.

28. Daniel Kadlec, "Buy (I Need the Bonus)," *Time*, May 20, 2002, p. 55.

29. Marcia Vickers and Mike France, "How Corrupt Is Wall Street?" *BusinessWeek*, May 13, 2002, pp. 37–42.

30. Richard Oppel, "Merrill Replaced Research Analyst Who Upset Enron," *New York Times*, July 30, 2002, p. A1.

31. Charles Gasparino, "Merrill Replaced Its Tyco Analyst After Meeting," *Wall Street Journal*, September 17, 2002, p. C1.

32. Peter Elkind, "Where Mary Meeker Went Wrong," *Fortune*, May 14, 2001, pp. 68–82.

33. Ibid.

34. Marcia Vickers and Mike France, "How Corrupt Is Wall Street?" *BusinessWeek*, May 13, 2002, pp. 37–42.

35. Leslie Boni and Kent L. Womack, "Solving the Sell-Side Research Problem: Insights from Buy-Side Professionals," Dartmouth College working paper, August 8, 2002.

36. Susanne Craig, "Securities Firms Do the Soft Sell in Their Ratings," *Wall Street Journal*, September 13, 2002, p. C1.

9 MORE FAILED MONITORS: CREDIT RATING AGENCIES AND LAWYERS

While the media has mostly concentrated on the failures of the executives, accountants, and analysts, we would be remiss if we didn't mention the failure of two other potential monitors: credit rating agencies and corporate lawyers. Both the credit agencies and attorneys should be considered as monitors in the corporate system. While corporate lawyers are hired and paid by the company executives, their fiduciary duty is to the corporation. It seems that most corporate attorneys have been more devoted to the executives than to the shareholders. One difference between credit agencies and other monitors is that they focus on protecting a company's bondholders and other creditors. This chapter details the role of credit agencies and lawyers in the corporate system and examines how credit agencies might have played a role in the business scandals.

CREDIT RATING AGENCIES

The level of safety in a bond is very important to investors. The very best return a bondholder can get is to receive the interest payments and get the principle back. Therefore, bond-holders focus on safety. Corporate bonds are given a safety rating so that you can tell if a firm's debt is safe or risky. At least one of three firms, Moody's Investors Service, Standard & Poor's, and Fitch Ratings, conduct a credit analysis and give a firm a grade. This grade tells investors how risky the bonds of the firm are.

A BRIEF HISTORICAL PERSPECTIVE

To understand how the credit industry works and how important it is, a brief history is in order. John Moody invented credit ratings in 1909 when he published a manual of ratings on 200 railroads and their securities.[1] He made his money by charging investors for the book. By 1916, the Standard Company, the predecessor to Standard & Poor's, started rating bonds. Fitch started bond ratings in 1920. By the 1970s, photocopy equipment was so prevalent that too many investors were obtaining the ratings without paying for the published books. However, the demand for the ratings was so great that the rating companies were able to give the ratings to investors for free and earn money by charging the bond issuers fees to rate their bonds.

After the stock market crash of 1929 and the following Great Depression, the government was looking for ways to restore confidence in the banking system. The securities acts of 1933 and 1934 went a long way toward increasing regulation of the banking and securities industries. These laws are discussed in Chapter 7. However, in 1936, the government expanded the role of credit ratings by requiring that commercial banks only hold high-quality debt. Specifically, the U.S. Comptroller of the Currency decreed that the banks could only own "investment-grade" bonds. The categories of ratings are illustrated in the next section. Because one large and influential type of investor (commercial banks) needed credit ratings on securities in order to buy them, all bond issuers wanted to be rated. Today, anyone who wants to issue debt securities in the United States needs to get them rated. This applies to companies, state and local governments, and even foreign governments.

This fee arrangement creates a conflict of interest. While a credit rating is supposed to help investors understand the riskiness of a bond issue, it is the company that pays the bill. In other words, a company planning a bond issue could discuss it with several credit agencies and see which one would rate it at the highest grade. A high-quality rating for a company means that it could offer bonds at a low interest rate and still easily sell them all. A lower-quality rating would require offering the bonds at a higher interest rate. A lower rating would cost the firm millions of dollars more in interest payments. Unscrupulous rating agencies could sell high ratings to firms that were willing to pay higher fees to get them. In the wake of the 1975 scandalous bond default of Penn Central Corporation, the SEC designated three ratings agencies as the only ones that satisfy rating regulations. The three anointed agencies, called Nationally Recognized Statistical Rating Organizations, are Moody's, Standard and Poor's, and Fitch. The SEC later designated four more agencies as valid. However, mergers between the firms have left only the three original firms. Only having three agencies creates an uncompetitive environment for the industry.

The situation of having a small number of firms in the industry is called an oligopoly. The SEC rules protect the three firms from further competition by preventing any other firms from joining the industry. Other, small credit rating agencies have tried and failed to get the SEC designation. For example, Egan-Jones Rating Company rates debt securities. Since the SEC does not recognize it, debt issuers will not pay Egan-Jones to rate their securities. Therefore, the company must count on investor subscribers to generate revenue.[2] Sean Egan runs the small agency and cannot get the SEC designation until his firm is bigger, but the company cannot afford to get bigger without the designation.

With a lack of competition by new entrants, the three credit rating agencies operate in a very profitable business. The credit analysis process does not require expensive factories or machine tools. The low expenses and low level of competition lead to highly profitable business. Moody's profit margin is estimated to be 50 percent and Standard & Poor's' is closer to 30 percent. Regardless, these three firms have been immensely rewarded in the protected environment.

THE RATINGS

To assess the worthiness of companies' credit, the credit agencies employ financial analysts who examine a firm's financial position, business plan, and strategies. This means that the analysts carefully go over the public financial statements issued by the company. However, the SEC has also granted the agencies an exemption from disclosure rules so that companies can reveal non-public or sensitive information to the agencies in confidence. Companies are under no obligation to reveal special information, but they often do so in order to convince the agencies that their debt should be rated highly. Because of the importance of credit ratings, the credit analysts often get to directly question the CEO and other top executives when conducting a review of a company.

The rating systems of Moody's and Standard & Poor's are shown in Table 9–1. Notice that the two rating agencies have similar systems.[3] Although not shown in the table, both agencies can partition the ratings further. Moody's includes 1, 2, or 3 after the rating to show that the firm is near the bottom, middle, or top of the scale within the category. Standard & Poor's uses a – or + sign. Consider two companies that want to borrow $1 billion by issuing bonds. The first company is rated in the "high quality" category by the rating agency. This firm will have to pay 6.9 percent (or $69 million) in interest every year. The second firm is rated "Non-Investment Grade" and would have to pay $99 million annually. This difference is substantial. Riskier companies pay higher interest.

If a company becomes financially stronger over time, the bond rating will also improve. Therefore, the interest rate demanded by investors will fall, as illustrated in the table. When interest rates fall, bond prices rise. So if a firm becomes safer, the price of its bonds will increase. This is what the bondholders desire. Alternatively, if the firm becomes riskier, bond prices fall. The worst-case scenario for a bondholder is for the issuing company to default on the bonds and file for

TABLE 9–1 Ratings of Bond Safety and Example Bond Yields

	MOODY'S RATING	STANDARD & POOR'S RATING	EXAMPLE BOND YIELD
Best Quality	Aaa	AAA	6.4%
High Quality	Aa	AA	6.9
Upper Medium Grade	A	A	7.1
Medium Grade	Baa	BBB	7.8
Non-Investment Grade	Ba	BB	9.9
Highly Speculative	B	B	10.5
Defaulted or Close to It	Caa to C	CCC to D	20 to 90

bankruptcy protection. Bondholders typically receive only a small portion of their principal back if a firm defaults.

The ratings that the three main credit agencies issue have historically been good predictors of the default potential of a debt issuer. Only 0.5 percent of the firms rated at the highest level (best quality) default.[4] This percentage increases to only 1.3 percent for issuers rated as high quality. However, the increase in the default rate substantially increases to 19.5 percent in the non-investment grade bonds and 54.4 percent in the CCC category.

When a firm begins to struggle financially, the credit agencies begin to downgrade the ratings on its securities. A bond issue rated AAA– might be downgraded to AA+ or even AA. If the business operations or cash position of the firm continues to decline, the rating could fall further. Each downgrade signals investors that the bonds are becoming riskier. In response, the price of the bonds declines and the investors experience a capital loss. The term *investment-grade* in the regulations is interpreted as ratings of BBB– or higher. If a bond slips to BB+ or lower, it is not considered investment-grade. In fact, the popular term for non-investment grade bonds is *junk bonds*. For additional protection of a bondholder's principle, many modern debt offerings include a rule (or covenant) that requires the company to increase the interest payment made on the bonds if the rating slips to junk status. Some bond covenants require the company to pay back all the principle if the rating slips to junk. While this sounds like a good idea for bond investors, in practice it often triggers the very bankruptcy filing that bondholders are trying to avoid. A firm's debt is downgraded to junk bond status because the company is having some financial difficulty. If the firm suddenly owes higher interest payments or even hundreds of millions of dollars in principle, it is pushed into a more financially precarious position. The very covenants that try to protect the interest of bondholders can actually drive a company toward insolvency.

CRITICISM

One of the criticisms of the credit agencies is that they have started to enter the consulting business. Being both consultants and credit raters creates a conflict of interest similar to the one that occurs when auditing firms are also consultants for a company. If the credit agency is earning lucrative fees consulting for a firm, it might not be able to give unbiased analysis of the firm's financial position. Just as auditing firms should not be allowed to audit companies for which they are acting as consultants, credit agencies should not rate the debt securities of companies they consult for.

The credit agencies have also been given the same First Amendment rights as the media. When disgruntled companies or investors have sued the credit agencies, agencies have been successful in using free speech protection as a defense. The combination of regulated protection from new competitors, exemptions from disclosure rules, and First Amendment protection in court make the credit agencies nearly invincible. That is, it is nearly impossible for market forces (like competition) or the court system to discipline them.

The credit rating agencies are also criticized for rating decisions on individual issuers. Take, for example, Moody's downgrade of Japan's government debt on May 31, 2002. The change in ratings took the grade down two notches to A2 from Aa3. Japanese government officials were furious at the move.

They argued that Japan has the second largest economy in the world and the highest savings rate. The new debt rating suggests to investors that Japan's creditworthiness is on par with Israel, South Africa, Poland, and Cyprus, but is below that of Hungary, Botswana, Chile, and the Czech Republic.[5] Japanese officials argue that it is absurd for their ratings to be below that of developing countries where Japan provides economic assistance.

While the total record of the credit agencies is pretty good, they have made some dramatic mistakes. For example, the agencies completely missed the financial trouble and bankruptcy filing of Orange County, California, in 1994. In the early 1990s, the economic output of Orange County would have ranked it among the top ten countries in the world. By every standard, the county was one of the wealthiest in the United States. As such, the credit agencies rated the municipal bonds of the county as very safe—a grade of AA–.

Much of the money raised with bond issues in the county and other places in California was invested by Orange County until it was needed to build the school, hospital or other project the capital was raised for. The county treasurer, Robert Citron, invested the funds. The investment of municipal money is usually done in very safe instruments. However, Citron was using some complicated interest rate derivative securities that carried higher risks.[6] Those risks became real to the county when it had to announce a "$1.5 billion paper loss" on December 1, 1994. On December 7, the county filed for bankruptcy protection. The credit rating agencies responded by downgrading many of the bonds from "high quality" to "close to default." That is quite a large downgrade! However, it was too late for bond investors. The agencies had rated the county as good investment-grade debt right up to the bankruptcy filing.

Another questionable call by the credit agencies occurred at the issuance of WorldCom bonds in May 2001. WorldCom issued an American record $11.9 billion of bonds, of which $10.1 billion was new financing. WorldCom, and the massive debt issue, was rated investment grade—A3 by Moody's and BBB+ by Standard & Poor's.[7] The massive offering by World-

Com should have come with a robust analysis by the investment banks, as the underwriters, and the credit rating agencies.

One year later, in May 2002, the credit agencies downgraded WorldCom debt to junk bond status. The rationale behind the downgrade was that Worldcom's $30 billion in total debt was too high.[8] While this is true, why didn't the debt level concern the agencies in the previous year when WorldCom increased its debt by 50 percent with the massive bond issue? It seems incredulous that the agencies could have put their seal of approval on the giant bond issue and then use that same issue one year later as a reason to downgrade the company. It was the high rating given by the agencies that allowed WorldCom to borrow so much money in the first place. It was the very next month, on June 25, 2002, that WorldCom disclosed it had improperly booked $3.8 billion as capital investments instead of operating expenses over the previous five quarters. Several more billion dollars in accounting fraud was discovered over the next couple of months.

ENRON

The credit agencies are not blameless in the corporate scandals. Indeed, their special relationship with companies allows them to get private information that other monitors, like independent analysts, might not receive. Of the outside monitors, credit rating agencies might have been in the best position to detect corporate fraud and warn investors. Yet, in some cases, they were one of the last to respond to the troubles. The collapse of Enron is a good example.

The decline in Enron's stock price should have been a big warning that something was amiss. The price was $90 per share in August 2000. By April 2001, the stock price had fallen to $60 per share. In the late summer, the price continued to fall to less than $40 per share. Even in November 2001, just before Enron declared bankruptcy, the stock was down to less than $5 per share. As it turned out, the credit agencies might have been more of an enabler than a watchdog.

The investment banking chapter illustrated how deeply involved JPMorgan Chase and Citigroup were with the Enron partnerships. The banks had raised capital for the partnerships used by Enron to falsify loans as profits. The banks had invested hundreds of millions of dollars of their own money in Enron and its associated partnerships. The banks knew that if Enron filed for bankruptcy protection, their losses would be enormous. The banks also knew that if the credit rating agencies were to downgrade Enron to non-investment grade status, at least $3.9 billion in debt repayment would be immediately required. Enron would be forced to declare itself insolvent.

On November 8, 2001, the news about the partnerships and the massive losses became public. The stock price was down to less than $10 per share. The banks needed to act quickly or take massive losses. On that day, Robert Rubin, the former Treasury secretary under the Clinton administration, called Peter Fisher. He asked Fisher, the current undersecretary of the Treasury, if he would talk with the credit agencies about the Enron situation.[9] Rubin wanted the credit agencies to work with Enron and the bankers to see if there was an alternative solution to an immediate downgrade. What was Rubin's interest? He was working for Citigroup, one of the bankers. Fisher rightly decided that it was not a good idea and did not make the calls.

Nevertheless, it appears that the SEC-designated credit agencies delayed in downgrading Enron to non-investment grade. At first, they merely downgraded the firm to the lowest levels of investment-grade ratings. Non-designated credit agencies like Egan-Jones downgraded Enron's debt to junk status, but the big three waited. Since companies seek a rating on debt they issue and investment banks help them issue the debt securities, banks and credit agencies frequently work together. The bankers may have used this relationship to convince the credit agencies to give them some time to save

Enron. That is, the bankers wanted some time to get additional cash for Enron and even find a buyer for the company.

To locate a buyer, investment banks Merrill Lynch and JPMorgan just looked across town from the headquarters of Enron and found Dynegy. Enron and Dynegy executives went into negotiations for a merger during November 2001. If they could agree, Dynegy would infuse Enron with $1.5 billion of cash to tide them over until the final merger could take place. The credit rating agencies knew that if the merger did not take place, Enron would be in deep financial trouble. Yet, instead of communicating this enormous risk to bondholders via a downgrade to junk bond status, they waited. Given what the agencies knew, this was a big gamble for bondholders. If the merger went through, the financial situation would be improved, but if it didn't, Enron would likely go into bankruptcy. This might be the kind of risk that investors take in speculative stocks, but not in investment-grade bonds. The stock price had fallen to less than $5 per share. The credit rating agencies failed to warn investors how risky the situation had become.

On November 26, 2001, the Enron merger with Dynegy was dead. Enron was still discovering how vast the problems with the partnerships were becoming. Dynegy claimed that it wasn't being told about all the problems. No one could tell how much Enron was really worth. The designated credit rating agencies downgraded Enron to junk bond status on November 28, 2001. Enron's stock price fell to $0.61 per share. On December 2, 2001, Enron filed for bankruptcy protection. Bondholders had to wait in line at bankruptcy court with other creditors and hope to get some of their principle back.

In defense of their actions, the credit rating agencies claim that Enron executives lied to them. While this might be their defense, it is no excuse. The agencies have unusual access to executives, but it is not their job to believe what the CEO of a company says. It is their job to validate the information they receive and then analyze it to form their own conclusions. What good are they as independent monitors if they simply follow the lead of the company executives?

SUMMARY OF CREDIT AGENCY PROBLEMS

The credit agency's purpose is to be a monitor of debt issuers in the protection of public investors. However, the way the industry is structured creates a situation in which the agencies do not often deal with the investors whom they are protecting. Instead, they are paid by the debt issuers to give a rating. They work with the issuers and the investment bankers to obtain information about the debt issue. Most of their business relies on the interactions with corporate participants, not with investors. Over time, this situation may warp the agencies' best intentions and lead them into acting in the best interest of companies or bankers instead of investors. The Enron case is an example of this.

This may not be a big problem if other forces were able to monitor and discipline the agencies when they get off track. However, the government has made them a closed and uncompetitive industry. Therefore, typical market forces are not at work. In addition, the government does not regulate the industry. Lastly, they seem to have unusual immunity in the court system under the First Amendment that prevents investors from seeking damages when they make errors. The lack of disciplinary forces can make the agencies lax in their watchdog duties.

These problems may become even more important. The new Basel proposals for commercial bank capital requirements may use the type of ratings used by the credit agencies to assess the riskiness of a bank's entire portfolio.[10] Indeed, since the agencies' ratings on bonds tell these banks which ones they can buy, it is likely that the agencies will be involved with rating the portfolios.

ATTORNEYS

Companies frequently consult with attorneys outside the firm on the deals and actions they plan to take. The corporate executives hire the outside counsel for the corporation. However, since the lawyers deal nearly exclusively with the executives, they may feel that their attorney-client relationship is with them. The executives are agents of the corporation, which is owned by the shareholders, so the corporate lawyers must remember that they really represent the corporation, not the CEO. This may be hard to remember considering that they negotiate their fees and interact with the CEO, not the board of directors or the shareholders. The outside attorneys could be monitors of the corporation, but they do not always act like they are.

Typically, law firms act as legal enablers for companies. As enablers, they take no position on the wisdom of business decisions. That is, they provide recommendations that are morally neutral and provide the legalese to justify whatever decisions the executives want to make. Consider the predicament that the law firm Vinson & Elkins is in for its work with Enron. Vinson & Elkins did some of the legal work that set up the offshore partnerships (discussed in Chapter 7) that Enron used to hide debt and falsify revenue. The investment banks found investors to fund the partnerships. Included in this process is a legal opinion letter that effectively states that the transaction in question appears legal and proper. The letter (actually more like a ten-page document) is called a true sale opinion. Vinson & Elkins wrote these opinions for Enron.[11] We don't want to suggest that Vinson & Elkins was the only law firm involved in the offshore transactions. There were other law firms participating, like Milbank, Tweed, Hadley & McCloy, and Kirkland & Ellis. In truth, none of the outside counsels to Enron and the partnerships seemed to sound a warning.

Just as we argued that the investment banks (in Chapter 7) had to know that Enron was misleading the public and even committing fraud, the outside counsels also had to know. After all, they were in the middle of setting up the legal structures and negotiated the deals that were used in the deception. Yet they did not warn the board of directors or regulators about the situation.

Indeed, Enron's vice president Sherron Watkins warned her bosses in August 2001 that the firm could implode from an accounting scandal. In response, Enron hired a law firm to review her allegations and investigate the partnerships. They hired Vinson & Elkins. Watkins was upset about hiring Vinson & Elkins because of the conflict of interest it presented. How could the law firm be unbiased in its findings when it was involved in the partnerships themselves? Indeed, two months later, Vinson & Elkins issued a report.[12] It showed concern that the deals looked bad and would invoke bad publicity if made public, but it stated that the deals were sound and no further investigation was needed. Typical attorney opinion—it's bad, but it's good. The executives could then decide that the opinion would support whichever decision they made. Enron collapsed just a few weeks later.

PROTECTING LAWYERS

Like the credit rating agencies described earlier, law firms enjoy some special privileges that reduce the chance they will be disciplined for wrongdoing. For example, it is unlikely that the law firms will bear much legal responsibility for the recent corporate fraud—even though outside counsels were an integral part of the process. This is partly due to a 1994 Supreme Court ruling that law firms cannot be sued for merely helping companies commit accounting or financial fraud. Then, in 1995, Congress passed a law that made it harder to sue lawyers directly involved in financial fraud. As a consequence, outside counsel may be less worried about moral and ethical issues when advising company executives.

These laws are being challenged in the aftermath of the scandals as investor groups sue the law firms involved. However, successfully suing lawyers is difficult because much of the evidence is not admissible in court. For example, plaintiffs can subpoena all Enron documents at the accounting firm Arthur Andersen. However, many of the documents shared by Enron and law firms are protected under the attorney-client privilege. Also, the work-product doctrine permits lawyers to withhold documents created in anticipation of litigation. It remains to be seen who the courts deem to be the "client" in this case. If the board of directors and shareholders are the clients, plaintiffs should get the documents. If the executives are the clients, the plaintiffs probably won't get the documents. These protections allow attorneys to develop legal rationalizations for corporate decisions without fear that the work will be reviewed later in court.

SUMMARY OF ATTORNEY PROBLEMS

In contrast, corporate lawyers could be trusted counselors who prevent clients from committing criminal or immoral acts. As trusted counselors, lawyers would act as officers of the court to protect the stakeholders of a firm. However, this would require a significant shift in the profession. Several things need to change. First, it must be clear that when a company hires attorneys, it is the shareholders (represented by the board) who are the clients. While the lawyers mostly interact with the company's executives, their fiduciary duty is to the shareholders. Second, members of the profession need to be held more accountable for their actions. If attorneys aid a firm in committing financial fraud, they should be held responsible for their role. Once the law firms become focused on the real client, shareholders, and are held accountable for their actions, they are more likely to become trusted counselors instead of legal enablers.

ENDNOTES

1. Amy Borrus, Mike McNamee, and Heather Timmons, "The Credit-Raters: How They Work and How They Might Work Better," *BusinessWeek*, April 8, 2002, p. 38.

2. Leslie Wayne, "Credit Raters Get Scrutiny and Possibly a Competitor," *New York Times*, April 23, 2002, p. C1.

3. Ratings categories are from *Moodys.com* and *standard andpoors.com*.

4. These estimates are provided by Standard & Poor's using data from 1987 to 2001.

5. Akiko Kashiwagi, "Japan's Credit Rating Cut by Two Notches," *Washington Post*, June 1, 2002, p. E1; Valerie Reitman, "Asia: Moody's Downgrade Infuriates the Government, Which Had Protested the Action," *Los Angeles Times*, June 1, 2002, p. C1.

6. John Nofsinger, *Investment Blunders of the Rich and Famous* (Upper Saddle River, NJ: Financial Times Prentice Hall, 2002).

7. "WorldCom Smashes Records with $11.9bn Blowout Bond," *Euroweek*, May 11, 2001, p. 4.

8. Gregory Zuckerman and Shawn Young, "Leading the News: WorldCom Debt Is Slashed to 'Junk,'" *Wall Street Journal*, May 10, 2002, p. A3.

9. Peter Behr and April Witt, "Hidden Debts, Deals Scuttle Last Chance," *Washington Post*, August 1, 2002, p. A1.

10. "Finance and Economics: Badly Overrated; Rating Agencies," *The Economist*, May 18, 2002, pp. 69–70.

11. Riva Atlas, "A Law Firm's 2 Roles Risk Suit by Enron, Experts Say," *New York Times*, January 29, 2002, p. C1.

12. Richard Oppel, "Lawmakers Contend Lawyers for Enron Should Have Raised Concerns," *New York Times*, March 15, 2002, p. C7.

3 SHORTCOMINGS IN ENFORCEMENT AND INVESTOR ACTIVISM

10 THE SECURITIES AND EXCHANGE COMMISSION

For a while, everyone was enjoying a tremendous bull market. Business seemed to be booming. Investors were excessively speculating in the stock markets, optimism was very high, and some people were even pondering early retirement. Then, all of a sudden, quite dramatically, all of it changed. Large corporations began going bankrupt. Corporate officers were found to be deceiving the public. Executives became engaged in courtroom battles that grabbed the nation's headlines. As a result, investors became leery of corporations and the stock market plummeted.

While this may sound like 2002, we are actually describing the way things were during the late 1920s and early 1930s. This period spawned the Great Depression. There are many examples of fraudulent behavior that can be used to illustrate the condition of those times, including unethical activities by corporate executives, securities analysts, large investors, and even newspaper reporters (who hyped their own stocks). Instead of dwelling on such examples, we simply point out that our nation has been in a similar situation before. That is, it has experienced a crisis in investor confidence. In a revealing comment in 1932, Charles Schwab of U.S. Steel stated, "I don't know, we don't know, whether values we have are going to be real next month or not."[1] Does this comment seem vaguely familiar?

What did the United States do to try to fix the crisis during the early 1930s? It did something quite dramatic. It decided to federally regulate the securities markets, and it also created the SEC. The SEC would become an advocate for investors by putting them on equal footing with the corporations in which they invested, and it would become a type of corporate police force. In fact, the SEC was created specifically to restore investor confidence. When President Franklin D. Roosevelt signed the Securities Act of 1933 into law, he stated, "The Act is thus intended to correct some of the evils which have been so glaringly revealed in the private exploitation of the public's money." Seventy years later, why are we again in the midst of an investor confidence crisis? Was the creation of the SEC not the solution that we were looking for? Was the SEC caught off-guard? Is the SEC partly to blame for the crisis today?

It is important to point out that U.S. corporations are regulated by many governmental agencies. For example, the Fair Trade Commission (FTC) regulates advertising by businesses, and the Food and Drug Administration (FDA) approves drugs for sales by pharmaceutical companies—all of which is done for the protection of consumers. What makes the SEC different from other business overseers (thus making it the focus of this chapter) is that it is assigned the role of protecting investors.

Interestingly enough, in the wake of recent corporate scandals, the SEC is not being criticized too badly. In the summer of 2002, there were some who called for the resignation of Harvey Pitt; at the time, he was the SEC chairman appointed by President Bush. Those demands were mostly based on the fact that Pitt was once one of the top attorneys representing the accounting profession. At one time or another, as a lawyer for the firm Fried Frank Harris Shriver & Jacobsen, Pitt had represented all of the Big 5 accounting firms. Thus, some felt that he had a conflict of interest. After all, how will he be expected to be critical of those individuals and companies that he once protected? In addition, there are also others, mostly Democrats, who are skeptical of Pitt's desire for more regulation. Due to the role of the SEC chairman in government and business, it often becomes a political lightning rod.

For the most part, however, investors feel that the SEC was fooled along with everyone else. Even though no one is pointing fingers at the SEC, it is certainly in the spotlight. There is a call from investors for reform and a tougher regulatory stance. This chapter will provide an overview of the SEC, its role in our business environment, and its potential weaknesses. We will also discuss Pitt's predecessor Arthur Levitt, who many believe tried to warn us that this crisis could happen, and the challenges that had faced Pitt.

THE SECURITIES ACTS

There are generally six laws that govern the securities industry that the SEC is responsible for overseeing.[2] The first of these laws is the Securities Act of 1933. This act requires firms to register securities intended for public sale. In the registration, important information regarding the securities for sale and the firm (e.g., its financial statements, its business operations, and its management) must be disclosed. No information can be fraudulent or deceitful. All statements are made publicly available.

The Securities Exchange Act of 1934 created the SEC and gave it authority to oversee the securities industry, including large shareholders (defined as a 5 percent shareholder), brokerage firms, securities dealers, and the stock exchanges. Corporations are required to submit accurate annual reports (the 10-K) and quarterly reports (the 10-Q). The act also allows the SEC to govern the proxy process (the process used to solicit shareholder votes) and insider trading. This act, along with the Securities Act of 1933, was specifically designed to restore investor confidence.

The Trust Indenture Act of 1939 applies to the sale, and formal agreement between buyer and seller, of debt securities. The Investment Company Act of 1940 regulates investment companies, such as mutual funds, by requiring the disclosure of their financial condition and their investment policies. The

Investment Advisors Act of 1940 currently regulates investment advisors who manage more than $25 million or who advise a registered investment company. Finally, the Public Utility Holding Company Act of 1935 regulates the holding companies of gas and electric companies.

All of the acts taken together, especially the first two, boil down to the following. They force corporations to tell the public about themselves without lying. This allows investors to make informed decisions. In addition, the spirit of the acts is to put the investors' interests first.

ORGANIZATIONAL STRUCTURE OF THE SEC

The SEC has 11 regional and district offices, including offices in Chicago, Denver, Los Angeles, and New York City. The headquarters is located in Washington, D.C. The commission consists of four divisions and 18 offices, and employs almost 3,000 people.

At the top of the organizational chart are the commissioners. There are five of them, each serving a five-year terms appointed by the U.S. President with subsequent approval by the Senate. The appointments occur annually and there is one appointment per year, as the terms are on a staggered basis. No more than three commissioners can belong to the same political party. One commissioner serves as chairman, the SEC's top executive, who is also designated by the President. The very first SEC chairman was Joseph P. Kennedy (John F. Kennedy's father) appointed by President Franklin D. Roosevelt. Harvey L. Pitt, who resigned on November 5, 2002, was appointed by President George W. Bush.

Figure 10–1 shows that the four divisions are the pillars of the SEC. The Division of Corporate Finance oversees corporate disclosure, making sure that the public has all of the rele-

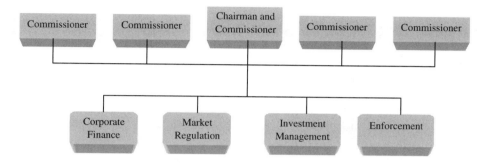

FIGURE 10–1 SEC organizational structure.

vant information necessary to make its investment decisions. Full corporate disclosure encompasses the registration statements of securities for sale, annual and quarterly reports, proxy materials, and annual reports to shareholders. The Division of Market Regulation oversees the participants of the securities markets, such as the brokerage firms and their agents and the stock exchanges. The Division of Investment Management primarily regulates investment companies. Finally, the Division of Enforcement investigates possible violations of the securities laws. The SEC only has civil enforcement authority, but it can play a crucial role in helping federal agencies pursue criminal charges for severe law violations. Each year, the SEC prosecutes between 400 and 500 individuals and companies for wrongdoing, with most of these prosecutions being settled out of court. Most of these violations involve accounting fraud, insider trading, and deception regarding securities.

The 18 offices are mostly for the internal affairs of the SEC, such as personnel, or they are set up to serve as advisors (e.g., general counsel and economists) for the divisions and the SEC commissioners. The other responsibilities of these offices are varied, including the handling of compliance inspections, investor education, and international affairs.

ASSESSMENT OF THE ACTS
AND THE SEC

Opinions regarding the SEC are varied. For the most part, it's pretty obvious that businesses and the securities industry aren't exactly enamored with having the SEC around. The costs of reporting and following SEC regulations, in general, are tremendous. Byron C. Radaker, CEO of Congoleum Corporation, took his company private in the early 1980s, citing that this would save his firm between $6 and $8 million dollars per year in reporting costs.[3] Furthermore, what firm would want to be policed? However, while companies may not appreciate the SEC, can investors do without it? In order to consider this, let's first think about the thrust of the acts, which is for corporations to honestly tell the public about themselves.

Many people, especially academics, believe that the stock markets are efficient. What is meant by this? The notion of market efficiency is that current stock prices reflect their correct value. Believe it or not, this concept actually means that stock prices are never wrong. To understand this concept, consider this: We have millions of participants in the stock markets. The average of their beliefs and opinions, based on current and past information, is going to be reflected in the current stock price. For example, if the stock price were too low, at least some people out of the millions would recognize the error in pricing and rush in to buy the stock. Because of the buying, the stock price would get pushed up and not be mispriced for long. Because information is continuously being processed by millions of market participants, which, in turn, makes the markets efficient, do we really need the SEC? Consider the fact that the SEC only requires quarterly and annual reporting. By the time these reports are made public, the information is already old. Are the disclosures therefore useful?

What about SEC regulations that state that firms cannot lie? Again, in the context of market efficiency, if companies do hide facts and/or lie, someone is bound to find out because there are so many people involved! There are brokers, analysts, directors, employees, accountants, creditors, investors, and even state regulators. So the inevitable revelation of fraud will cause the stock price to subsequently plummet. Besides, companies that lie and get caught cannot last for long anyway. We have always had a climate in which consumers and investors have cast a suspicious eye toward big businesses. Again, do we really need the SEC? This question cannot be answered with ease. For one, none of us can recall what life was like before 1933. So we don't know if things have improved.

Some finance scholars have attempted to empirically assess the importance of SEC regulation to our financial markets. In 1964, George Stigler, who would later go on to win the Nobel Prize in economics, published a famous study in which he compared new securities being issued in the 1920s to those issued in the 1950s to determine whether or not the existence of the SEC had improved the securities markets.[4] He found no difference, and he contended that SEC regulation did not improve the quality of the securities markets. However, professors Irwin Friend and Edward S. Herman subsequently debunked Stigler's study, citing that there was now less securities fraud because the SEC was around.[5] This debate continues today. In 1995, in response to complaints by market participants regarding regulatory costs and excessive regulatory burdens, an SEC committee was formed to study the feasibility of making it less burdensome for established public firms to issue securities.[6] In 1998, the SEC issued such a proposal, but it subsequently went nowhere.

Overall, we may never know for sure if the SEC makes our securities markets better. Perhaps markets would still be efficient without the SEC. However, it is also just as possible that the very existence of the SEC contributes to making our markets efficient. Or perhaps the very idea of a securities regulator is a good one, but the current implementation may be ineffective.

SEC PROBLEM AREAS

One thing that people are wondering about is whether or not quarterly and annual reporting is enough. If the information provided in these documents is useful, perhaps there needs to be more frequent reporting. We now live in a world in which technology permits us to access information, especially up-to-date information, on a continuous basis. Why not take advantage of this? Of course, frequent reporting will cause an outcry by corporate America, which already complains about the costs of reporting as it is, but there may be several viable ways to address this. One is to force companies to submit their reports earlier, which is something that is currently being considered.[7] Instead of providing a 90-day deadline to file annual reports after the fiscal year, it could now be 60 days. For quarterly filings, the deadline could be shortened to 30 days instead of 45. However, these suggestions may not be ideal—the frequency of the reports is still the same, and only the timeliness is improved. Also, as pointed out in a *BusinessWeek* commentary, this proposal may only add to concerns about the hastiness, and thus the accuracy, with which the reports get compiled.[8] Another way to address the problem of infrequent reporting (and one that is also currently being considered) is to force companies to reveal, as soon as it is known, any material information that investors would deem important as part of the disclosure requirements.[9] Such information could include the selling and buying of insiders—information that currently can take many months before it is filed.

Others believe that the SEC may be too weak because it cannot prosecute criminally. If we believe that criminal prosecution can serve as a key deterrent to corporate crime, there may be some truth to the notion that the SEC doesn't really have the policing power necessary to do its job. However, this may not really be a critical problem. The SEC can easily persuade prosecutors to bring criminal charges once it has evidence that a case is merited. Also, it is important to keep in mind that it is difficult to prosecute corporate criminals to begin with. As pointed out in an article in the July 1, 2002, issue of *BusinessWeek*, securities laws are ambiguous, sophisticated financial concepts are difficult to grasp, and executives have plenty of tricks up their sleeve to absolve themselves of responsibility (e.g., "I didn't know that the books were fraudulent").[10] Therefore, given the current difficulties that we already have with criminal charges, it may not make sense to give an additional agency, such as the SEC, the additional responsibility of bringing criminal charges.

Another problem may be that the SEC is underfunded. Being underfunded has two repercussions. First, the SEC may be hindered in its ability to hire and retain the best staff. One estimate has SEC attorneys and examiners as being paid up to 40 percent less than their peers at comparable federal agencies.[11] In 2001, Congress gave its approval to the SEC to pay its lawyers and accountants salaries that are competitive with other government banking agencies, such as the Federal Reserve. However, Pitt felt that Bush's proposed $29 million dollar increase (6.6 percent), announced in February 2002, wouldn't be enough to significantly raise salaries.[12] The increase in budget from the passage of the Public Company Accounting Reform and Investor Protection Act of 2002 ended up being much larger—more than $300 million! For a long time, the SEC has had the distinction of being an important stepping-stone for many young, ambitious, and talented attorneys and accountants who can usually count on the experience to command much higher salaries elsewhere. These talented people gain experience and a name for themselves at the SEC. Then, they get hired away by the very law firms that represent companies, auditing firms, and individuals who are working against the SEC. According to one estimate, the SEC employee turnover rate is at 30 percent, which is double the rate for the rest of the government.[13] Losing talent shortens the SEC's institutional memory and the average experience of its key employees. Losing talent also increases the time and money needed to train new hires. Even Pitt joined the SEC fresh out of law school in 1968, and, despite becoming the youngest general counsel in SEC history at the age of 30, he himself also parlayed that experience to join a law firm in 1978.

The second repercussion to being underfunded is being understaffed. Since 1993, the SEC's workload has increased by 80 percent, but staffing at the SEC has been stagnant.[14] Former SEC commissioner Laura S. Unger once admitted that there were only about 100 lawyers who reviewed the disclosure documents of the 17,000 public firms.[15] An SEC chief accountant stated that only 1 out of 15 annual reports gets reviewed.[16] While it may be impossible for the SEC to ever be able to thoroughly pursue and investigate all possible violations, a larger staff will definitely be able to do more. In light of the recent crisis, Pitt had tripled the number of SEC probes.[17] However, over-working the current staff cannot last forever. Fortunately, the Public Company Accounting Reform and Investor Protection Act of 2002 mandated that the SEC hire hundreds more people. Of course, it takes time to hire, train, and effectively use so many new employees. In fact, while the increased funding started in 2002, the SEC had plans to hire only 100 new people that year and planned to delay the hiring of an additional 200 people until future years.[18] Therefore, the higher funding might be too little and too late for many investors.

Finally, does the SEC have enough clout in the securities markets? For example, does it have the authority to regulate corporate executives, directors, and auditors? Again, the SEC's main purpose is to ensure corporate disclosure, so the easy answer to this question is "no." We have traditionally relied on shareholders and directors to police their own executives' conduct, and we have let the accounting profession police their own activities as well. However, as we have seen the actions of officers, directors, and auditors having detrimental effects on investors, whom the SEC is supposed to protect, perhaps it is time for the SEC to expand its authority. The Responsibility Act gives the SEC a bigger stick to wield, but is this the right solution? We will discuss this later. At this point, with the mentioning of auditing, it may be insightful to discuss Pitt's predecessor, Arthur Levitt, who left the SEC in 2001 while adamantly believing that things were wrong—especially with the accounting profession.

ARTHUR LEVITT'S I TOLD YOU SO

As Wen Stephenson of PBS's *Frontline* pointed out, Pitt was perhaps the most controversial and embattled SEC chairman since ... his predecessor, Arthur Levitt.[19] Levitt was a Clinton appointee who served as the SEC chairman from 1993 to 2001. While Pitt was criticized for his professional closeness with big business and the accounting profession, Levitt was often criticized for just the opposite, since he was often attacked by both corporate America and the accounting profession. This is probably why a September 2000 issue of *BusinessWeek* dubbed Levitt the "Investor's Champion."[20]

Unlike Pitt, Levitt was known as a tough regulator, and his victories included the censuring of the National Association of Securities Dealers for collusive pricing practices, which resulted in Nasdaq dealers having to pony up more than $1 billion to settle the case, and the adoption of Regulation Fair Disclosure, which put an end to corporate officers tipping off analysts. Toward the end of his tenure, one of his main causes was to clean up the accounting profession. In a famous speech delivered at New York University on September 28, 1998, Levitt called for an end to the "numbers game."[21] Corporate managers, auditors, and analysts participated in the process of managing earnings by using a variety of tricks (Levitt called them "nods and winks") to meet earnings estimates—all at the expense of high-quality, full disclosure. He felt that this had to stop to make numbers more reliable and to have the trust of the investing public.

Levitt felt strongly that one way to clean up the accounting profession, which at the time was facing a slew of accounting scandals such as those involving Cendant, Sunbeam, and RiteAid, would be to separate the accountants' role as auditors and consultants for the same firms. Levitt felt that this was a huge conflict of interest. After all, if an accounting firm relies on a client for consulting fees, will it really wreak havoc on the accounting books in its auditing role? Toward the end of Levitt's tenure at the SEC, slightly more than half of the revenue of the Big 5 accounting firms came from consulting. Of course, there was a tremendous backlash from corporate America, which claimed that accountants who consult for it are in the best positions to audit it, and from the accounting industry, which didn't want to see its profitable consulting practices taken away. Less than two years later, on June 27, 2000, the SEC unanimously approved issuing Levitt's proposal. In the end, Congress defeated the proposal with the help of Harvey Pitt, who represented the American Institute of Certified Public Accountants (AICPA) in fighting the proposal.

Considering that Enron's auditor, Arthur Andersen, was also an important and well-compensated Enron consultant, many people now believe that an accounting firm providing both auditing and consulting services represents a serious conflict of interest. Senator Robert Torricelli, a New Jersey Democrat, told Levitt on January 24, 2002, "We were wrong. You were right."[22] However, there are still many people who believe that this conflict of interest is not problematic and is hardly at the heart of the problems plaguing the business environment today. On the other hand, many people also believe that separating consulting and auditor services will solve the problems. We feel that neither solution will be effective, and we discuss these ideas in Chapters 12 and 13.

THE MAN IN THE MIDDLE: HARVEY PITT

In a much-anticipated May 7, 2002, speech, President Bush responded to the lawmakers who demanded new and tough laws by stating, "I call upon the Securities and Exchange Commission to take action." In other words, he was asking Harvey Pitt to take care of it. When Pitt was confirmed as the new SEC chairman on August 1, 2001, he probably had no idea of what he was getting himself into. At the time, almost no one questioned that he was the right man for the job. Even a Democratic senator, Charles Schummer, stated at the confirmation hearings, "His reputation, deservedly so, has achieved—at least in securities law—almost godlike proportions. He could well be described as the Zeus of his field."[23] Indeed, as we have already mentioned, he had worked for the SEC for ten years (1968–1978), and his latter years there were spent as general counsel. He spent the next 24 years as a Washington, D.C., lawyer representing, on one occasion or another, each of the Big 5 accounting firms and various financial fraud defendants, including Ivan Boesky. As such, and in response to critics who question his loyalties, he knows the workings of the accounting profession—and of accounting chicanery. In addition, Pitt also responded that he now worked for "the most wonderful client of all—the American investor."[24] Thus, he may indeed have been, as Bush contended, the perfect person for the job. Here, we discuss two things: Pitt's reasoning for why he did not believe the dual role of auditor and consultant was a problem and his proposed multi-pronged plan for the SEC in the wake of the current scandals.

Two weeks before the Enron scandal, Pitt was giving a talk to the AICPA governing body and said, "The agency [the SEC] I am privileged to lead has not, of late, always been a kinder and gentler place for accountants. I want to have a continuing dialogue, and partnership, with the accounting profession, and we will do everything in our power to evidence a new era of respect and cooperation."[25] Talk about bad timing. However, Pitt stood firm that auditor independence, especially with regard to a potential conflict of interest with consulting practices, was not the cause of these current problems. To his credit, he may have been right. When Levitt battled against auditors engaged in consulting services, it was based on hearsay evidence rather than on any proven cases.[26] Even Levitt's blue-ribbon committee, the Panel on Audit Effectiveness, reported that among the 126 audits that it studied, the quality of the audits were actually better in 25 percent of the cases in which the auditor also provided consulting services, and in no cases was there a conflict.[27] Pitt had pointed out that independence is important, but taking away consulting was not getting at the issue of independence. He stated that the mere fact that auditors rely on their clients' fees made them non-independent.[28] However, he had made some recommendations (some pertaining to the accounting profession), but they were not in the form of new rules or regulations. Instead, his solutions took on the appearance of a free-market agenda.[29]

Basically, Pitt called for stronger enforcement, stronger penalties for corporate wrongdoing, better financial disclosure, and some reform of auditing.[30] Specifically, with regard to stronger enforcement, Pitt proposed a new oversight board, the Public Accountability Board, that would be made up of mostly non-accountants and would oversee the accounting. Currently, the accounting profession polices itself via the AICPA. Also, he wanted a stronger SEC, which he felt needed a budget that was almost 20 percent larger than it already was.

With regard to stiffer penalties for corporate officers, Pitt wanted them to be more liable for their books, he wanted to force them to disclose insider stock sales within 48 hours, and he wanted to punish them for wrongdoing by imposing more severe penalties, such as restricting eligibility to serve as directors in the future and making them give back gains based on deceptive earnings. He also wanted to step up activities to catch corporate wrongdoing. On the disclosure front, Pitt wanted the Financial Accounting Standards Board to move faster and make rules clearer. Finally, with regard to auditing and auditor independence, Pitt thought that each firm's audit committee should decide for itself whether or not its auditor is truly independent rather than just simply preventing auditors from consulting, as we have previously discussed. Further, Pitt felt that there should be more focus on auditor compensation to ensure that auditors are independent. For example, does an auditor get a bonus if his or her firm's books grow? If so, are auditors really independent?

Are these good plans? Several of the ideas were adopted in the Responsibility Act of 2002. For example, the new law created a new accounting oversight board and increased penalties for white-collar crime. However, the act also mandated a separation between auditors and consultants. Thus, Pitt's recommendation for the audit committee of a given corporate board to handle the problem was not taken. Given the problems of boards of directors' independence (as discussed in Chapter 6), that might be for the best.

However, the implementation of the laws that Congress passed in the summer of 2002 was a problem for Pitt. These laws are described in Chapter 12. Congress only provided a general framework for which the SEC must fill in the details. For example, Congress mandated the creation of a board to oversee the auditing industry. However, it is up to the SEC to do the actual hiring and to set up the organization. Pitt was highly criticized for how he handled this process.

In one instance, he was accused of withholding important information in the nomination process for the chair of the oversight board.[31] He wanted William Webster, former chief of the CIA and the FBI, to head the new board. Others in the SEC wanted John Biggs, head of TIAA-CREF, to head the panel. In a close vote of SEC commissioners, Webster won 3–2. A week later, Pitt was accused of not telling the commissioners that Webster had headed the audit committee of U.S. Technologies, the firm that is being investigated for financial misrepresentation. If this had been known, the SEC commissioners may not have voted for him to head the oversight panel. This criticism led to Harvey Pitt's resignation on November 5, 2002. His resignation will delay the SEC's progress toward getting the oversight board up and running.

Summary

The United States has experienced a confidence crisis before, which is one of the reasons why the SEC was created in 1934. The SEC's main function is to oversee the federal securities acts, which essentially boil down to forcing public corporations to honestly tell the public about themselves. However, is what the SEC requires of our corporations enough? Or, on the other hand, is the SEC even necessary in the first place? Former SEC Chairman Arthur Levitt wanted the SEC to be stronger. While nobody seems to be blaming the SEC for the current crisis, many people, including former SEC Chairman Harvey Pitt, seemed to believe that the SEC now has to do more. Some SEC reforms are on the table, and while they all seem well intended, perhaps the key question that we have to ask ourselves is, "How much will such reforms contribute to restoring investor confidence?" This question especially warrants consideration if the size of the SEC's role in the current crisis is questionable to begin with.

Increasing the SEC's budget and hiring new employees will surely increase enforcement in the short term. However, we feel this is only a short-term solution. Years from now, after investor confidence has been restored, who's to say that those budgets won't be cut back again? The government tends to spend money where the public and the media have their attention and cut budgets elsewhere. In the 1990s, the number of investors in the stock market quadrupled, but the SEC budget hardly grew. In 1996, a Senate committee initially tried to cut the SEC budget by 20 percent. It ended up keeping the budget at the existing level. In 1998, Chairman Levitt appealed to Congress for an emergency $7 million for special bonuses to stem the high turnover of the SEC's attorneys and investigators. Congress rejected the proposal. Finally, in 2001, Congress agreed to increase the SEC budget, but it never appropriated all of the money for the increase. What will happen to the SEC's budget, and its ability to regulate several years from now when the public focus has moved elsewhere?

ENDNOTES

1. Joel Seligman, *The Transformation of Wall Street* (Boston: Northeastern University Press, 1995), ch. 1.

2. Most of our factual information on the SEC comes from its website, *www.sec.gov*.

3. Eugene F. Brigham and Michael C. Ehrhardt, *Financial Management*, 10th ed. (Cincinnati: South-Western Publishers, 2002), p. 759.

4. George J. Stigler, "Public Regulation of the Securities Markets," *Journal of Business* 37 (1964): 117–142.

5. Irwin Friend and Edward S. Herman, "The SEC Through a Glass Darkly," *Journal of Business* 37 (1964): 382–405.

6. Hyun-Han Shin, "The SEC's Review of the Registration Statement and Stock Price Movements During the Seasoned Equity Issuance Process," an unpublished dissertation paper, Ohio State University.

7. Judy Mathewson, James L. Tyson, and David Evans, "Harvey Pitt: Odd Man Out on Enron," *Bloomberg Markets*, March 2002, pp. 51–56.

8. Mike McNamee, "The SEC's Accounting Reforms Won't Answer Investor's Prayers," *BusinessWeek*, June 17, 2002, p. 28.

9. Judy Mathewson, James L. Tyson, and David Evans, "Harvey Pitt: Odd Man Out on Enron," *Bloomberg Markets*, March 2002, pp. 51–56.

10. Mike France and Dan Carney, "Why Corporate Crooks Are Tough to Nail," *BusinessWeek*, July 1, 2002, pp. 35–38.

11. Joseph Nocera, "System Failure," *Fortune*, June 24, 2002, pp. 62–74.

12. Mike France and Dan Carney, "Why Corporate Crooks Are Tough to Nail," *BusinessWeek*, July 1, 2002, pp. 35–38.

13. Joseph Nocera, "System Failure," *Fortune*, June 24, 2002, pp. 62–74.

14. Mike McNamee and Amy Borrus, "The Reluctant Reformer," *BusinessWeek*, March 25, 2002, pp. 72–81.

15. Joseph Nocera, "System Failure," *Fortune*, June 24, 2002, pp. 62–74.

16. Ibid.

17. Mike McNamee and Amy Borrus, "The Reluctant Reformer," *BusinessWeek*, March 25, 2002, pp. 72–81.

18. Michael Schroeder, "SEC Gets a Raise, but Will It Be Enough?" *Wall Street Journal*, August 12, 2002, p. C1.

19. Wen Stephenson, "A Tale of Two Chairmen," *Frontline,* June 20, 2002, *http://www.pbs.org/wgbh/pages/frontline/shows/regulation/lessons/two.html*.

20. Mike McNamee, Paula Dwyer, and Christopher H. Schmitt, "Accounting Wars," *BusinessWeek*, September 25, 2000, pp. 156–166.

21. The full text of Arthur Levitt's speech, titled "The Numbers Game," is available at *http://accounting.rutgers.edu/raw/aaa/newsarc/pr101898.htm* (September 28, 1998).

22. Judy Mathewson, James L. Tyson, and David Evans "Harvey Pitt: Odd Man Out on Enron," *Bloomberg Markets*, March 2002, pp. 51–56.

23. Ibid.

24. Mike McNamee and Amy Borrus, "The Reluctant Reformer," *BusinessWeek*, March 25, 2002, pp. 72–81.

25. Judy Mathewson, James L. Tyson, and David Evans, "Harvey Pitt: Odd Man Out on Enron," *Bloomberg Markets*, March 2002, pp. 51–56.

26. Mike McNamee, Paula Dwyer, and Christopher H. Schmitt, "Accounting Wars," *BusinessWeek*, September 25, 2000, pp. 156–166.

27. Ibid.

28. Mike McNamee and Amy Borrus, "The Reluctant Reformer," *BusinessWeek*, March 25, 2002, pp. 72–81.

29. Ibid.

30. Ibid.

31. Michael Schroeder, "As Pitt Launches SEC Probe of Himself, Criticism Mounts," *Wall Street Journal*, November 1, 2002, pp. A1, A7.

11 INVESTOR ACTIVISM

Given the corporate scandals, the failure of various monitoring systems, and the dramatic downturn of the markets, shareholders are naturally upset. Individual shareholders have been viewed as the innocent and helpless victims of this mess, and they rightly deserve our sympathies. After all, they lost a lot of their hard-earned savings at the hands of others. Individual investors have become nervous about investing in the markets—perhaps rightly so. However, what about the larger institutional shareholders like insurance companies that also invest in stocks? Should we feel sorry for them, too? We think so. They also lost a ton of money, but many of these institutional investors, such as pension funds and mutual funds, are actually investing money on behalf of many smaller individual investors. Don't these large shareholders have a fiduciary responsibility to the smaller investors who invest with them? The answer is yes. So where were they during all of this? Robert Monks, a well-known advocate of shareholder activism, asks the same question when he wonders where Enron's owners were.[1]

In the midst of our shareholder confidence crisis, there is a uniform cry from shareholders, both individuals and institutions, for more protection. It is this very need for more protection that has everyone, from the stock exchanges to the SEC to the U.S. President, scrambling around trying to find ways to protect investors. However, one question that begs asking is, "Why can't shareholders *also* take care of themselves?" That is, why can't they take more responsibility for the stocks that they own? Is it right for investors to blame everyone else *but* themselves?

People who own homes will often take precautions to safeguard themselves against potential burglary. The various ways to protect a home are wide-ranging, from forming neighborhood watches, buying a watchdog, or installing a security system to doing something as simple as locking doors each night. Of course, homeowners also rely on the local police to protect their homes, but the police obviously can't *guarantee* that all homes will be perfectly protected. This is just as true with shareholders.

No one can guarantee the integrity of our business system, and no one can ensure the soundness of our investments. So then, why don't shareholders, like homeowners, do more to protect themselves—even if it's merely the equivalent of locking the door at night? Even on the SEC website (*www.sec.org*), the following statement appears, "...stocks, bonds and other securities can lose value. There are no guarantees. That's why investing should not be a spectator sport; indeed, the principal way for investors to protect the money they put into the securities markets is to do research and ask questions."

There are valid reasons why individual investors don't pay more attention to what they own. Those reasons were briefly discussed in Chapter 2. Most individual shareholders don't own enough stock in any one company to be able to influence its management. Nor do most shareholders think it would be worth their time and effort to do anything because the gains (e.g., stock price increases) from their efforts would be shared by all other shareholders while they alone would suffer the costs. If they do anything at all, it is to sell shares that they are unhappy with—commonly known as doing the "Wall Street walk."

However, institutional shareholders that usually own many different stocks to begin with, and at the same time have some restrictions about what they can own, may not have so many opportunities to sell stocks. For them, it may be worthwhile to exert some of their ownership rights. Further, given the large amounts of stocks that they own, they may be able to effectively affect the decision-making of the firm. Finally, the potential benefits accrued from their activism may be large enough that it would be worth the effort. This being the case, perhaps there is more that institutional shareholders should have done to prevent recent scandals, especially given the fact that individuals seem to trust them to invest money on their behalf. According to the Survey of Consumer Finances, there are more individuals who own stocks through a fund than own stocks directly. In 1998, for example, 50.2 million individuals owned stocks through a fund as compared to 33.8 million individuals who only owned stock directly.[2] Therefore, if we really are concerned with restoring the confidence of the individual investor, it may be worthwhile to consider institutional shareholder activism as playing an important role.

This chapter discusses investor activism of various forms. For example, it describes ways that individual shareholders can exert some influence over the firms that they own. However, the focus of this chapter will be on activism by institutional shareholders who, by virtue of their enormous ownership stakes, have the potential and the power to be active and effective owners. We will also summarize anecdotal and academic evidence that suggests that their activities may be beneficial. Finally, and perhaps most importantly, we will also point out some of the problems and constraints that institutional shareholders currently face, which may explain why they were largely inactive before and during the recent corporate system failures.

WHAT IS SHAREHOLDER ACTIVISM?

We are not aware of any formal definition of shareholder activism. Loosely speaking, any time that a shareholder does anything in order to express his or her opinion or tries to affect or influence a firm, he or she is being an active shareholder. A shareholder who votes his or her shares, submits proposals to be voted on, and/or attends the annual share-holder meetings could certainly be considered an active shareholder. Even writing a letter to management regarding some aspect of the firm's operations or social policies could also be considered investor activism. For example, Lee Greenwood is a well-known active shareholder to the General Mills management. Greenwood once simply suggested that Wheaties should appear in airlines and hotels.[3] Among individual shareholder activists, however, Evelyn Y. Davis is perhaps the most well known and was once even featured in *People* magazine.[4] As the modest shareholder of around 120 firms, she attends about 40 shareholder meetings each year. What does she do at these meetings? As everyone from journalists to executives seem to put it, she "raises hell." She has berated executives for everything from questionable merger decisions to the enormous size of their pay. She even told Lee Iacocca, then CEO of Chrysler, to watch his diet.[5] Most individual shareholder activists use less dramatic methods. But there are enough people like Evelyn Davis who make themselves vigorously and frequently heard that they have been deemed "corporate gadflies."

Lewis Gilbert is generally credited with being the first individual shareholder activist.[6] In 1932, as the owner of ten shares of New York's Consolidated Gas Company, he attended the company's annual meeting. While at the meeting, however, he was appalled that he wasn't given a chance to ask questions. Subsequently, he and his brother pushed for reform. In 1942, the SEC created a rule to allow shareholders to submit proposals that could be put to a vote. Today, most shareholder proposals are governance-oriented, primarily attempting to forge an alignment between shareholder views and managerial actions. For example, proposals may address issues related to anti-takeover amendments, shareholder voting rules, or board composition.[7] Having these proposals passed, or even brought to the attention of the managers, can certainly have a potentially positive effect on a firm.

In reality, however, most proposals don't pass, especially those that go against management desires and those that involve obtaining a board seat. One reason for this is that it is difficult and expensive for one shareholder to communicate with all other shareholders. Also, most passive shareholders are reluctant to vote against the firm's management anyway. For example, during 2000, the stock price of Computer Associates had dropped from a $70 high in January to about $30 in September. In the following year, stockholder Sam Wyly sponsored a proposal to unseat four board members at Computer Associates.[8] After a highly publicized and expensive campaign, Wyly's proposal was defeated, primarily because it also sought to unseat the firm's co-founder and board chairman, Charles Wang. This doesn't mean, however, that proposals, and even defeats, are fruitless or that shareholders should give up. Robert A. G. Monks spent $250,000 to run for a board seat at Sears in 1991 that resulted in defeat, but the publicity eventually caused Sears to make its own massive changes.[9]

Proposals sometimes get majority support. John Chevedden sponsored a proposal in 2001 to change the way board members are elected at Airborne Freight and he received the support of 71 percent of the voting shareholders.[10] During the same year, Guy Adams beat tremendous odds with his bid for a board seat. As the owner of 1,100 shares of Lone Star restaurant's stocks, or 0.005 percent of the company, he was disgruntled that his stock had plummeted in value while at the same time the CEO's income rose. Consequently, he took it upon himself to run for a board seat. The seat was one held by the restaurant's CEO, Jamie B. Coulter. Despite the fact that Chevedden had never before served on a corporate board and had no restaurant experience, Chevedden actually won. What does he plan to do with his newfound authority and power? He says he will be a watchdog for other Lone Star investors.[11] Isn't that what we want all the board members to be?

One of the more dramatic forms of individual investor activism is to buy a significant stake in a firm and become one of its larger shareholders. Carl Icahn with RJR/Nabisco and TWA and Kirk Kerkorian with Chrysler are two popular names that come to mind in this regard. For example, Kerkorian purchased a significant stake in Chrysler in 1990, and over the next decade he was able use his voting power to influence the board and management to get dividends increased and stocks repurchased.[12]

No matter the size of the victories of individual shareholders, they are all nice because they show that individuals can make a difference in corporate policy, and they give other shareholders a free ride. That is, other investors do not have to conduct monitoring activities. But the bottom line is this: We definitely shouldn't have to rely on them! After all, independent shareholders do not have explicit fiduciary responsibilities to one another. Nor should we expect these apparent knights in shining armor to always appear and make us money. Perhaps most importantly, the odds are heavily stacked against individual shareholders for them to be able to make a difference.

But there are shareholders who have the potential to exert effective activism. They are the institutional investors. For example, one academic study finds that proposals sponsored by institutional shareholders have a much greater chance of success than ones sponsored by individuals.[13] And, fortunately, institutional shareholders, especially the public pension funds, have become more active in their oversight of companies. One reason for their increased activity is their increasing ownership stakes. The pie charts in Figures 11–1 and 11–2 show the percent of U.S. equities held by different shareholder types for the years 1970 and 2001.[14]

From these pie charts, it's easy to see that institutions now own more shares than they did in 1970. The most dramatic increases are with pension funds and mutual funds. In fact, according to John Bogle, retired founder of Vanguard, just 75 funds alone held 44 percent of the U.S. stock market at one point during 2001.[15] As such, these funds have the economic incentive to be more active, and some actually have been.

Further, both pension funds and mutual funds are actually managing the money on behalf of many smaller investors. As such, the individual investor has a right to push the institu-

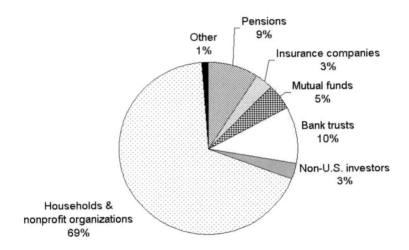

FIGURE 11–1   Shareholders of stocks by investor type in 1970.

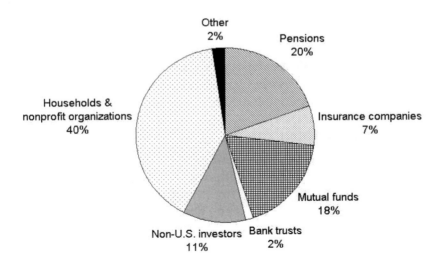

FIGURE 11–2   Shareholders of stocks by investor type in 2001.

tions to be more active shareholders. This may be especially true of pension funds, which have less restrictions on how much of a firm they can own. Pensions can take on a relatively large ownership stake and subsequently be engaged in a long-term active ownership role in the firm. Furthermore, under the Employment Retirement Securities Act (ERISA), pension funds have a fiduciary responsibility to their plan participants and beneficiaries. Therefore, it's not surprising that for the most part, it is the public pension funds that have been leading the way with regard to institutional shareholder activism.

Since the early 1990s, a few public pension funds have taken on a relational investor role with a long-run mindset. The primary ways that they have tried to influence the firms they own are through direct communications with management and with other shareholders and through something known as "targeting," a process in which they specifically identify poor corporate performers and push for reforms.[16] For example, the public pension fund California Public Employees' Retirement System (CalPERS), which has $100 billion in assets and serves 1 million members, has targeted Sears and Westinghouse in the past and has pushed for them to divest laggard divisions. Also, during July 2002, the chairmen of 1,754 major U.S. firms all received a letter from the Teachers Insurance and Annuity Association College Retirement Equities Fund (TIAA-CREF), the country's largest pension fund, asking them to account for stock options as an expense.[17] Activism by TIAA-CREF is quite common. It constantly monitors firms and makes numerous recommendations for reform.

To help further their influence, many pension funds also belong to a coalition called the Council of Institutional Investors (CII), which, as its primary objective, seeks to help members take an active role in protecting their assets. Given that they control more than one trillion dollars worth of assets, members certainly have an incentive to come together and exert influence as large shareholders. But before we get too excited about having this powerful ally on our side, there are two issues that need addressing: Does institutional activism pay off and do institutional activists face any hurdles to exert effective activism? The answer to the first question seems to be a luke-warm "yes" at best and more likely a "maybe." The answer to the second question, unfortunately, is a resounding "yes." We discuss each, in turn, next.

DOES INSTITUTIONAL SHAREHOLDER ACTIVISM PAY OFF?

It is usually difficult to determine whether or not activism results in anything positive because, more often than not, we cannot directly link good subsequent firm performance to increased activism. According to one study commissioned by CalPERS, Steven Nesbitt of Wilshire Associates conducted a before-and-after analysis of 42 firms that were targeted for reform by CalPERS. After being targeted, the aggregate stock returns of these 42 firms over a five-year period were 52.5 percent higher than the returns of the S&P 500 Index. Prior to being targeted, these same firms had underperformed the S&P 500 by 66 percent over a five-year period.[18] Michael P. Smith of Economic Analysis Corporation conducted an independent study of CalPERS activism, and found that the combined gain to CalPERS for its activities toward 34 targeted firms was $19 million during the 1987–1993 period, while the total cost to its monitoring was only $3.5 million.[19] His evidence suggests that CalPERS's activism pays off.

However, there is also plenty of counterevidence. For example, in one academic study, the authors found that the submitting of shareholder proposals did not lead to any obvious improvements in firm performance—even for those firms in which the proposals were passed.[20] Even the practice of targeting looks questionable. For example, in a study that examined the effects of targeting by the CII, the authors found no subsequent improvement for the targeted firms and very little evidence of the efficacy of shareholder activism.[21] Due to the inconsistent evidence, we find ourselves having to make the same conclusion. That is, we don't really know if activism pays off. Perhaps one of the main problems is that activism has its own set of shortcomings in the current environment, which may partially explain why it seemed absent before and during the recent corporate crisis. We discuss these shortcomings next.

POTENTIAL ROADBLOCKS TO EFFECTIVE SHAREHOLDER ACTIVISM

Mutual funds and pension funds are trying to make money. One of the shortcomings of chasing after financial gains may be that the process may be also harming the funds. For example, many active and anxious investors have a speculative or short-run view of the stock market. They make trading and investment decisions based on short-term trends. Therefore, should we really be surprised if some funds have the same short-run views?

Darrell K. Rigby of Bain & Company asserts that institutional investors might be interested in propping up results for the short term and then selling the stock to move on to something else.[22] John C. Bogle, founder of the Vanguard mutual funds, makes the same contention. He has been calling on mutual fund managers to engage in more activism, but instead he witnesses mutual funds engaging in speculative investing. He claims that during 2001, four out of every ten equity funds turned their portfolio over at an annual rate of more than 100 percent.[23] That is, if equity funds don't like the future prospects of a firm, they sell the stock instead of helping to change the firm.

In a *BusinessWeek* commentary, John A. Byrne was even more accusatory. He argued that shareholders deserve a good deal of the blame themselves. After all, it was the institutional investors, shareholder advocates, and corporate raiders who made popular the principle of "maximizing shareholder value."[24] He is not alone in this opinion. Beverly A. Behan of Mercer Delta Consulting makes the most damaging assessment by stating that "Institutional investors could just as easily turn a blind eye to accounting practices that might increase the stock price in the short-term."[25]

These accusations carry some weight. For example, prior to the onslaught of corporate scandals, where were these large shareholders? Why did they stand by while boards were obviously tainted? Why wasn't the independence of auditors questioned? In general, why didn't they more strongly impose better governance standards? Is it because they only care about making a quick buck? Linda E. Scott of the New York State Retirement Fund openly admits, "It's all bottom line. It's 'How much money did you make for us this past year?' We're not here to make sure that boards are composed of good directors. We're here to make sure boards make money for us."[26]

In fact, there were even some murmurings that CalPERS had known about Andrew S. Fastow's questionable self-dealing partnerships with Enron but remained silent.[27] Indeed, CalPERS invested $250 million in Enron's offshore partnership JEDI.[28] Later, CalPERS invested more money in the partnership JEDI II. What makes these investments even more interesting is the fact that they were recommended by the investment advisor Pacific Corporate Group (PCG). This is interesting because PCG's fee for its recommendation came from Enron.[29] How can an institutional investor—one that is trying to champion proper corporate behavior—neglect an obvious conflict of interest? Perhaps it was CalPERS's profiting $132 million on the first Enron deal that had something to do with it.

Another potential problem with funds is that they may be subject to the same problems that regular businesses are subjected to. For example, mutual funds and pension funds also have boards of directors. How do we know that they are meeting their fiduciary obligations? After all, corporate boards are rife with potential problems. In 2002, CalPERS was criticized for having questionable board members itself.[30] Specifically, CalPERS has a $1 million stake in Premier Pacific Vineyards, whose CEO is a major fundraiser for California Governor Gray Davis—who just happens to have assigned three of the CalPERS board seats. CalPERS also invested $700 million with a fund run by Ronald Burkle, who makes campaign contributions to two CalPERS board members. In fact, two other board members had previously worked for Burkle. Is this board a bit too cozy? How can CalPERS be expected to exert proper governance standards on the firms that it owns if it doesn't have a board that is squeaky clean?

Other than the activism of public pension funds, what about *private* (or corporate) pension funds? Are they active? Actually, they are extremely quiet on the activism front. Jamie Heard, CEO of Institutional Shareholder Services, is not aware of a single corporate pension fund that has become a governance activist.[31] This is too bad. In total, private pension funds own almost 50 percent more assets than public pension funds. As a group, private pension funds could be a strong monitoring force and exert influence to protect shareholders. However, private fund advisors face a huge conflict of interest problem—they are hired by corporate executives to manage the pension assets. If they take an aggressive approach with a firm's management, they probably won't be retained to manage the assets for very long. That is, no executives want to see activism by shareholders because it interferes with their activities. Therefore, executives would not hire pension fund advisors who are activists.

These corporate pension funds own many companies, so the conflict of interest intensifies because, as pointed out by Robert Monks, a well-known shareholder activist, one CEO can make an agreement with another CEO to have his or her respective pension funds not raise issues with each other's company.[32] This being the case, private funds usually just go along with a firm's management, even though their fiduciary duty is supposed to be with their beneficiaries, the employees and retirees. William Patterson, head of the AFL-CIO Office of Investments, argues that a large investment firm like Fidelity gets hired by a company like Enron to run its 401(k) plans. Therefore, it wouldn't endanger its own business activities by voting against a company's managers.[33]

Private funds can get away with their subtle violation of their fiduciary obligations because the votes of shareholders are not public information. While the firm knows how all of the shareholders voted, shareholders are not necessarily privy to how other shareholders voted because the company is not required to make this kind of disclosure. This may change. In a December 9, 1999, speech to the Investment Company Institute, SEC Commissioner Paul R. Carey urged for more disclosure by the funds.[34] Recently, some private fund managers, such as Bill Miller of Legg Mason Value and Chris Davis of Selected American, have actually been more forthcoming with voicing their displeasures.[35] But much more activism by private pension funds, given their size and ownership, may now be needed.

The regulatory and political environment may also hinder large institutional shareholders from engaging in activism. Under the Investment Company Act, mutual funds that own more than 10 percent of any one company must face additional regulatory and tax burdens. Half of the mutual fund assets must be vested in at least 20 firms (that is, a firm cannot constitute more than 5 percent of half of the fund's portfolio). These ownership restrictions apply to pension funds as well. Specifically, ERISA imposes a rather strict diversification standard on them. As stated by Benard S. Black, a Columbia law professor and well-known advocate of shareholder activism, "... pension funds are encouraged by law to take diversification to ridiculous extremes."[36] Why do these restrictions exist? In general, the public fears having single entities with so much power. This means that funds are limited in their ability to become a major shareholder of any one firm, and thus they are constrained in their ability to become stronger and more influential owners.

Bernard S. Black and another law professor, Mark J. Roe, have adamantly argued that legal restrictions stand in the way for large investors to engage in the beneficial oversight of corporations.[37] They contend that the legal and regulatory environment prohibits or discourages institutional investors from becoming too big, from acting together, and from becoming a significant owner. At the same time, these investors also face tremendous SEC paperwork if they do wish to accumulate a significant stake in a firm—while facing unfavorable tax ramifications in the process. Meanwhile, there are few laws that actually encourage or make it easier for institutions to be effective owners.

Finally, funds have too many different assets under management and are therefore unlikely to be able to effectively monitor all of their holdings. For example, CalPERS was completely blindsided by WorldCom's demise and lost $500 million in its holdings in this stock alone.[38] We shouldn't blame them because everyone else was caught off-guard, too, but it highlights the company's limitations in its ability to look out for the smaller investors. What's the lesson here? Large shareholders could make a difference because they are a more powerful version of the individual shareholder, but they also have significant limitations.

THE FUTURE ROLE OF SHAREHOLDER ACTIVISTS

We obviously can't have a stock market system in which investors just sell stocks as soon as they are unhappy with them. This would encourage a "if you don't like it here, then leave" mindset, which may undermine any chance of establishing a stable stock market. Instead, if we want a steady and trustworthy market for the long haul, we should try to fix it rather than leave it. For this to happen, we may have to start with the shareholders themselves. Regulatory reforms, after all, take time and are sometimes reversed later. With the ownership clout that institutions currently have (despite their inability to effectively monitor all of their assets and the existing legal limitations), they may need to be the key agents of a fairer market. Robert Monks has called on shareholders to unite. John Bogle is asking mutual funds to engage in long-run investing and more activism. Corporate governance expert Charles Elson believes that in the end, the best watchdogs are the investors themselves.[39]

Throughout this chapter, we have used the traditional terms *investor activism* or *investor activist* when discussing investors who actively monitor a firm and try to influence its direction. However, to many people, the term *activist* implies an adversarial role. The relationship between an investor and the executives and board members does not have to be adversarial. Indeed, the system would work best if all participants would work on the same team instead of on opposite teams. This is really the only solution that makes sense in the long run for the corporate system. Yet, how can we bring it about?

SUMMARY

Shareholders have lost a lot of money due to recent corporate meltdowns, and they are blaming everyone but themselves. It is true that most individual shareholders aren't able to do much to protect themselves to begin with. However, most of us have trusted larger shareholders, such as mutual funds and pension funds, to handle our money. Have they let us down? There are some public pension funds that earnestly try to engage in shareholder activism. However, for the most part, most institutions are not active shareholders. Why is this? Institutional investors face incentive problems, conflict of interest dilemmas, and regulatory constraints. Should these hurdles be closely reconsidered? The answer for restoring investor confidence *must* involve individual shareholders themselves.

ENDNOTES

1. Robert A. G. Monks, "Where Were Enron's Owners?" *Forbes*, February 11, 2002, *http://www.forbes.com/2002/02/11/0211opinion. html.*

2. "2001 NYSE Fact Book," New York Stock Exchange, 2002, *http://www.nyse.com/about/factbook.html.*

3. Lee Clifford, "Bring Me the Head of Your Board Chairman!" *Fortune*, October 2, 2000, p. 252.

4. Richard Jerome, "Evelyn Y. Davis for America's Most Dreaded Corporate Gadfly," *People*, May 20, 1996.

5. Ibid.

6. See "Ending the Wall Street Walk," a commentary on the Corporate Governance website, *http://www.corpgov.net/forums/commentary/ending.html* (1996).

7. Stu Gillan and Laura Starks, "Corporate Governance Proposals and Shareholder Activism: The Role of Institutional Investors," *Journal of Financial Economics* 57 (2000): 275–305.

8. David Shook, "Rebel Stockholders Are on the Move," *BusinessWeek*, September 6, 2001, *http://www.businessweek.com/investor/content/sep2001/pi2001096_073.htm*.

9. Robert A. G. Monks and Nell Minow, "Sears Case Study," 2001, *http://www.thecorporatelibrary.com/cgii/cases/cs_sears.html*.

10. David Shook, "Rebel Stockholders Are on the Move," *BusinessWeek*, September 6, 2001, *http://www.businessweek.com/investor/content/sep2001/pi2001096_073.htm*.

11. Grainger David, "Driving a Stake Into Lone Star," *Fortune*, August 13, 2001, pp. 32–33.

12. "Kerkorian's Bumpy Ride," *Detroit News*, November 28, 2000, *http://www.detnews.com/2000/autos/0011/28/a07-154513.htm*.

13. Stu Gillan and Laura Starks, "Corporate Governance Proposals and Shareholder Activism: The Role of Institutional Investors," *Journal of Financial Economics* 57 (2000): 275–305.

14. "2001 NYSE Fact Book," New York Stock Exchange, 2002, *http://www.nyse.com/about/factbook.html*.

15. Marc Gunther, "Investors of the World, Unite!" *Fortune*, June 24, 2002, pp. 78–86.

16. Stu Gillan and Laura Starks, "A Survey of Shareholder Activism," *Contemporary Finance Digest* 2 (1998): 10–34.

17. The letter is available for viewing on the TIAA-CREF website, *http://www.tiaa-cref.org/siteline/gen0207_064.html* (July 24, 2002).

18. See "Ending the Wall Street Walk," a commentary on the Corporate Governance website, *http://www.corp gov.net/forums/commentary/ending.html* (1996).

19. Michael P. Smith, "Shareholder Activism by Institutional Investors: Evidence from CalPERS," *Journal of Finance* 51 (1996): 227–252.

20. Jonathan M. Karpoff, Paul H. Malatesta, and Ralph A. Walkling, "Corporate Governance and Shareholder Initiatives: Empirical Evidence," *Journal of Financial Economics* 42 (1996): 365–395.

21. Wei-Ling Song, Samuel H. Szewczyk, and Assem Safieddine, "Does Coordinated Institutional Investor Activism Reverse the Fortunes of Underperforming Firms?" scheduled for publication in the *Journal of Financial and Quantitative Analysis* (2002).

22. John A. Byrne, "Investor Power Has Its Downside, Too," *BusinessWeek*, July 1, 2002, p. 48.

23. Remarks by John C. Bogle before the New York Society of Security Analysts on February 14, 2002. For the text of the speech, "Just When We Need It Most ... Is Corporate Governance Letting Us Down?" *http://www.vanguard.com/bogle_site/sp20020214.html*.

24. John A. Byrne, "Investor Power Has Its Downside, Too," *BusinessWeek*, July 1, 2002, p. 48.

25. Ibid.

26. John A. Byrne, "Putting Your Money Where Your Mouth Is," *BusinessWeek*, November 25, 1996, p. 106.

27. Christopher Palmeri, "Can CalPERS Afford to Throw Stones?" *BusinessWeek*, June 24, 2002, pp. 132–134.

28. Martha Mendoza, "CalPERS Fund Officials: Enron Deals a Mistake," *Associated Press*, July 18, 2002.

29. Christopher Palmeri and Ronald Grover, "Did CalPERS Bend Its Own Standards?" *BusinessWeek*, March 18, 2002, p. 80.

30. Ibid.

31. Marc Gunther, "Investors of the World, Unite!" *Fortune*, June 24, 2002, pp. 78–86.

32. Ibid.

33. Aaron Bernstein and Geoffrey Smith, "Can You Trust Your Fund Company?" *BusinessWeek*, August 8, 2002, *http://www.businessweek.com/bwdaily/dnflash/aug2002/nf2002088_7528.htm*.

34. Paul Carey's speech, "Remarks to the Investment Company Institute Procedures Conference," is available on the SEC website, *http://www.sec.gov/news/speech/speecharchive/1999/spch335.htm* (December 9, 1999).

35. Penelope Wang, "With All the Lobbying by Big Business, Who's Looking Out for the Small Investor?" *Money*, September 2002, p. 90.

36. Bernard S. Black, "Institutional Investors and Corporate Governance: The Case for Institutional Voice," in *Discussing the Revolution in Corporate Finance*, 3rd ed., Joel Stern and Donald Chew, eds. (Malden: Blackwell Publishers, 1998), pp. 316–337.

37. Ibid; and Mark J. Roe, "Political and Legal Restraints on Ownership and Control of Public Companies," *Journal of Financial Economics* 27 (1990): 7–41.

38. Penelope Wang, "With All the Lobbying by Big Business, Who's Looking Out for the Small Investor?" *Money*, September 2002, p. 90.

39. Ibid.

4 RESTORING CONFIDENCE

12 NEW RULES, REGULATIONS, AND POLICIES

As one corporate scandal after another broke in 2002, the drumbeat for corporate reform became louder. The scandals were front-page news in the national newspapers and the lead stories of the nightly news. The media seemed to demand reform. Even self-proclaimed opponents of nearly all new regulation, like CNN financial journalist Lou Dobbs, acknowledged that the government should step in.[1] Angry employees and upset investors expressed displeasure to their government representatives. People seemed to want action taken against those who were responsible for the fall in their investment portfolios.

Politicians and regulators heard the drumbeat. Indeed, politicians were especially attuned to their constituents' reaction because 2002 was an election year. In fact, the angriest people may be those citizens who had started planning their retirements. These people saw a significant decline in their retirement investments, which will have a large impact on their plans for retirement.[2] Also, these people are the most likely to vote! Therefore, politics and media grandstanding have been a part of the reform process. In responding to public outrage and scandal, Democrats are typically more inclined to offer government regulation and oversight as solutions to any problem. Republicans tend to offer punishment and enforcement as solutions to a problem. This can be seen from the debate of the 1990 and 1994 crime bills and the 1993 Brady Act. Corporate crime is no different. House Democratic Leader Dick Gephardt viewed the situation as an opportunity for his party to regain control of the House in the fall elections.[3] The Republicans recognized the potential political loss and also went on the offensive. Therefore, politicians from both parties wanted to appear tough on corporate crime. While fixing the problems in the corporate system was probably lawmakers' top priority, a secondary priority was to act quickly and maximize credibility with voters. Many politicians went on TV talk shows to express their anger at corporate executives. Each guest would demand tougher penalties and regulations than the previous guest. President Bush also spoke against the "evil doers." Even former SEC Chairman Pitt, who once said that he would change the SEC to become "kinder and gentler," tried to change his tune and enacted policies to toughen up the agency.

We recognize that our national lawmakers have a very difficult job. Consider the vast differences in recent legislative topics such as the economy, homeland security, international relations, human cloning, education, etc. Because the topics are so diverse, lawmakers can't possibly be experts in all of them. Therefore, they should take the time to thoroughly analyze the ramifications of any sweeping new legislation. A rush to enact laws to protect investors and punish white-collar crime may show constituents that lawmakers are doing something about the problem. However, rushed laws may not be the best and most effective laws. The Sarbanes-Oxley Act (discussed in greater detail later in the chapter) is an example of this. No politician wanted to be seen as opposing corporate responsibility legislation during the public outcry. Therefore, the bill sailed all the way through to a Presidential signature without serious debate on its effectiveness and ramifications.

To be most effective in fixing and enhancing the corporate system, lawmakers should first fully understand why the system is structured the way it is. Next, lawmakers must know how and where the failures took place. Then, and only then, can effective laws that punish crime and instill proper incentives be designed. This book has outlined the corporate system and its failures. The next section briefly reviews these problems.

A REVIEW OF THE CORPORATE PROBLEMS

Remember from Chapter 2 that the U.S. corporate system experiences the problem that the control of a public company is in the hands of one group of people (the executives), while the ownership of the firm is in another (the shareholders). This separation between ownership and control can lead to misbehavior by the executives. There are two mechanisms for influencing executive behavior—incentive systems and monitoring.

We examined the executive incentive systems in Chapters 3 and 4. The main device used in the incentive program is the stock option. Both stock and options compensation plans are used to try to align manager goals with shareholder goals. We demonstrated that stock options also create other incentives that are not aligned with stockholder interests. Owning a large amount of stock can also cause the misalignment of interests between the CEO and public investors. Specifically, the equity incentives like stock and options cause executives to benefit from "timing the market." By timing, we refer to maximizing earnings in a future period and then selling the stock before the ensuing earnings and stock price decline.

There are several different groups that monitor the decisions and behavior of company executives. Specifically, we discuss the monitoring role of auditors (Chapter 5), boards of directors (Chapter 6), investment banks (Chapter 7), analysts (Chapter 8), and credit rating agencies (Chapter 9). Of course, the SEC as the primary securities regulator is an important monitor (Chapter 10), and we also noted that even the investors themselves can monitor the firm and try to influence company management (Chapter 11). We provide a summary of the problems facing the corporate system in Table 12–1. It

TABLE 12–1   Summary of Problems in the Corporate System

INCENTIVE OR MONITOR	PROBLEM
Stock and Options	1. They give executives the ability to time the market and sell out at possibly artificially high levels. 2. They reward and punish executives for influences outside of their control (like a stock market bubble or an economic recession).
Auditors	1. If auditors provide consulting and auditing services to the same company, auditing quality is inhibited. 2. Auditors desire to maintain a long-term relationship with a company, and this inhibits auditing quality.
Boards of Directors	1. They lack independence from the executives. 2. They lack expertise in business and industry. 3. They lack the incentive to monitor. 4. Accepting consulting fees from executives creates the wrong incentives.
Investment Banks	1. The incentive is to raise capital for companies regardless of whether the firm deserves the capital or of its impact on shareholders and other firm stakeholders.
Analysts	1. Analysts' pay derives from investment banking services rather than accuracy of predictions. 2. Analysts are too dependent on relationships with corporate executives for information. 3. Analysts suffer serious conflicts of interest with their employers' investment banking business.
Credit Rating Agencies	1. Agencies have very little discipline because they are protected from competition by government regulations and are legally protected in lawsuits. 2. There is little interaction with customers (the investors).
SEC	1. The commission is underfunded and overburdened.
Shareholders	1. There is little incentive for small shareholders to monitor a firm. 2. Management-backed proposals nearly always pass. 3. Institutional shareholders have had only marginal success with investor activism.

is useful to review these problems now in order to see if the solutions proposed by the government and the stock exchanges actually address them.

SARBANES-OXLEY ACT OF 2002

On July 30, 2002, President George W. Bush signed into law the Sarbanes-Oxley Act, otherwise known as the Public Company Accounting Reform and Investor Protection Act of 2002 (henceforth, the Act). The new law sets up a new oversight body to regulate auditors, creates laws pertaining to corporate responsibility, and increases punishments for corporate white-collar criminals. The following discussions detail each aspect of the Act and comment on its ramifications and probable effectiveness given the problems that we have identified in the corporate system.

PUBLIC COMPANY ACCOUNTING OVERSIGHT BOARD

The Act establishes a nonprofit corporation called the Public Accounting Company Oversight Board to oversee the audit of public companies and to protect the interests of investors and the general public by improving the accuracy of audit reports. The board will operate under the discretion of the SEC. Indeed, the SEC was charged with filling in the details and actually getting the board running. The duties of the board are to

1. register public accounting firms
2. establish or adopt auditing quality control, ethics, independence, and other standards
3. conduct inspections of public accounting firms
4. conduct investigations, disciplinary proceedings, and sanctions of accounting firms when justified
5. promote high professional standards and improve the quality of audit services

6. enforce compliance of the rules of the board, professional standards, and securities laws in regard to auditing
7. oversee the budget and manage the operations of the board

The five members of the board will be employed full time by the board and will exhibit independence from the public accounting firms being regulated. Only two of the board members can be (or can have been) a CPA. To a large degree, the board is an extension of the SEC. The SEC has oversight and enforcement authority over the board. For example, the SEC has authority over all rules proposed or changed by the board and all sanctions set.

Increasing regulation is a typical response from the government after the occurrence of ethical scandals. Politicians want to appear to be tough on crime, and one easy way to accomplish this is to vote for more law enforcers. This is probably a good reaction when there is a lack of regulators. In other words, the securities acts in 1933 and 1934 that created the SEC were helpful because there were no significant regulators to protect the public investor. However, too much regulation can stifle innovation, risk-taking, and general business activities. It is hard to know how much is too much.

In this instance, we believe the action to create new regulators is overkill. There isn't much the new oversight board will do that the SEC couldn't have done before if it really wanted to. The board will regulate accounting standards and the auditing process. But recall how quickly the combined team of the SEC and Justice Department took down Arthur Andersen. Arthur Andersen was indicted and found guilty very quickly—long before any hint of indictments of Enron employees. Indeed, Arthur Andersen had been found guilty before Congress passed this new Act. The SEC could already act quickly and decisively against accounting firms when it wanted to.

Other activities of the new board deal with the process of adopting accounting standards and overseeing professionalism in the accounting industry. These tasks are already being accomplished through another private-sector body called the Financial Accounting Standards Board (FASB). Both Congress and the SEC have the ability to influence FASB's policies on creating GAAP. Essentially, this part of the Act simply moves responsibility from one private body to another. It also moves some of the enforcement function from the SEC to the new oversight board. However, since the SEC still retains the top-level regulating responsibility, the board just becomes another layer in the regulatory system.

Since we already have government regulators and private bodies overseeing accounting, we don't feel that the additional layer of regulations will solve much of anything. It still boils down to a very small number of regulators watching a very large number of accounting activities. Changing how those regulators are organized will not add much to their effectiveness. We advocate solutions that change the incentives and relationships of the people in the corporate system. This part of the Act does nothing to change the incentives and relationships identified in Chapter 5 and in Table 12–1.

AUDITOR INDEPENDENCE

The Public Company Accounting Reform and Investor Protection Act also attempts to protect investors by breaking the relationships among auditors, consultants, and the public company being audited. To accomplish this, the Act

1. prohibits accounting firms from providing both auditing and consulting activities for the same firm
2. gives the audit committee of the company's board of directors more authority over auditing activities
3. forces the lead audit partner in an audit team to change at least every five years
4. disallows auditing by an accounting firm if any of the top executives of the pubic company were employed by the accounting firm within the past year
5. requires a study to be conducted that investigates the potential outcomes of mandatory rotation of accounting firms conducting audits

This aspect of the Act addresses one of the problems with auditors as monitors of a firm. The consulting fees earned by accounting firms often greatly exceed the auditing fees they earn. Therefore, auditors of a firm have little incentive to question the aggressive methods of the company when their own consulting wing of the firm proposes those methods. Indeed, accountants conducting an audit could find themselves removed from the job and even fired for jeopardizing the lucrative consulting fees.

We applaud the lawmakers' attempt at addressing a conflict of interest problem through creating new or breaking old incentives. However, this solution does not address the other conflict—the long-term relationship between the public company and the auditing firm. We feel that the best solution to fix the problems with auditing is hinted in number 5 above—rotate auditors. In the next chapter, we describe in detail how this solution would actually solve both conflicts of interest for auditors and increase competition in the accounting industry. The Act only has the SEC conducting a study of this idea instead of actually implementing it.

CORPORATE RESPONSIBILITY

The Act attempts to increase the monitoring ability and responsibilities of boards of directors and improve their credibility. Specifically, the Act

1. makes the audit committee of a board of directors both more independent from management and more responsible for the hiring and oversight of auditing services and the accounting complaint process

2. forces CEOs and CFOs to certify the appropriateness of the financial statements filed with the SEC

3. deems it unlawful to mislead, coerce, or fraudulently influence an accountant engaged in auditing activities

4. requires that the executives of a firm forfeit any profit from bonus or stock sales resulting in earnings that needed to be restated as a result of misconduct

5. prohibits executives from making stock transactions during the time in which the employee pension plan blacks out employee stock transactions

This portion of the Act has several very different types of ideas. The first section strives to make a board's audit committee more independent from the management team. While we believe more independence is good, why stop at just the audit committee? Why not strive to make the board in general more independent? The board is a critical monitoring mechanism in the system, and it needs more independence.

The second section states that CEOs and CFOs must certify the appropriateness of their public financial statements. The SEC initially implemented this policy by requiring certification from 695 of the largest companies. The first time this certifying process is done, it brings much publicity and media attention. However, after a year or two, the certification becomes old news and business goes back to usual. In a way, the purpose of the certifying process is a bit mystifying. Isn't a company's annual report started with a letter from its CEO? That letter summarizes in words and aspirations what the accounting numbers show later in the statements. From the investor's point of view, the CEO has always certified the numbers in effect, if not in legalese. It seems that the only real advantage of this policy is in prosecuting offenders and preventing, for example, the "I didn't know" defense used by executives in Congressional investigations of the Enron collapse.

The third section deals with specifying that accounting fraud is indeed fraud. Existing laws about committing fraud against public investors already cover accounting fraud. It might be useful to clarify a few points about the laws with this policy, but it doesn't add much to existing law or have a very real effect on behavior. After all, those who are perpetrating accounting fraud know it is wrong and do it anyway.

The fourth policy in the section of the Act requires executives to give back ill-gotten gains. Consider the CEO who gets a big bonus for good company performance or cashes in options at high stock price levels. If it is later discovered that the company's performance wasn't so good after all and the stock price was artificially inflated, that compensation must be paid back. This law lets executives know that they will not keep any money that they received by being deceitful. In this regard, the law is useful. However, it will not solve all of the compensation problems identified in Table 12–1. In other words, executives can still cash in all of their stock and options at the end of a long economic expansion. When the stock price falls in the ensuing recession, investors will still be angry that the executives received big paydays even though the stock did not hold up. The gains made by the executives are not ill-gotten if the stock price falls because of a recession.

Finally, the prohibition against executives making stock transactions during a time in which employees cannot make changes in their pension plans is a good idea. If employees can't sell their stock, why should the executives be able to? This will give executives and pension fund advisors the incentive to work hard to shorten blackout periods.

ENHANCED FINANCIAL DISCLOSURES

The new law tries to make executive actions more transparent to shareholders. Specifically, the Act

1. requires the disclosure of off-balance sheet transactions and corrections in reporting identified by auditors
2. decreases the time an executive has to report company stock (and other equity) trades to the SEC to two days
3. prohibits the lending of money by public companies to executives except for the use of home loans
4. requires increased internal financial controls and review by a board of directors

5. encourages a code of ethics for senior officers of the company and reports changes and exemptions to the SEC
6. requires a financial expert on a board of directors' audit committee

The outcome of the first two laws is to increase transparency. That is, corporate monitors and investors will have better information about executive actions and compensation. Transparency is very important and useful.

The prohibition against lending an executive money is an example of fighting a symptom instead of the disease. In several of the scandals, executives appeared to abuse the loans they were given. This is less of a problem with loans as it is a problem with the monitoring by the board of directors. Loans, like compensation and other perks, can only be abused if the board lets the executives do it.

The last three rules are designed to increase the effectiveness of boards. We endorse them wholeheartedly, although most (if not all) companies already have a code of ethics. It is more a matter of following and enforcing it!

Analysts' Conflicts of Interest

The role of securities analysts and their failure to monitor a company is detailed in Chapter 8. In recognizing this failure, the Act tasks the SEC to develop rules for making sure that analysts are separated from investment banking activities and that any conflicts of interest that analysts may have are fully disclosed. As we discussed in Chapter 8, both the National Association of Securities Dealers and the NYSE have already made proposals along these lines, and the SEC approved of these proposals on May 10, 2002. Under the Act, the SEC is given one year to develop these rules further.

SEC Resources and Authority

One limitation that the SEC has had over the years is that the organization is small compared to the industry it regulates. The SEC regulates tens of thousands of public companies, investment banks, auditors, and other participants in the stock and bond markets. In order to help the SEC expand its monitoring and investigative capabilities, the Act appropriates more money for the SEC and mandates the hiring of at least 200 more employees. Will this be enough? Keep in mind that the Act simultaneously imposes many new responsibilities on the SEC.

CORPORATE AND CRIMINAL FRAUD ACCOUNTABILITY AND PENALTIES

To make it easier to prosecute executive criminal behavior in the future, the new law spells out new or altered definitions of criminal behaviors and stiffens penalties. For example, the destruction or falsification of documents in a federal investigation or bankruptcy can be punished with a fine and/or imprisonment of up to ten years. Destruction of audit materials is punishable by a fine and/or imprisonment of up to five years. The statute of limitations for securities fraud is changed to two years after the discovery of the facts or five years after the violation. The bill also protects employee whistle blowers from retaliation by the company or its executives.

In most cases, the penalties for committing white-collar crimes were generally increased from a maximum of five years imprisonment to 20 years. While this pertains to just the *maximum* prison sentence, federal sentencing guidelines are also to be amended. That is, the intent is for the actual *average* white-collar prison sentence to increase, not just the maximum. The company CEO, CFO, and chairman are required to certify the appropriateness of the financial statements. If they willfully violate the integrity of the disclosures, they can be fined up to $1 million and serve up to ten years in prison.

SUMMARY OF THE ACT

This bill passed the House and Senate with overwhelming majorities and was signed very quickly by President Bush. There was a lack of the serious kind of debate that accompanies hotly contested bills. No one wanted to appear as if he or she were defending greedy executives. Therefore, it should not be surprising if we find that the new law does not directly address many of the problems in the corporate system. The bill was rushed, so we can almost expect it to be far from perfect and filled with holes. For example, there is nothing that helps shareholders influence the direction of their firm. Also, the bill does not address the problems with investment banks, credit rating agencies, and corporate attorneys. Even the lawmakers themselves seemed to recognize that more work needs to be done. Much of the Act directs the SEC to create the details within the general guidelines it provides.

The Act addressed many of the problem areas in the corporate system. Much of the new law includes more regulation and more penalties for white-collar crime. This is a common response of lawmakers during a time racked by scandal and public outrage. We feel that the stiffer penalties were warranted, but the increased regulation was not. Instead, we believe that setting up the right incentives would better influence behavior. If the Act promoted better behavior, other benefits would arise. For example, we wouldn't have to worry as much as to whether or not the SEC is overburdened. In some cases, the corporate problem areas of the incentive system and the monitoring system were improved by altering incentives, but, in other cases, the new law will have little or no effect.

OTHER PROPOSALS FOR CHANGE

The government is not the only organization that proposes changes in the corporate governance system. Indeed, groups like the Business Roundtable (made up of corporate executives), the U.S. Chamber of Commerce, and the Securities Industry Association made their own proposals for change. One particularly influential group is the NYSE. The NYSE can enact standards for firms that choose to list on the exchange. As the NYSE is generally considered the most prestigious exchange in the world in which to be listed, it has the power to influence the corporate system.

NEW YORK STOCK EXCHANGE

Former SEC Chairman Pitt asked the NYSE to review its corporate governance standards for listing on February 13, 2002. The exchange responded four months later with detailed recommendations of changes to the standards. On August 16, 2002, the NYSE approved changes to listing standards. Companies listed on the NYSE were given two years to make some of the changes to their governance system (like altering board composition) and six months for others (like adopting a code of ethics).

While there are many monitors of a firm, the NYSE can really only influence the part of the corporate system that is inside the corporation. In other words, it can influence the function and the structure of the board. It can influence compensation systems and how auditing firms are selected and monitored. It does not, however, have much influence over the actions of outside monitors such as credit rating agencies, investment bankers, financial analysts, and auditing firms. Therefore, its listing standard changes deal with the areas with which it has the most influence. Some of its proposals were also adopted in the Sarbanes-Oxley Act. We focus here on those changes that were not adopted by the Act but were adopted by the NYSE.

Most of the new changes have to do with the structure, function, and incentives of the board of directors. Specifically, the NYSE mandates that companies have a *majority of independent directors*. Of course, the definition of "independent" is very important and the NYSE tightens the previous definition. A director is not independent if he or she (or his or her immediate family) has worked for the company or its auditor within the past five years. The board members who are not also executives of the company *must meet regularly* without the presence of management. This move to increase the independence of boards is long overdue and we certainly endorse it. However, we feel that company executives serving as board members present a problem—especially when a CEO holds the leadership position of chairman of the board. Indeed, of the 30 companies in the Dow Jones Industrial Average, only 8 have a separate chairman and CEO. The NYSE has not made any recommendations about this.

The NYSE also requires some functions of the board. For example, the *nominating committee of the board must be composed entirely of independent directors* and perform certain duties. This is also true of the compensation committee. Otherwise, the executives would have undue influence on their own compensation. The audit committee must also be independent. However, the members of this committee will have an *increased authority and responsibility to hire and fire the auditing firm*. To handle this expanded responsibility, the audit committee members are to have necessary experience and expertise in finance and accounting. To help maintain the independence of audit committee board members, members are not to receive pay (especially consulting fees) from the company outside of their regular director fees. Again, we endorse making boards more independent—particularly the audit and compensation committees. However, we question why only audit committee members must refrain from earning consulting fees. When the CEO of a company hires a board member as a consultant, they develop a special relationship that inhibits the board member from being independent. That is, the board member will be less likely to make decisions against the CEO's desires if that CEO is paying him or her a consulting fee. Why aren't all board members prevented from this type of relationship with the company's executives?

Lastly, the NYSE will require that *shareholders approve all executive equity-based compensation plans*. That is, there will be a shareholder vote on whether a CEO gets a certain number of stock options or restricted stock shares. This rule creates more transparency because each shareholder will receive a proxy statement detailing the compensation proposal. In general, we support increased shareholder control and higher transparency. However, we have some concerns. First, the rule does not seem to recognize that management-approved proposals nearly always pass. While shareholders will be more aware of a CEO's compensation, that compensation may not be altered much by this process. Second, the rule may inhibit a board from hiring a good CEO to run a company. When hiring a new executive, a board cannot guarantee a compensation package in an offer to a qualified candidate. The package must be voted on by shareholders first. They must either hold a special meeting for the vote (which is costly) or wait until the regularly scheduled annual meeting. If the shareholders reject the compensation package, the newly hired CEO will leave and another search will have to be made. This rule seems to handicap a board in hiring good executives. We would prefer to let the equity-based compensation be more transparent in the financial statement of the firm and strengthen the independence of a board so that it can do its job.

Overall, the NYSE changes to its listing standards do a good job of strengthening a board's ability to monitor executives. However, more can be done.

EXPENSING STOCK OPTIONS

Several organizations and people have promoted the idea that the cost of stock options issued to employees and executives should be treated as an expense on the financial statements. Some people, like legendary investor Warren Buffett, have been promoting this idea for quite a while. It appears that there are three reasons that expensing stock options are being promoted.

The first purpose is to have better disclosure and account for the real cost of using options as compensation. The expensing would cause the compensation to be more directly observable to shareholders because it would be reported in the income statements. Also, the expensing would identify that there is a cost to a firm for issuing options. Expensing options will lower the earnings of a firm. As we discussed in Chapter 3, there is a real economic cost to shareholders when executives convert tens (or hundreds) of millions of dollars in options into common stock and then sell it in the stock market. Prior to the push for expensing, this economic cost was not well accounted for on the financial statements of a given firm. In other words, this reason for expensing options argues that the economic cost of options should be more transparent.

The second reason for some groups and people to be proposing option expensing is that it may reduce the amount of options that executives receive and thereby reduce their total compensation. The media attention on the tens (or hundreds) of millions of dollars that executives received in the late 1990s brought this topic to more of the public's attention. Let's face it: Getting paid $200 million (or even $20 million) for working a few years seems obscene. Without recording the cost of stock options in some way, a board has an incentive to use options in a very generous way to reward its CEO. If the cost of the options is expensed and thereby reduces a firm's earnings, its board may not be quite so generous.

The third reason for expensing stock options is the impression of the public and politicians that options owned by CEOs and other executives contributed to corporate scandals. That is, the public's perception seems to be that options gave executives a mechanism for benefiting from using accounting chicanery to artificially pump up the price of the company stock. If options are not as attractive for firms to issue, maybe there will be less of an incentive for executives to misbehave.

We agree that options have an economic cost to a firm and that this cost should be identified more clearly in the financial statements. This added disclosure would move the option issues from the footnotes to the main statements and make the process more transparent for shareholders. This is good. However, we also have some major concerns about expensing stock options.

Our first concern has to do with how companies will respond to having to expense options. Some industries, like technology, use options as compensation for many employees, not just executives. For example, Microsoft issues options to most of its employees. Indeed, more than 2,000 Microsoft employees have become millionaires because of the option programs.[4] Even some non-tech companies, such as department store chain Kohls Corp., use options to pay middle and lower managers. Also, it is common for start-up companies to partially pay employees in stock options to help compensate for low salaries. Using this type of pay system, a young company can conserve one of its most precious resources—cash—and motivate employees to work hard. What happens to these compensation systems if options are expensed? The cost to earnings will cause the companies to curtail option programs. This could inhibit the growth of new companies. It could even have an impact on the economy since new companies are an important source of new jobs.

It seems likely that expensing options will have a greater impact on middle and lower management than it will on the top executives. We foresee that a few years from now the top executives will cash in options for millions and the other managers will get nothing. Will we feel better that a CEO only received $100 million instead of $200 million? Not likely! Indeed, the gap between top executive pay and lower management pay may increase because lower levels of management may no longer get options.

Lastly, we do not believe that expensing options solves any of the problems identified in Table 12–1. Expensing options does not alter the incentives of the executives who own them. That is, executives will still have stock options—although possibly not as many. Therefore, they still have the incentive to manage earnings to maximize the stock price over the short term (a few years) instead of the long term.

Currently, dozens of firms have decided to expense stock options. Other firms announced that they would not. At the time of publication, whether a firm expenses its options is purely voluntary. This is just one more illustration of how the accounting standards do not really seem to be standard.

In general, we are a bit puzzled why expensing options have been pushed so hard and have attained such exposure in the media. We feel that the ramifications of expensing options will be to increase the difference in pay between CEOs and other employees in some firms. In addition, the expensing does nothing to change how stock options are used to reward top executives or how those executives will behave. Expensing stock options is not a solution to the corporate governance problems. So, again, why all the hubbub?

MORE CHANGE

The drumbeat for corporate reform seemed to continue after the Sarbanes-Oxley Act became law and after the NYSE voted to change its listing standards. At the time of publication, some Congressmen have expressed an interest in investigating investment banks. Others have expressed a desire to reform the pension regulations to better protect employees. The SEC must also determine how much of the Act will be implemented. Clearly, there could be more laws and regulations developed. We urge lawmakers and regulators to target their efforts on the problems (like those identified in Table 12–1) and not on the symptoms. We also encourage the development of laws that create good incentives instead of simply providing stiffer punishment. In the next chapter, we discuss these issues and offer suggestions for changing the corporate incentive system and the corporate monitoring system in ways that will enhance them and alter behavior.

ENDNOTES

1. Lou Dobbs, "Reform Wall Street," *Money*, July 2002, pp. 65–66.
2. Susan Page, "Worried Investors Become Target of Election," *USA Today*, July 22, 2002, p. 1A.
3. Tom Curry, "Can Congress Protect Investors?" *MSNBC*, July 19, 2002, *http://stacks.msnbc.com/news/781440.asp*.
4. Timothy Egan, "Microsoft Spawns a New Upper Class," *Seattle Post Intelligencer*, June 19, 1992, p. B3.

13 CREATE GOOD INCENTIVES FOR LONG-TERM SOLUTIONS

Many of the new laws will make it easier to prosecute the future offenders and punish them more harshly. This is good. However, they may not be effective in deterring behavior. When talking about the recent scandals, prosecution and punishment are very important. We think that prevention is a better strategy for the future. However, not the kind of prevention that more regulators bring. To prevent market-wide problems in the future, long-term solutions need to be implemented. We want to see solutions that set up the right relationships among shareholders, executives, and monitors. Various solutions could create incentives for these participants to work hard in the right activities, not the wrong ones.

THE POWER OF INCENTIVES

Incentives can be a powerful tool for creating desired behavior. However, the wrong incentives can cause undesired behavior. Consider the efforts of the U.S. military to cut the supply line of the North Vietnamese in the Vietnam War. To cut or slow down the supplies from the north that fortified the offensive in the south, the U.S. military decided to attack the supply line on the Ho Chi Minh Trail using airpower. The best way to determine the effectiveness of the strikes was through aerial photography. A successful strike was one that rendered the various trucks and vehicles inoperable. Probably the best way to destroy these lightly armored vehicles was with the gun cannons, bombs, or rockets used by the planes. After all, a few bullets or bits of shrapnel in an engine block would permanently ruin it. However, bullet holes in the hood of a truck are hard to see from a photograph. Photographic intelligence specialists could really only see when the truck was burned. Therefore, a "kill" was recorded when the vehicles appeared burned. This inferior measure of a kill caused the Air Force to switch tactics and bomb the supply lines with Napalm, which causes fires. However, a burned truck is not necessarily an inoperable truck. If the top of a truck was burned, a person might still be able to drive it. The inferior performance measure of the goal created the wrong incentive. Instead of using the most effective weapons, the Air Force used inferior ones.

Throughout this book, we have identified situations in which the incentives or measurement of performance was inferior. This has lead to inferior and undesirable outcomes. For example, auditing firms are hired by a public company and want to maintain a long-term relationship with the company. This gives auditing firms an incentive to accommodate the company's desires instead of challenging them. Under such an incentive, auditing firms become passive monitors instead of active monitors. Or consider how a company's stock price is a poor measure of the performance of its CEO. Over the long term, a CEO's actions will impact the price of the stock. However, in the short term, the price is strongly influenced by the economy, the mood of investors, and other influences outside of the CEO's control. Yet, the way equity-based compensation plans are currently designed, managers are rewarded simply when the stock price of the company for which they work increases. Often, the outcome is that ineffective managers can be rewarded in a bull market and good managers are not rewarded in a bear market. Poor measures of success lead to ineffective compensation.

It is our intent to suggest solutions to the corporate governance problems that better align incentives and better measure performance. We do not claim to be the originator of every solution we propose. We have designed our own solutions and we have also searched for good ideas elsewhere. The following proposals meet our goals of (1) fixing the problems and not just addressing the symptoms, (2) improving incentives or performance measures, and (3) avoiding excessive regulation.

OUR RECOMMENDATIONS

In this section, we present our recommendations for improving the corporate governance system. In some cases, we briefly repeat the proposals of others (see Chapter 12) to put our recommendations in perspective. The following recommendations are presented in the same order of the incentives and monitoring participants that we have discussed in this book.

STOCK AND STOCK OPTION INCENTIVES

The purpose of granting shares of stock or stock options to executives is to align their interests with those of the shareholders. If the executives can create value for a firm, the stock price will rise. The added stock wealth makes shareholders richer. The executives can then cash in their stock or options for a big profit and also become richer. We have argued that this equity-based compensation partially aligns management's interests with those of shareholders. However, it also creates a short-term focus in which executives manage earnings (fraudulently or otherwise) to maximize the stock price in the short run, not the long run. In this way, executives can cash out their rewards quickly and at a high price. Unfortunately, this may be at the expense of the future financial health of the firm.

We have also identified the problem that stock options reward managers for increases in the stock price. However, the stock price is not the best measurement of managerial performance. Poor measurements lead to the wrong incentives and, ultimately, to the wrong behavior. We address these problems in the next two subsections.

Insider Equity Sales. To better align the interests of insiders to those of the average shareholder, we propose that *insiders announce their intent to sell equity and must spread out their sales over a three-year period*. Specifically, the insiders would file a schedule with the SEC showing a plan for equally distributing the total number of shares to be sold quarterly over a minimum of three years. For example, when a CEO decides to sell one million shares of stock, he or she would file a form with the SEC stating that 83,333 shares will be sold each quarter over the next three years.

Consider how this rule changes the incentives of insiders. When managers can cash out all at once, they end up having a short-term focus. They may try to maximize the stock price at one point in time, and they can do this by being aggressive in accounting methods by moving future sales to the present. For example, Enron would make a deal to sell energy over the next 20 years to a client. Then it would book all the profit over the 20 years into the current quarter or year. Enron called this marking-to-market. It sure makes the present year look good—but at the cost of mortgaging the future. Then the executives cashed out hundreds of millions of dollars in profits while the stock price was artificially high. If those executives were forced to sell over a three-year period, their incentives would change. They would no longer be willing to sacrifice the future for the present because much of their own profit would have to be obtained in the future. Many of the recent corporate scandals originated with executives who were trying to maximize the stock price at a given point in time to exercise their stock options. They hired consultants and investment bankers to figure out ways to do this. The boards weren't watching and the auditors either missed it or were hampered by their own conflict of interest. If the executives had a different incentive, like maximizing the stock price for the long term, they would have acted differently. Our recommendation better aligns the managers' motives with the shareholders' goals. After all, shareholders want high stock prices too, but they want high prices without having to worry about managers' myopic motives.

We consider insiders to be the top executives and the board of directors of a firm. This definition should also apply to insiders' family members and people who have been (but no longer are) insiders of a firm at any time during the previous three years. That is, leaving the company does not absolve someone of the requirement to sell over a three-year period. After all, we don't want the CEO to quit when the company is facing tougher times just so he or she can cash out.

It is always suspicious when an insider of a firm sells equity right before a big stock price decline. Did the insider have information about the future that was not publicly disclosed? Did he or she trade on the information? If insiders had to announce their equity sales and spread them over three years, there would be no need to be concerned that insiders were making investment decisions from private information. That information would become public during the three years the insider was selling. President Bush and Vice President Cheney would not be under the vale of suspicion that they are now under because they would have sold their stock over time instead of all at once near a market peak. Martha Stewart would still be under suspicion because she could still have dumped her ImClone stock (she would not be considered an insider of that firm). However, under our proposed insider selling regulation, CEOs like ImClone's Sam Waksal might become less willing to divulge inside information.

Changing Option Structure. Stock options give the executives of a firm the incentive to manage the firm in such a way that the stock price increases. This is also what the stockholders want. Therefore, stock options are believed to align managers' goals with shareholders' goals. This alignment helps to overcome some of the problems with the separation of ownership and control (Chapter 2). Using stock options to align managers' interests with shareholders' interests has become very popular over the last 30 years. However, there are problems with the way that these options are being used. One problem was addressed in the previous section. That is, options lead to a market timing incentive. There are other problems that can be fixed by altering the structure of options issued.

Specifically, options are a poor, merit-based compensation scheme because managers only have partial influence over stock prices. Stock prices are affected by the performance of a company. However, many other factors influence prices that executives have no control over. When the economy thrives, stock prices rise—even for those companies that are poorly run. This may richly reward executives through their options when they do not deserve rewards. For example, consider the fate of Nabors Industries. From 1995 to 1997, the oil and gas drilling company's stock increased by 386 percent. This seems impressive, doesn't it? However, the oil and gas drilling industry rose in value by 424 percent over the same period. Nabors Industries actually underperformed the industry. Yet, Nabors Industries executives cashed in equity compensation worth nearly $48 million.[1] Quite a payday for a firm that was a laggard in the industry!

Alternatively, the stock market may fall because of poor economic conditions or investor pessimism. A company with management that is able to outperform its competitors may still find that its stock is falling—and thus not be rewarded for success. Companies have responded to this last situation by repricing the executives' options. If the options give a CEO the right to buy at $40 per share (the strike price) and the stock is currently trading at $20 per share, the options are underwater. To give the CEO more incentive, the board may reprice those options to a strike price of $20 per share.

Repricing options is not a very good solution to the problems with options as compensation. First, repricing only attempts to solve one of the two problems we just identified. Second, and more importantly, it creates bad incentives for executives. If repricing becomes common, the CEO knows that he or she can take some risk with the firm. If risky decisions pay off, the stock price will soar and the CEO cashes in for megabucks. If those decisions fail, the stock price plummets. The CEO negotiates for repricing and is ready to take another big risk with the firm. Repricing options takes away the risk for the CEO![2] With no risk to his or her own future wealth, the CEO has an incentive to gamble with the firm (heads, the CEO and shareholders win; tails, the shareholders lose and we try again).

We think a better solution is to use indexed options. That is, *executive options should be linked to an industry index*. Traditional options fix the price at which executives can buy shares of stock. A bull market will increase the stock price to a level much higher than the fixed price (or strike price). A bear market will sink the stock price to a level far below the strike price. Therefore, the price of the stock might be more related to the type of stock market (bull versus bear) than to the results of a CEO's decisions. Indexed options take into account the type of stock market and reward executives for outperforming their industry—even in a bear market.

The following describes how indexed options work. Consider, for example, that the stock of a company is currently trading at $50 per share. The CEO is given indexed options with a strike price at $50 that is linked to the industry. Over the next few years, the company's stock price increases to $75 per share. With traditional options given to CEOs, he or she could buy stock for $50 per share with the option and sell it for $75 per share, thus making a $25 profit on each option owned. However, the price at which the CEO can buy the stock is linked to the industry index in an indexed option. For example, let's assume that during the same period, the entire industry also increased such that the indexed option strike price moved to $65 per share. The CEO did indeed manage the firm well. The industry increased in value by 30 percent while the company increased 50 percent. The executive is rewarded through the options with a $10 per share profit (=$75–$65). If he or she has options for 1 million shares, the profit would be $10 million. However, if the industry did better than this company, the strike price might rise to $80 per share. Since the company's stock only rose to $75 per share, the CEO did not manage the firm as well as the other firms in the industry were managed by their CEOs. He or she should not be rewarded for his or her sub-par performance. And, indeed, the CEO is not rewarded by the index-linked stock options (–$5=$75–$80).

Now consider the effect of a bear market. If the stock price were to drop to $30 per share, normal stock options have no exercisable value and are said to be underwater. However, the index-based option may still have value for a good manager. If a firm's industry index dropped to $25 per share, the manager has beaten the index and deserves some reward. The indexed option pays $5 per share (=$30–$25).

The advantage of indexed-linked options is that they reward managers for outperforming their industry regardless of good or bad economic times. In this way, only good managerial performance is rewarded, and it is rewarded in both bull and bear markets. This type of option compensation creates a better alignment between managers and shareholders and avoids the problems of option repricing. Although indexed options are a more recent evolution of executive compensation, their option pricing and valuation dynamics have been worked out. For example, there is another advantage for companies that expense options. Option valuation models show that the initial value of the indexed options is lower than the value of the traditional options.[3] Therefore, indexed options cost a company less to issue!

AUDITING FIRM INCENTIVES

The auditing process is an important part of the monitoring system in corporate governance. We describe the history and situation of auditing firms in Chapter 5. Two problems are identified. The first problem is the conflict of interest that occurs when auditing firms also provide lucrative consulting services to a company. The second problem is that auditing firms want to provide auditing services to a company for many years. That is, they want to keep the public company as a long-term client. This makes the auditors less willing to challenge the company's accounting methods.

The government's response to these problems is to mandate that a consulting firm cannot provide auditing services to any company it consults with, which effectively solves the first problem, and to increase the regulation in the auditing industry. The Public Company Accounting Reform and Investor Protection Act creates another regulatory organization called the Public Company Accounting Company Oversight Board to oversee the auditing industry. The oversight board operates under the discretion of the SEC. However, we foresee that the board will find that it has the same problem as the SEC and any other regulator—it has few regulators watching many auditors, who, taken together, are conducting tens of thousands of audits. The first of the government's solutions actually changed auditor incentives. However, the creation of the new regulators does little to change incentives. Accounting fraud has always been illegal. There have been private organizations (like the new board) formulating policy and setting standards for many decades.

Instead of the government's two solutions, we propose one solution that changes incentives for auditors and solves both problems (and others!). We recommend that *companies must change auditors every two years*. When we refer to auditors, we are referring to both the auditing firm and the individual people who conduct the audits. After Arthur Andersen collapsed, other accounting firms hired many of the Arthur Andersen auditors. The same individual auditors ended up auditing the same firms—only under a different auditing firm's logo. We want to avoid this way of sidestepping our recommendation. Consider the incentives that our recommendation could create. If you are an auditor, you do not want to be blamed for any errors or questionable practices in the company's past. Therefore, you will work hard to ferret out any problems of the past while you can still blame the previous auditor. Indeed, you had better do a good job because a different auditor will be examining your work in one or two years. That is, you would have an incentive to challenge the company's accounting practices when necessary because you know you cannot have a long-term relationship with the company and the next auditor will be closely reviewing your work.

The real beauty of this recommendation is that it provides incentives for the thousands of auditors to monitor each other! That is, outsider audit regulators wouldn't even be necessary under our proposal because auditors are far more equipped to monitor each other than a handful of regulators. Thus, the system itself would become more self-sufficient.

By rotating the auditor every two years, it doesn't really matter if this year's auditing firm is also providing consulting services. All parties know that a different auditing firm will be hired soon and it will be closely examining the decisions made this year. Therefore, this solution also has a positive impact on the conflict of interest that occurs when both auditing and consulting are provided by the same firm to a company.

Our solution will also open up the industry to competition again. Over the past couple of decades, accounting firms have merged and consolidated. This has created a situation in which very few firms conduct the auditing services for the vast majority of corporations. Not too long ago, we referred to these major accounting firms as the Big 8. Recently, with the collapse of Arthur Andersen, there are only four big firms left (the Final 4). While there are many medium-sized and small accounting firms, it is hard for them to expand because of the long-term relationships these four firms have with their clients. Our recommendation breaks these long-term relationships and gives the medium-sized accounting firms the chance to compete for the business of the larger clients. Over time, this will give more accounting firms the opportunity to grow and will eventually increase the number of major accounting firms. We want to see this increased competition in the industry.

Critics of our recommendation will claim that the long-term relationship between a company and an auditing firm makes the auditing process more efficient. That is, the auditing team already knows the accounting systems and business operations of the firm, existing auditors do not have to relearn these systems every year, and the increased work will cause the auditing service to be more costly to the company. However, we argue that being too familiar with the systems and procedure makes the auditors more complacent. For example, auditors missed WorldCom's capitalization of billions of dollars of ordinary expenses (see Chapter 5). It appears that this occurred for several years—perhaps because auditors were too complacent.

We do indeed expect that the cost of auditing services will initially increase if our recommendation is implemented. However, two factors will operate to eventually bring the cost of auditing services back down. First, the market will adjust to the new problems of providing an audit. That is, companies will change to accounting methods that are more likely to be easily understood and approved by auditors. Also, new standardized software and procedures will be developed to improve the ability of new auditors to get up to speed. However, the most important factor will be an increase in competition. As the number of major accounting firms increases, so will competition for auditing. The increased supply should lower auditing fees.

BOARDS OF DIRECTORS

Compared to the boards of corporations 100 years ago, modern board structure and function has improved considerably. So, while there has been general improvement, the recent collapse of several companies and other corporate scandals have shown that there is obviously room for improvement. Many of the proposals by the NYSE and some of the new laws in the Public Company Accounting Reform and Investor Protection Act address problems with boards of directors. In general, we feel these proposals are good. If anything, they do not go far enough. The following are some additional ways that boards can be improved.

1. The NYSE proposals recommend that all of the boards of key subcommittees, such as the audit committee, compensation committee, and director nominating committee, should be comprised entirely of *independent directors*. The criterion for being an independent director was also improved. We wholeheartedly approve of these recommendations.

2. *Increase the level of financial and accounting exper-tise* of board members should be increased. The NYSE proposals and the act mandate that members of an audit committee should have significant knowledge of accounting and financial practices. However, more experience in these areas would be useful for a large portion of the board. For example, when board members have banking expertise, they can provide valuable opinions regarding the debt market.[4]

3. The NYSE also recommends that *independent board members should meet frequently* without management present. We recommend going a step further. Independent directors should *become more involved* with the firm so that they get a better understanding of the firm. Directors need to take the initiative to occasionally talk with employees. For example, Home Depot's board policy requires directors to regularly visit its stores to better appreciate the business.

4. *Pay a significant portion of directors' pay in stock* so that they have a personal interest in the firm's success. We recognize that this recommendation could give board members the same short-term focus and market timing incentive as executives. Therefore, in order to make it effective, board members would have to be restricted in selling the stock in a manner recommended in the "Insider Equity Sales" section of this chapter. The restriction gives board members a materially long-term focus and incentive to actively monitor the firm.

5. *Separate the CEO and board chairman positions.* The chair has a strong influence on a board's agenda and the information that is distributed to the board members. Also, the effectiveness of the board is obviously undermined when the person who is the chairman is also the same person who the board is supposed to evaluate. In fact, it should not be surprising that there is some evidence that shows that a manager who is both the CEO and chairman rarely gets fired even when the firm's performance is poor.[5]

6. *Make boards smaller.* This suggestion may seem counterintuitive (more heads are better than one?), but smaller boards are actually more active and effective (too many cooks spoil the broth!). Imagine that you are one board member out of 20. You are more likely to think that other directors are doing the monitoring and you do not have to work so hard. However, if you are one of ten directors, it is more obvious that each director must be an effective monitor for the board to function properly. In fact, there is evidence that suggests that firms with fewer directors have higher market values, which indicates their effectiveness.[6]

INVESTMENT BANKS AND ANALYST INCENTIVES

Many of the problems with the behavior of investment banks and analysts have to do with their association with one another. As we discussed in Chapters 7 and 8, sell-side analysts have become salesmen for the investment banking business. Once this happens, analysts' recommendations and analyses become biased—they go from research to advertising. The American public already knows not to trust what is said on a TV commercial. Yet the advertisement disguised as unbiased research is trickier.

Some good recommendations have been made to separate analyst research and investment banking activities. Indeed, analyst conflicts of interest came under scrutiny before the investigations of the other corporate governance system participants. On May 10, 2002, the SEC approved rule changes proposed by the National Association of Securities Dealers (NASD) relating to research analyst conflicts of interest. The NASD Rule 2711 recommendations establish standards governing analyst relationships with investment banking activities. Of particular interest are the following rules:

- Analysts cannot be supervised or controlled by investment banking departments.
- Analysts' compensation cannot be tied to specific investment banking transactions.

- Analysts are not to provide favorable research to acquire banking business.
- Analysts must report conflicts of interest in research reports and public appearances.

These are good ideas because they attempt to break the relationship between analysts and bankers and change the incentives of analysts. If the rules work well, analysts' reputations could increase over time. However, buy-side analysts seem to be skeptical whether the rules can be credibly implemented and/or enforced.[7] While analysts might not work for an investment banking department, their departments will still be in the same firm. At some point up the chain of management, someone will be in charge of both services. Thus, pressure to conform for the good of the company can still be felt.

In addition to implementing these rules, the SEC has one additional recommendation. A new proposal by the SEC called Proposed Regulation Analyst Conflicts would require that analysts include in their research reports a statement certifying that the views expressed accurately reflect their personal views about the company that they are analyzing. This is like the certifying of annual financial statements that the SEC requires of CEOs. Analysts have always signed their names to their research reports. This certifying process does nothing except make regulators feel better—especially since most retail investors don't even read the reports. Of the information provided by analysts, most investors use the buy/sell ratings. Investors often access these ratings from financial Internet sites that compile multiple analysts' recommendations and report summary information. In other words, investors see the ratings, but they rarely see the analyses or reports.

We advocate the goal of increasing the research produced by independent analysts. The trick is to find a source of revenue for independent analysts. Institutional investors can afford to pay for independent research, and they often do. The recommendations of both buy-side analysts and independent analysts are confidential and not public. Therefore, retail investors only see sell-side analysts' recommendations. It would be ideal if independent analysts' recommendations were public. That way, retail investors would get unbiased analysis. Of course, independent analysts sell their research to institutional investors, and thus want it private. We want to create a group of analysts that is willing to make public recommendations but that does not work for the brokerage or banking firm underwriting a stock issue.

One possibility is to require each new stock issue (especially IPOs) that is underwritten to have security analysis reports from three analysts who do not work for the bank or brokerage firm doing the underwriting. These reports and recommendations would be publicly disclosed. We propose that an organization organize a pool (or list) of analysts who want to conduct this type of analysis for pay. When a firm issues a security, the investment bank would pay (with fees from the firm) the organization to obtain three independent reports from analysts who specialize in that industry. Independent credit agencies have been serving this function for bond issues for many years. These ratings are paid for by the issuing companies. The companies pay to get rated because they want to get a fair price for their issues. Why not improve and expand on this idea? Independent analysts like the ones we're suggesting will have no other incentive but to provide accurate assessments of each stock issue. Eventually, good firms will want good independent analysts to evaluate their stock issue as a way of proving the quality of the offering. Here, both potential investors and the firm are better off.

While the SEC could be the organization to create this pool of analysts, we feel that it would be better for the analysts' private association to do it. Analysts seek the Chartered Financial Analyst (CFA) designation from the self-governing body, the Association of Investment Management Research (AIMR). AIMR already has databases of analyst characteristics, and it is very concerned about professional ethics. It has been working with the SEC, Congress, and others to improve the integrity of analyst recommendations. Indeed, many of the new rules enacted by the SEC have been advocated by AIMR.

When investment banks try to take unworthy firms public, as they did in the late 1990s, they will find that it is hard to market an IPO when the analysts' reports are negative. In the past, they could underwrite any IPO and have their own analysts tout the firm. If investors were not paying as close attention as they should (as in the late 1990s), they would succumb to the marketing campaign of the banks, which included analysts' recommendations that were only disguised ads. The investment banks take on risk when they underwrite a security. If the true prospects of a firm will become public during the issue process, they will take more care in the quality of the issues that they underwrite.

Our recommendation has several good incentive outcomes. First, investment banks will be motivated to bring only quality stock issues to market. Second, investors will have access to unbiased analyst research and recommendations for free. Third, our recommendation lowers the chance that a stock market bubble will occur—especially in the IPO market. And fourth, the stature gained by analysts in the industry's and the public's view of them will be earned through quality research and a history of accurate predictions.

CREDIT RATING AGENCIES

Credit rating agencies can be an integral part of the corporate monitoring system. However, there are some structural problems with the industry that could be improved. For example, government regulations are keeping the number of agencies to only three. In addition, they have been able to protect themselves from lawsuits by claiming their right to free speech. The lack of competition and the high degree of legal protection combine to create a situation in which credit rating agencies do not have a disciplinary mechanism. Without the possibility of being disciplined, these agencies can easily become complacent and have little incentive to be thorough in their analyses.

The SEC needs to create a process by which additional credit rating agencies can gain the coveted Nationally Recognized Statistical Rating Organization designation. Currently, a firm must be considered large enough to be a credible, nationwide firm. However, a small credit agency cannot grow to be large enough without the designation. This catch-22 has ensured that only three firms remain in the industry. We recommend *giving promising small credit rating agencies a limited designation*. For example, the SEC could approve them for rating one type of security, like asset-backed securities. These debt instruments are mostly purchased by institutional investors who are more able to make their own judgments about risk than individual investors. Therefore, there is low risk to the general public in giving younger agencies this area to grow. If a new agency proves itself with a good track record in its ratings and sustains solid growth in the asset-backed securities area, the SEC can either expand the agency's designation to other securities or give it full recognition. Increasing the industry competition by adding trustworthy firms provides more incentives for the credit rating agencies to be diligent in their monitoring role.

SHAREHOLDERS

We want investors, especially the large institutional investors, to have more ability and desire to influence the strategy of the companies they own. However, there is a fine line between investor activism designed to improve the performance of a firm and activism designed to further other objectives. For example, the origin of modern investor activism in the United States occurred in the 1970s. Early activists were interested in furthering their agenda for social justice. Therefore, their shareholder proposals involved resolutions on topics like South African apartheid, community development, and gender and racial equality. Many people with environmental agendas entered the shareholder activism arena after the 1989 *Exxon Valdez* oil spill disaster. There are many people who would like to use shareholder proposals to force companies to use union labor. Other people would like to use proposals to force companies to avoid union labor.

On the other hand, as indicated in Chapter 11, many institutional investors now coordinate their activism efforts through the Council for Institutional Investors to improve corporate governance. The ability to improve corporate governance through investor activism should be enhanced. These institutional investor activists first try to change things through dialogue with the managers and board of directors of a company. If that fails, they can make a shareholder proposal (also called a resolution) for the shareholders to vote on. However, there are often impediments to this process that make it difficult to achieve success. The following recommendations help to overcome some of the obstacles.[8]

1. *A majority of shareholders approving a proposal should amend the company's bylaws.* Some firms have supermajority rules that require a two-thirds approval for shareholder proposals. If more than half of the owners approve a proposal, it should be implemented. The higher approval hurdle is simply too high to get anything to pass because many shareholders do not even bother to vote.

2. *The vote of each investor should be kept confidential.* That is, company managers should not know how each investor voted. Institutional investors want to keep a dialogue going with managers. When managers see that an investor has voted against their wishes, they sometimes refuse to talk with him or her. This possibility pressures institutions to simply vote with management in order to keep the dialogue going.

3. *Companies should avoid anti-takeover defense bylaws.* Examples include poison pills and greenmail (payment by a takeover target to a potential acquirer, usually to buy back at a premium acquired shares that the potential acquirer already owns; in exchange, the acquirer agrees not to pursue the takeover bid). Anti-takeover defenses help prevent an investor or another company from taking over the company. These measures help members of management stay entrenched in their jobs. The corporate takeover market is an important disciplinary force for managers. If they run the firm poorly, it may get taken over by people who think that they can run the firm more profitably. The former

managers get fired. Many firms enacted these bylaws in the 1980s when there was a trend of hostile takeovers. Takeovers are usually good for investors because the purchaser buys the firm for more than the current stock price (usually 20 to 30 percent or higher). This is a good return for investors who have seen their company perform poorly.

Having good corporate governance bylaws and policies helps allow institutional investors to influence a firm on those rare occasions when it might be appropriate. Are companies with good corporate governance actually good investments? The answer appears to be yes. In a recent academic study, financial economists ranked approximately 1,500 companies into ten groups based on their corporate governance policies. The group with the highest shareholder rights outperformed the group with the lowest shareholder rights by 8.5 percent per year during the 1990s.[9] Given that management compensation is predominately in stock or stock options, managers should want the company for which they work to have these good governance policies. However, since managers feel that their jobs may be at risk with these bylaws, they usually do not support them.

SUMMARY

We have provided recommendations for improving the corporate governance system that are based on creating proper incentives. We hope that these ideas are thoroughly discussed and even improved upon. It will take effort by many participants in the corporate system to make the changes we recommend. The government and regulators must implement some of these ideas. Other recommendations will have to be enacted by corporate boards of directors. It is in everyone's long-term interest to improve the system and restore investor confidence. However, it will take more than just fixing the system to restore investor confidence. We discuss this issue in the next chapter.

ENDNOTES

1. Jennifer Reingold, Richard Melcher, and Gary McWilliams, "Executive Pay: Stock Options Plus a Bull Market Made a Mockery of Many Attempts to Link Pay to Performance," *BusinessWeek*, April 20, 1998, p. 2.
2. Viral Acharya, Kose John, and Rangarajan Sundaram, "On the Optimality of Resetting Executive Stock Options," *Journal of Financial Economics* 57 (2000): 65–101.
3. Shane Johnson and Yisong Tian, "Indexed Executive Stock Options," *Journal of Financial Economics* 57 (2000): 35–64.
4. James Booth and Daniel Deli, "On Executives of Financial Institutions as Outside Directors," *Journal of Corporate Finance* 5 (1999): 227–250.
5. Vidhan Goyal and Chul Park, "Board Leadership Structure and CEO Turnover," forthcoming in the *Journal of Corporate Finance*, 2002.
6. David Yermack, "Higher Market Valuation of Companies with a Small Board of Directors," *Journal of Financial Economics* 40 (1996): 185–212.
7. Leslie Boni and Kent Womack, "Solving the Sell-Side Research Problem: Insights from Buy-Side Professionals," Dartmouth College working paper, August 8, 2002.
8. Recommendations are adapted from "U.S. Corporate Governance Principles," CalPERS website, *www.calpers-governance.org*.
9. Paul Gompers, Joy Ishii, Andrew Metrick, "Corporate Governance and Equity Prices," forthcoming in the *Quarterly Journal of Economics*, February 2003.

14 REGAINING INVESTOR CONFIDENCE

It is important that long-term solutions to the corporate governance problems are implemented. The governance changes proposed or enacted into law are detailed in the previous two chapters. Many of the solutions that have been implemented are not necessarily going to be effective over the long term. For example, the SEC has been given significantly increased funding to expand its investigations. But prior to the summer of 2002, its funding was totally inadequate to monitor firms and protect investors. The intense focus on these issues will start to wane over time. As the public shifts its focus, so will politicians. Five, ten, or twenty years from now, elected officials will be looking to reduce the size of government. Or they may be looking for places to cut spending in order to fund other areas that have caught the attention of the public. How long will it be before the SEC's funding is reduced again? When we are experiencing the glow of another prolonged economic expansion and bull market, will anyone care about those regulators who are always trying to ruin the fun? In fact, the governance problems will probably be totally forgotten by the height of the next bull market. When the bull is raging, people who are seeing big investment profits rolling in are likely to overlook a new round of infectious greed.

PROTECTING INVESTORS (NOT)

The government continually tightens and loosens its laws regarding the investment industry just as it continually raises and lowers income taxes. After each major bear market or scandalous period, the government enacts new laws to protect investors. Consider the new laws shown in Table 14–1. The securities acts passed in 1933 and 1934 followed the corporate governance problems of the late 1920s, the 1929 stock market crash, and the beginning of the Great Depression. The Investment Company Act and the Investment Advisors Act of 1940 followed a bear market that diminished the value of the stock market by 25 percent. The late 1960s experienced a 30 percent bear market. In 1970, the government created the Securities Investor Protection Corporation (SIPC). Investor protection laws also followed the bear market of the early 1970s and the Black Monday market crash of October 19, 1987. And, of course, the recent corporate scandals combined with the severe stock market decline spawned the 2002 Public Company Accounting Reform and Investor Protection Act.

Unfortunately, the laws that are enacted to protect shareholders and investors are often repealed during times of economic strength and stock market euphoria. The 1920s and the 1990s had many similarities. Both decades experienced strong economic expansions and powerful bull markets. Indeed, investors at the end of each decade could have been called irrationally exuberant. In the middle (or toward the end) of the excitement over stocks, the government changed its laws that protected investors.

Consider the examples in Table 14–2. In 1927, the stock market was close to the end of a bull market that increased values more than 200 percent. There were many new companies conducting IPOs that were not really strong enough to be offered to investors. Investors did not seem to care and rushed in to snap them up. The commercial banks were prevented from getting into the investment banking activities and sharing in the lucrative fees. They lobbied the government to change the rules and succeeded. Commercial banks began helping

TABLE 14–1   Major Laws Created to Protect Investors

ACT	PURPOSE	PRECEDED BY
1933 and 1934 Banking Act and Securities Exchange Act	Separates commercial and investment banking; creates SEC as market regulators	Stock market crash of 1929 and ensuing bear market removes nearly 90% of Dow value
1940 Investment Company Act and Investment Advisors Act	Regulate investment companies and advisors	Market decline of 25% from October 1939 to May 1940
1970 Securities Investor Protection Act	Creates Securities Investor Protection Corporation and insurance from broker defaults	Market decline of 30% from April 1969 to June 1970
1974 Employee Retirement Income Security Act	Regulates pension funds	Long bear market from December 1972 to September 1974 takes the Dow down 40%
1988 Insider Trading and Securities Fraud Enforcement Act	Increases penalties and liabilities for insider trading and fraudulent activities	Stock market crash of 1987 takes Dow down more than 40%
2002 Public Company Accounting Reform and Investor Protection Act	Increases regulation of auditors, lengthens punishment for white-collar crimes, and creates more corporate fraud laws	Two-and-a-half-year bear market reduced Dow by 35%; Nasdaq declines 75%

companies issue securities. Unfortunately, the stock market crash of 1929 left commercial banks with many losses that jeopardized people's bank deposits. The people panicked and

TABLE 14–2   Repeals of Some Investor Protections

ACTION	PURPOSE	PRECEDED BY
1927 Government agency policy allows commercial banks to issue securities	Allows commercial banks into investment banking activities	Stock market rose more than 200% from 1925 to 1928
1995 Private Securities Litigation Reform Act	Limits the ability and available damages of investors suing for corporate fraud in federal courts	Dow increased 60% from 1993 to 1995
1998 Securities Litigation Uniform Standards Act	Precludes plaintiffs from bringing securities actions to state courts	Dow increased 125% from 1996 to 1999
1999 Financial Services Modernization Act	Allows commercial and investment banking activities to be combined	Dow increased 125% from 1996 to 1999

demanded their money back. Of course, banks did not have the cash to return all of the deposits at once because the cash was loaned out. The banks therefore had to close their doors.

Now, examine the three law changes in the 1990s. The Private Securities Litigation Reform Act limited the ability of investors to sue companies and executives for damages due to corporate fraud in federal courts. This law was enacted in the midst of a strong bull market that increased the value of the Dow Jones Industrial Average by 60 percent. It was followed three years later with a similar act that applied to state courts. The Financial Services Modernization Act allowed commercial banks to associate themselves with investment banks again. This is similar to the 1927 capitulation. Again, this reduction in investor protection occurred toward the end of a market rally that increased the Dow by 125 percent.

Another recent example is not listed in the table. In 1997, the SEC proposed new rules that would have severely limited the ability of shareholders to introduce corporate resolutions. The procedure for the SEC to enact a new rule is that the regulator proposes a new rule and then provides a time period in which people can comment on the rule. A consortium of investor activists lobbied strongly against the proposed rule. In the end, the SEC decided not to enact the new limitations. Even though the new limitations were defeated, they are an example of how investor protections are often reversed or limited during an extended bull market.

Our point is that laws are frequently made to protect shareholders and investors. This usually occurs after people become angry over scandals and a bear market. However, these protections can also be reversed in the midst of good times. A strong economy and a good bull market lead to pressure being put on lawmakers to loosen restrictions on corporate participants. The loosened restrictions have the potential to help push the stock market from a bull market to a bubble market. When a bubble occurs, a crash will inevitably follow. This leads to more scandals and more investor protection laws. We need to avoid this cycle. Yet, the social mood can be represented by stock prices. The level of the stock market indicates what kind of mood the people are in. This dictates the tone and character of the resulting action by government, regulators, and investors.[1] The relationship we show between how the stock market has performed and the resulting legislation illustrates this point.

It also doesn't help that lawmakers and regulators are so tightly tied into the business community. We have already detailed how President Bush and Vice President Cheney have been criticized for their own behavior as a corporate board member and as an executive, respectively. Former SEC Chairman Harvey Pitt was a corporate lawyer before taking on the role of chief regulator. In addition, the accounting profession contributed nearly $7 million to national political campaigns during the 2001–2002 election cycle (data available through July 2002).[2] The top three individual recipients of this money were Charles Schumer (D–Senate), Michael Enzi (R–Senate), and Max Baucus (D–Senate), who received $75,000, $59,000, and $49,000, respectively. In the presidential election cycle of 1999–2000, George Bush received $1,100,000, Al Gore $400,000, and Bill Bradley $352,000 from the accounting profession. Both political parties accept big contributions from participants in the corporate system.

The accounting profession is not even a big contributor to political campaigns compared to other participants in the corporate system. Securities firms and investment banks contributed $34 million, lawyers and law firms contributed $50 million, and businesses contributed $75 million in the 2001–2002 election cycle. With this kind of money flowing to political campaigns, it is no wonder that there is a cycle of strengthening and reducing investor protection laws. After scandals, politicians listen to the anger of the voters and pass tough laws to protect investors. When the next good economic period arrives with a strong bull market, voters focus their attention elsewhere. Then these big contributors get a politician's ear and laws are passed that are more advantageous for the business participants.

Or, take the IPO process. Chapter 7 discusses how investment banks used hot IPOs as a carrot to get companies to use their investment banking services. That is, a bank would allocate a large number of shares of a popular IPO company to executives of a company that might be issuing its own securities in the near future—a tactic called spinning. The grateful executives would be more likely to hire the bank to underwrite their own issue. But investment banks don't just allocate IPO shares to company executives. They also allocate scarce shares to celebrities and, yes, politicians. All of the IPO shares that go to these VIPs mean that it is more difficult for the average investor to get these shares.

Indeed, the very lawmakers who investigate this investment banking practice have also flipped their own IPOs. For example, Senator Barbara Boxer, a member of the Senate

Commerce Subcommittee, received five IPO allocations in 2000 that earned her thousands of dollars in profits.[3] The Senator (or her husband) was able to purchase stock from one such IPO, Avenue A, for $24 per share and sell it the next day for $72 per share.

Other lawmakers investigating investment banks participated in the IPO market as well. Some of these people claimed that their broker made their investment decisions for them. Others claimed that they received no special treatment. We are not suggesting that Senator Boxer, or any other politician, has done anything illegal. However, having people who are themselves privileged investigate spinning is not as comforting as a Senate investigation could be. This is just one more reason for investors to be less than ecstatic when politicians try to argue that they truly want to change the system.

INVESTOR CONFIDENCE

Much has been said about the crisis in investor confidence. Much has been said about the need to restore investor confidence. But how can investor confidence be restored? Indeed, what is investor confidence?

Two synonyms for the word *confidence* are trust and faith. It takes a lot of trust to invest in corporate securities. When you think about it, what investment do you actually *hold*? Most people hold a piece of paper with a mutual fund's name on it. This statement has a name and account number on it. It takes trust to believe that the piece of paper is actual wealth. How many investors have actually seen a stock certificate of a company they own? Unlike gold or real estate, when you invest in corporate securities, you hold only paper. It takes a great deal of faith in the system to convert your hard cash to financial statements from brokerages and mutual funds. Indeed, investor trust is the foundation on which the entire securities market is built.

Not only is trust a requirement for entering into the securities markets, it is also a force in decision-making for many investors. Consider two types of investors—the *assessing investor* and the *trusting investor*. The assessing investor uses analytical tools to evaluate the value of an investment. He or she does not trust what the CEO of a firm says or what analysts recommend. The assessing investor makes decisions on what to buy, when to buy, and when to sell after exhaustively gathering and analyzing all relevant information.

On the other hand, the trusting investor makes decisions based on the level of trust that has been achieved.[4] Trust is built over time. To know the degree of trust deserved, the trusting investor looks to the past. If a person, company, or mutual fund behaved in a particular way in the past, the trusting investor assumes the behavior will continue in the future. Psychologists and behavioral finance experts call this a representativeness bias. The events of the past represent what to expect in the future. The trusting investor will buy and own securities when the past behavior meets his or her threshold for trustworthiness. This investor is induced to invest after a company has shown a history of good performance and the stock has provided good returns. Because trust is built over time, trusting investors tend to be momentum investors. That is, it takes good returns over time to build up the trust to induce investment. Trusting investors buy the securities that have increased in price over time.

Notice the difference in behavior between assessing investors and trusting investors. After a stock price has risen, the trusting investor is likely to buy. The assessing investor determines whether the stock has risen too much (and is thus overvalued) or still has some upside. When stock prices fall, the trusting investor begins to lose faith. If the price falls too far, he or she loses confidence and sells the security. The assessing investor again trades on the basis of whether or not the stock is undervalued or overvalued.

Are there any assessing investors? Probably. Many books discuss how to conduct security analysis. Tens of thousands of people are trying to become certified as a Chartered Financial Analyst (CFA) by taking the rigorous tests on securities analysis. This analysis is also taught in business schools everywhere.

Are there any trusting investors? While there are many investors who know about security analysis, there are probably many more who do not. These investors make decisions based on other factors. How many people buy the stock of a company when they really are not sure how that company makes money (take Enron, for example)? How many people actually know what stocks are owned in their mutual funds or in the funds in their 401(k) plan? Indeed, how do people pick mutual funds? The decision for many investors is usually based on past return. The mutual funds that ranked in the highest 20 percent in performance last year are receiving nearly all the new investment money this year.[5] Trusting investors put their money in the funds that have earned their trust by performing well in the past. They also take their money out of mutual funds that performed poorly.

Faith in securities markets also applies to asset classes. The great bull market of the 1990s brought millions of new investors into the stock market. The market earned their confidence by producing good returns. Most of these investors did not learn how to conduct security analysis before buying stocks. They still do not know how to conduct analysis—they are trusting investors, not assessing investors. These investors lost confidence during the bear market of 2001–2002 and the corporate scandals. Most trusting investors had had enough by the summer of 2002 and sold their stock. Looking for another investment class that they can have faith in, they noticed that bonds had earned a solid return while stocks experienced a bear market. Sure enough, record flows of investment money poured into bonds in the summer of 2002. This is more likely the money of trusting investors rather than that of assessing investors. Assessing investors are more likely to find that securities are undervalued after a market decline and overvalued after a price increase. Bond prices had risen and stock prices had fallen. As a result, assessing investors were more likely to buy stocks rather than bonds. Even investors just rebalancing their portfolio would be selling bonds (because they had increased to a larger portion of the portfolio) and buying stocks (which had decreased in portfolio allocation).

Trusting investors do not necessarily have to trust a company's CEO or a particular analyst. They may learn to trust the corporate system of incentives and monitors to continue behaving as it did in the past to continue producing the good returns. A history of favorable experiences strengthens trust.

A history of unfavorable experiences makes trusting investors distrustful. The large decline in the stock market and a series of corporate scandals have given trusting investors many reasons for losing confidence.

FAILING TO REGAIN CONFIDENCE

The trusting investors are very important to the stock market. There are many of them and their capital is needed to expand companies' operations and to expand the economy. The media and politicians are correct when they state that there is a crisis in investor confidence. They are right when they advocate a need to restore investor confidence.

What happens when the trusting investors lose all faith? Most of them never regain it. Consider the stock market crash of 1929 and the ensuing Great Depression. It took nearly 25 years for the stock market to recover to its pre-crash highs (it did so in 1954). Why 25 years? In part, the recovery was delayed because the majority of the trusting investors of the 1920s never invested in the market again. It took another generation of people to slowly gain trust and begin investing.

American investors are not alone in occasionally losing confidence. For example, Japan experienced its own stock market crash in 1990. In December 1989 and January 1990, the Nikkei 225 Index peaked at nearly 39,000. By the end of 1990, the market had fallen 43 percent to 22,000. Although it has experienced both ups and downs, the Nikkei has mostly fallen ever since. In the fall of 2002, the index had fallen to less than 9,000—more than a 75 percent fall since early 1990. In other words, it had been more than 12 years since the Nikkei's peak, and the index still stands at only 25 percent of its former value. The previously trusting investors will not be coming back to the Japanese stock market. How long will it be before a new generation will begin to trust the securities markets there?

REGAINING THE CONFIDENCE

Can investor confidence in the United States be restored? Can it be restored before the current trusting investors lose all faith and never return to the stock market? We believe the answer to both questions is yes. However, rebuilding trust will require time and effort. Trust is not gained overnight. It is gained through a history of good behavior. Unfortunately, the recent history is one of poor behavior.

Politicians and regulators will not be able to regain the lost confidence through talk. For example, President Bush proposed solutions for the governance problems in a speech delivered on July 9, 2002. He recommended that punishment be increased and laws be enacted to make it easier to punish corporate criminals in the future. His focus seemed to be on personal ethics and accountability. On the day he presented his proposals, the Dow Jones Industrial Average fell 178 points. The next day, the Dow fell 282 points. This was not exactly the reaction the administration was looking for. However, there wasn't much in the speech to increase confidence. After all, ethical behavior is not motivated through prosecution and punishment.

Senator Paul Sarbanes introduced Bill S.2673, a proposal to create a Public Company Accounting Oversight Board. Recall that this bill seeks to (1) oversee the audit of public companies, (2) establish audit report standards and rules, and (3) investigate, inspect, and enforce compliance relating to registered public accounting firms. The proposal was for more regulation, and it was eventually passed as the Public Company Accounting Reform and Investor Protection Act of 2002. The bill's history shows that it was first introduced in Congress on June 18, 2002, and it then began making its way through the political process. During the ensuing weeks, senators appeared in the news and on political shows talking up the bill. The Senate passed it on July 15, 2002. Over the four weeks between the bill's introduction and its passage in the Senate, the Dow fell 1,048 points. The day after the bill passed, the House passed a similar bill and Alan Greenspan spoke to Congress. He seemed to have two important things to say: First, he was upbeat about the economy; and, second, he agreed with proposals that executives should be held accountable to accurately state the financial condition of their firm. On this day, the Dow fell 166 points.

So neither talk alone nor enacting laws restores confidence. How is confidence regained after the trust has been broken? To answer this question, we should remember that trying to restore trust is a frequent occurrence in our society and in our lives. Restaurants work to regain a community's trust after an outbreak of food poisoning. A professional sport has to recapture fans' faith after a players' strike or an owner's lockout. And, of course, broken trust in a personal relationship (like in a marriage or between a child and parent) can happen to anyone. Unfortunately, restoring confidence in the corporate system is more difficult than it is in a personal relationship. This is because there are so many different participants in the system. While some are working hard to restore confidence, others are stonewalling the system and denying any wrongdoing.

There are several steps that need to occur in order to restore investor confidence. *The first step is admitting that the trust was broken.* Investors know that they lack confidence in the system. Politicians and the media have also expressed their anger at the breaking of trust. Regulating agencies like the SEC and the NYSE admit problems. While all this is useful, it is those groups that are directly involved with the scandalous behavior that need to step forward the most. Executives, auditors, boards, banks, and analysts must admit to the public that mistakes were made. Many of these groups and people are working within their own associations and professional groups to refocus themselves on their monitoring roles.

In addition to these efforts, they need to address investors (the public) more directly. Quietly working to improve things is not enough. They need to be as creative and persistent in marketing their own participation in the solutions as they are in promoting their firms' products and services.

The individuals who are being investigated will not admit their crimes. Their lawyers will not let them unless it is in conjunction with a plea deal with the Justice Department. Anonymous people associated with the scandalized firms will not speak for fear that the spotlight will turn on them. Therefore, it is up to the executives at the good firms to speak. It is up to the ethical auditors and moral investment bankers to speak out against their colleagues. When these people keep quiet, the investor thinks that they are either protecting their colleagues in a "good-old-boys" network or have worries of their own. Neither belief leads to trust.

The second step is to fully explain how and why the trust was broken. In the rush to fix investor confidence, many public leaders forgot to actually find out what was wrong with the system. They were quick to blame one group or another—such as auditors. In general, this approach leads to enacting laws that treat the symptoms and not the disease. The new laws for auditors are a good example. The Public Company Accounting Reform and Investor Protection Act tries to anticipate every problem with conducting an audit and assigns a law or regulator to overcome it. However, taking the time to learn how the entire system operates—or fails—would allow public leaders to address the system of problems instead of the multitude of symptoms.

We hope that this book helps investors identify all the participants in the corporate system and explain their participation in the breaking of the trust. We urge public leaders, regulators, and the media to do more than just look down their noses at the unethical evildoers and educate investors on the incentives for this behavior. When investors truly understand why the scandals occurred, they will be more willing to accept the fact that the problems can be fixed. The system really can become trustworthy again.

The third step is to punish the criminals and restore a measure of restitution. Before investors can truly get over their anger and mistrust, they need to feel that the people involved in the scandals are being severely punished. By severely punished we mean fines and prison terms that are greater than those received by the white-collar criminals of the 1980s. The infamous junk bond king Michael Milken served only 22 months in jail. Arbitrageur Ivan Boesky served only two years in prison. Charles Keating of the savings-and-loan disaster served four and a half years in prison. Oh, and by "prison" we actually mean a cushy, no-walls jail often referred to as Club Feds. Contrast this with another financial crime. Coleman Nee robbed two banks for $500 each in Boston and received a sentence of nearly five years.[6] Yet, his ill-gotten gains wouldn't have even paid for the $6,000 shower curtain Tyco's former CEO Dennis Kozlowski charged to his shareholders.

These corporate scoundrels could never repay the losses experienced by investors. Therefore, true restitution is not possible. However, for investors who lost a great deal of their wealth, like Enron employees, it is not comforting to see the wealth that white-collar criminals of the previous era were able to keep. For example, while Milken paid $1 billion in fines, penalties, and civil settlements, he was allowed to keep $125 million. His family members were allowed to keep more than $300 million.[7] Boesky was allowed to keep his foreign bank accounts.

The government appears to want to severely punish the corporate scoundrels. As we discussed in Chapter 12, the new laws passed in the summer of 2002 provide for stiffer maximum penalties and increased average sentences. However, having so many scandals to investigate and prosecute at the same time takes its toll on the system. Both the Justice Department and the SEC are working on more cases than ever—and they are doing so with overworked employees. These cases are complicated, and it is hard to know exactly what charge to make and if it will stick. With all that Arthur Andersen contributed to the Enron collapse, it was convicted of only one count of obstructing justice. Of course, that was enough to bring down the firm, but is that action enough to enact severe punishments on the scoundrels?

The fourth step is to fix the system so that these problems won't happen again. Finding solutions to fix the corporate governance system is difficult. As we have argued, some proposed solutions would not have much effect, and other solutions could inhibit capitalism too much. Choosing the right balance is challenging. We advocate creating good incentives to motivate the corporate participants so that they will want to work hard to do the right thing. Laws that simply make bad behavior illegal sometimes get watered down during the next big economic expansion. Regulators find that over time, their budgets do not grow with inflation and sometimes even get cut. We thoroughly discuss government action and other proposals in Chapter 12 and our recommendations in Chapter 13. The solutions are not easy. Yet, just fixing the system is not enough. Investors have to be convinced that the solutions will really work. That is, the people have to first have confidence in the solutions before they will have confidence in the market. To have confidence in the solutions, the people will need to understand both the causes of the problems and how the new laws and regulations solve the problems. Therefore, investors should not just be educated in the failures of the corporate governance system, but they should also be made aware of how the solutions actually prevent failures in the long term.

Confidence can only be regained over time. Therefore, *the last step is to prove that the system is trustworthy over time through good behavior.* Remember, trusting investors began to invest in the stock market only after a history of good performance. They stopped investing only after a history of poor performance and a string of scandals. To expect investor confidence to be restored quickly is naïve and does not recognize the process of building trust.

Before we can witness the better behavior by the participants in the governance system, the system has to really be fixed. Many of the laws enacted in the summer of 2002 will take time before they can be implemented. It will be even longer before they affect behavior. Consider, for example, the Public Company Accounting Oversight Board that Congress created to oversee the auditing profession. By mid-fall of 2002, the SEC had not yet found the people to sit on the board. Indeed, the board has yet to hire staff, create bylaws and policy, or certify auditors. This process is going to take a while to get right. Also, consider the new listing standards that the NYSE has enacted. The NYSE allows up to one year for its listed companies to make the changes it wants to their boards. The solutions take time to implement. Afterward, investors can witness the behavior of the corporate system. If the system earns the trust of investors again, investors will regain confidence in the market.

SUMMARY

All of the participants in the governance system need to work hard to restore investor confidence. Just having regulators and politicians work to fix the system is not convincing. Corporate participants are clever enough to eventually undo or avoid many of the rules and policies that the government can enact. Therefore, investors want to see the corporate participants themselves working for improvement. Investment banks need to persuade us that they are aligning themselves better with the needs of investors who purchase the securities they help issue. Through executive groups and associations, CEOs need to both speak out against scandalous behavior and begin to police themselves. Analyst and accounting membership organizations must be vocal with their apologies and solutions. While these groups have been working in the background to improve incentive systems, they are far too quiet about it publicly. It is important to communicate the solutions for fixing the system and restoring confidence. However, in the end, it is a history of behavior and actions that truly gain trust. Investor confidence will be restored when the corporate governance system has proven itself trustworthy.

ENDNOTES

1. Robert R. Prechter, Jr., *The Wave Principle of Human Social Behavior and the New Science of Socioeconomics* (Gainsville, GA: New Classics Library, 2002).

2. Data is from the Center for Responsive Politics, *http://www.opensecrets.org/industries/index.asp* (2002).

3. Christine Whelan and Tom Hamburger, "IPO Largess Flowed to Capitol Hill," *Wall Street Journal*, September 6, 2002, p. A4.

4. The idea of the trusting investors comes from Lynn A. Stout, "The Investor Confidence Game," UCLA School of Law, Research Paper No. 02-18, 2002.

5. Erik Sirri and Peter Tufano, "Costly Search and Mutual Fund Flows, *Journal of Finance* 53, no. 5 (1998): 937–958; David Franecki, "Fund Ratings and Recent Results Diverge," *Wall Street Journal*, May 3, 2000, p. C27.

6. Steven Syre, "Waiting for Corporate Criminals' Time to Fit the Crimes," *Boston Globe*, September 1, 2002, p. E1.

7. Joe Loya, "Corporate Fraud; Keating and Me," *Los Angeles Times,* August 4, 2002, p. M6.

INDEX

8 reasons why you should read the Financial Times for 4 weeks RISK-FREE!

To help you stay current with significant
developments in the world economy ...
and to assist you to make informed business
decisions — the Financial Times brings you:

1 Fast, meaningful overviews of international affairs ... plus daily briefings on major world news.

2 Perceptive coverage of economic, business, financial and political developments with special focus on emerging markets.

3 More international business news than any other publication.

4 Sophisticated financial analysis and commentary on world market activity plus stock quotes from over 30 countries.

5 Reports on international companies and a section on global investing.

6 Specialized pages on management, marketing, advertising and technological innovations from all parts of the world.

7 Highly valued single-topic special reports (over 200 annually) on countries, industries, investment opportunities, technology and more.

8 The Saturday Weekend FT section — a globetrotter's guide to leisure-time activities around the world: the arts, fine dining, travel, sports and more.

FT FINANCIAL TIMES
World business newspaper